CRITICAL INSIGHTS

Flash Fiction

CRITICAL INSIGHTS

Flash Fiction

Editors
Michael Cocchiarale
Widener University, Pennsylvania
& Scott D. Emmert
University of Wisconsin—Fox Valley, Wisconsin

SALEM PRESS
A Division of EBSCO Information Services, Inc.
Ipswich, Massachusetts

GREY HOUSE PUBLISHING

Publisher's Cataloging-In-Publication Data
(Prepared by The Donohue Group, Inc.)

Names: Cocchiarale, Michael, 1966- editor. | Emmert, Scott, 1962- editor.
Title: Flash fiction / editors, Michael Cocchiarale, Widener University,
      Pennsylvania, & Scott D. Emmert, University of Wisconsin-Fox Valley,
      Wisconsin.
Other Titles: Critical insights.
Description: [First edition]. | Ipswich, Massachusetts : Salem Press, a division
      of EBSCO Information Services, Inc. ; Amenia, NY : Grey
      House Publishing, [2017] | Includes bibliographical references
      and index.
Identifiers: ISBN 978-1-68217-270-4 (hardcover)
Subjects: LCSH: Flash fiction--History and criticism.
Classification: LCC PN3448.F55 F53 2017 | DDC 809.3/1--dc23

First Printing

Contents _____

Critical Contexts _____

Critical Readings _____

Resources

Michael Cocchiarale and Scott D. Emmert

FLASH—like a lightning bolt, a very short story can flare intensely and linger in the mind's eye, stunning the senses and imprinting itself upon the memory. Although very short stories have a long history and have appeared under a number of labels, flash fiction is now the preferred term, one that describes an established genre that continues to grow in popularity. To date, however, relatively little scholarship has been published on it. The present volume seeks to address that deficiency while introducing students and teachers to the genre and to a number of its finest practitioners.

After our introductory essay, "On Flash Fiction," which sets out some of the genre's history and development, the volume offers four Critical Contexts chapters to deepen this background. Pamelyn Casto provides an extensive recounting of the major anthologies of flash fiction, from the 1920s to the present. Along the way, she also introduces readers to a number of recent musicians and filmmakers who have adapted flash fiction pieces for an ever-expanding audience. The scholarly response to flash is then taken up in Randall Brown's essay, which delineates how writers and theorists have grappled with the workings of very short stories to define flash as distinctive from longer fiction whose narrative conventions do not always apply to flash stories. Kristen Figgins then examines contemporary flash fiction through the critical lens of the fable, which offers narrative conventions similar to those found in flash fiction. Figgins argues convincingly that writers of flash have borrowed from fables a number of storytelling techniques to "quickly and efficiently affect the reader." Megan Giddings continues the discussion of narrative technique in flash by comparing a flash piece by Donald Barthelme, a canonical flash writer, and Amelia Gray, a talented contemporary author. Giddings discusses how first person point of view and tense help each writer to compress narrative time while amplifying suggested meanings.

Following the context chapters, the volume turns to ten essays that take up individual flash fiction authors. These Critical Readings chapters reveal not only flash fiction's extraordinary range, examining a remarkable array of authors with diverse themes and styles, but also its long history as an international phenomenon. In the first of these essays, Robert C. Evans discusses Kate Chopin, whose very short stories, such as "The Story of an Hour" and "Ripe Figs," are often assigned in high school and college literature courses. However, the careful structure of Chopin's very short stories may be less well studied. Evans grounds his insights on Chopin's formal mastery in flash fiction theory and upon deft close readings of selected stories to demonstrate fully their "impressive moral and artistic complexity."

The next three chapters focus on significant international writers of flash fiction. In "Against Short Attention Spans: 'Fragmentary' Fiction for 'Fragmentary' Lives," Santino Prinzi discusses the flash fiction of two Western European writers—Franz Kafka and his early twentieth-century contemporary Robert Walser—to challenge the dismissive criticism that very short stories appeal to very short attention spans. On the contrary, Prinzi argues from the examples of Kafka and Walser that flash stories engage readers in a particular way, one that "complements, rather than diminishes, our contemporary lifestyles." Next, Eric Sterling studies very short stories by Isaac Babel, who employed a minimalist style to represent the oppression of Jews in Russia both before and after the communist revolution of 1917. Intense and open-ended, Babel's flash fiction raised a voice against anti-Semitism in Russia, but as Sterling's moving essay shows, these subtly brief stories were still too loud for the Russian authorities, who murdered Babel to silence him. In the next essay, Laura Hatry continues the focus on international flash fiction, shining considerable light on flash by the Argentinian writers Julio Cortázar and Luisa Valenzuela. Hatry details how these innovative writers have created memorable flash stories by deploying absurdist humor and witty wordplay and, in the process, pushed the entire genre in new, delightful directions.

The final six chapters delight in the artistry of some of flash fiction's most audacious contemporary practitioners. Perhaps most prominent among these is Lydia Davis, the subject of a searching essay by Julie Tanner. Tanner traces Davis's development as a flash fiction writer who finds thematic and emotional liberation in this shortest form, one that rewards her considerable linguistic skill. In the essay that follows, Laura Tansley provides equally astute observations about the work of flash writer Amy Hempel. Tansley demonstrates how the brevity of Hempel's flash stories deepens our understanding of human motivations and character by focusing on the inner lives of female characters and the suggestive possibilities of what they do not or cannot think. The illumination of character is also the focus of Matthew Duffus's essay on the masterful flash writer Diane Williams. Duffus explains how Williams's flash stories "elicit emotional responses from readers at the same time that they refuse to provide easy solutions to the problems [her characters] encounter."

In the next essay, Randall Brown revels in the artistry of influential flash fiction writer Kathy Fish. With considerable insight, Brown demonstrates how Fish employs and refashions traditional narrative strategies to create condensed stories with intense conflicts, high stakes, and deep meanings. In the essay that follows this, David Swann explicates the complex flash fiction of Mary Robison, a writer who dazzles with "prose [that] has been distilled to its essence." Swann explains how Robison creates drama by resisting hero-worshipping plots to better value characters that are "damaged and vulnerable." In the final essay of the volume, Jarrell D. Wright explores the limits of flash fiction by imagining a point at which a story may be too condensed to be considered literature. Wright then demonstrates how Lou Beach in his "nanofictions" can flirt with this limit and still convey psychological complexity.

This volume, then, provides an informed introduction to an exciting and vibrant literary genre, and it covers a number of the most important flash fiction writers. Teachers and students will also benefit from an extensive list of flash writers, collections and anthologies, literary journals, and writing guides that concludes the volume. As teachers and readers of flash fiction, we hope the present volume is both illuminating and memorable, encouraging greater readership and inspiring further study.

We thank Randall Brown and Ashley Chantler for their help with the bibliography and Tara Masih for her advice and ideas at the early stage of this project.

On Flash Fiction

Michael Cocchiarale and Scott D. Emmert

We live in a world that constantly tells us that "bigger is better." Mega stores and supermarkets, sprawling all-you-can eat buffets, gas-guzzling vehicles, blockbuster movies—what's not to like when there is so much more to buy or eat or drive or see? This love of bigness also bears an implicit criticism of smaller things. Locally owned mom-and-pop stores, often hailed by politicians as the epitome of the American dream, stand little chance in the looming shadows of the superstore chains and franchise eateries that fill strip malls from coast to coast. The tiny house movement is praised by opinion writers as a model of efficiency and environmental consciousness. However, many see these miniature structures in a condescending manner. Sure, they're quaint, they're cute, but they are hardly big enough for that wall-covering plasma screen TV. In art, too, bigger is often seen as much better. A small-budget film, for example, may earn critical praise and win significant awards, yet show on very few big screens and fail to attract the public's attention.

It is in this context that we consider flash fiction—works of imaginative literature typically less than 1,000 words. Flash has enjoyed an incredible renaissance in the last thirty years, aided mightily by developments in technology. The shorter the piece, the easier it is to read on the laptop or phone. While flash aficionados argue vigorously for the worth of these short short fictions, others openly dismiss these works, seeing not literary quality but blatant pandering by writers attempting to reach readers with ever-decreasing attention spans. Writing for *Politico* in 2012, Jacob Silverman presents just such a critique:

> The problem with flash fiction is that much of it isn't very good. Boosters like to say that So-and-so packs more into a thousand words than most writers do into a novel, but that's almost never true—particularly when you consider that time spent with a novel, and all

of the mental and emotional investment that that requires, is one of its principal features. Instead, most flash fiction is too brief and self-satisfied to strike more than one note. Often, it's a joke told too long or a conceit that doesn't become anything else. It's literary tokenism, stories to be consumed between commercial breaks.

Undoubtedly, there is some truth to Silverman's argument. A lot of flash fiction is being published these days, and not all of it is good. However, this sweeping criticism is harsh and unfair; it condemns an entire genre and reveals a clear bias—an assumption that length is synonymous with depth, that the longer the piece the more readers become engaged with it. The dismissive judgments apparent in words and phrases such as "self-satisfied," "a joke," "literary tokenism" would never be applied to other brief literary works, such as sonnets or haiku, the latter of which is one of the most compressed literary forms of all. Dylan Thomas's "Do Not Go Gentle Into That Good Night," one of the most highly regarded villanelles ever composed, is 168 words. Shakespeare's "Sonnet 73," another literary masterpiece, is a mere 119 words. Never are these works dismissed because of their brevity.

To further counter Silverman's argument, we would do well to consider Henry James's important essay "The Art of Fiction" (1884), in which he argues that readers

> must grant the artist his subject, his idea, what the French call his donnée; our criticism is applied only to what he makes of it. Naturally I do not mean that we are bound to like it or find it interesting: in case we do not our course is perfectly simple—to let it alone. We may believe that of a certain idea even the most sincere novelist can make nothing at all, and the event may perfectly justify our belief; but the failure will have been a failure to execute, and it is in the execution that the fatal weakness is recorded. If we pretend to respect the artist at all we must allow him his freedom of choice, in the face, in particular cases, of innumerable presumptions that the choice will not fructify. . . . (56).

Accepted on their own terms, many flash fictions are full of beauty, insight, and nuance. They are worthy of the attention of literary scholars in the way that great novels and dramas and sonnets are worthy of our attention. It is the job of literary critics to grant writers their donnée not only in terms of content but of genre as well. Some brief works are admittedly slight—not worth a second read (and perhaps not worth a first). Others—many others—are worth another look. The best flash fiction is like a great poem. The thing to remember is this: Art (whether it takes the form of literature or painting or music or theater) is not supposed to do what readers or viewers want it to do. As James argues, "[a]rt derives a considerable part of its beneficial exercise from flying in the face of presumptions" (56).

* * *

Antecedents of flash fiction date to ancient times. The fables credited to Aesop (620–564 BCE) offer brief moralistic tales featuring animals as characters. "The Tortoise and the Hare"—one of the most famous—is a mere 200 words. The "Parable of the Prodigal Son," which appears in the Bible in the Gospel of Luke (70 CE), tells of a father who forgives his wasteful son in the space of about 500 words. "The Fisherman and the Jinni," a popular work from *The Thousand and One Nights*, packs significant drama into a roughly 1,000-word package. More "recent" examples can be found in Alan Zielger's *Short* (2014), a collection of extremely brief fiction and nonfiction from the likes of Michel de Montaigne, Friedrich Schlegel, Charles Baudelaire, Kate Chopin, and Robert Louis Stevenson, not to mention work by many twentieth and twenty-first century practitioners of the genre.

The twentieth century is filled with antecedents of recent flash fictions. Perhaps the most familiar of early twentieth-century practitioners is Ernest Hemingway, the larger-than-life author of such staples of American literature as *The Sun Also Rises* (1926) and *The Old Man and the Sea* (1952). Hemingway's first major work, however, was *In Our Time* (1925), a collection of interrelated short fictions, many dealing with Nick Adams, the book's protagonist.

Interspersed among more traditional-length stories are several vignettes, brief scenes of war and bullfighting, that serve to create a larger context for Nick's coming of age. One frequently anthologized flash-length fiction is the aptly named, "A Very Short Story," about a wounded soldier in Italy who falls in love with a nurse during his convalescence. The story begins with a summary of their romance and the explanation of their desire to be married "so they could not lose it" (Hemingway 65). However, "there was not enough time for the banns" (65) before the soldier has to return to the front. After the war, he goes home to Chicago, planning for their life together. Meanwhile, the nurse has fallen in love with an Italian major and sends the soldier a "Dear John" letter. The solider is despondent— his idealized, quasi-religious love for the nurse crushed. Instead of stating this point directly, Hemingway presents a devastatingly unromantic ending, one in which the man "contracted gonorrhea from a sales girl in a loop department store while riding in a taxicab through Lincoln Park" (66). This story is very short, but both the anonymous sex and the sexually transmitted disease make it far from sweet.

On the other side of the world, Japanese author Yasunari Kawabata (a contemporary of Hemingway) penned a number of "palm-of-the-hand" stories over a forty year span. These stories are small enough to fit into the palm of one's hand, and perhaps it is for that reason that Lane Dunlop, one of the translators of these brief pieces, said that, initially, "I mistook their subtlety for slightness, their lack of emphasis for pointlessness" (xi). Kawabata's work is often mysterious—an evocative mixture of reality and dream. In "Love Suicides," for example, a husband who has left his wife writes a series of letters with instructions about how to raise their daughter. In one letter, he says, "Don't let the child bounce a rubber ball . . . . It strikes at my heart" (Kawabata 56). In another, he tells the wife not to let the girl wear shoes because the sound of them "tramples on my heart" (56). In the third letter, he tells her not to let "the child eat from a porcelain bowl" because "[i]t breaks my heart" (56). At the end of the flash, another letter arrives, telling them "Don't make any sound at all . . . don't breathe" (57). As she's done before, the wife follows these directions, resulting in the death of mother and daughter. The last line of the story provides an image of an ironic reunion, with Kawabata writing, "And strangely enough, the woman's husband lay down beside them and died, too" (57). The extreme concision of this piece, coupled with its fairy tale-like style, makes it powerfully moving. In just a few pages, Kawabata is able to deeply explore the complex entanglements of familial love.

The work of Hemingway and Kawabata—along with that produced by such pre-"flash fiction" era writers as Franz Kafka, Jorge Luis Borges, Julio Cortázar, Italo Calvino, Donald Barthelme, and others—legitimated short-short fiction long before it was given the name it often goes by now. However, in the past thirty years, flash fiction has truly come into its own, with numerous literary journals (both print and online) and anthologies eagerly soliciting and publishing it. In addition to deeply committed flash fiction writers, such as Diane Williams, Kim Chinquee, and Pamela Painter, many better-known, more heralded writers of our time— including Joyce Carol Oates, Robert Coover, John Updike, Robert Olen Butler, John Edgar Wideman, Lydia Davis, and Amy Hempel, among others—have produced fascinating and enduring examples of the form. Flash fiction, as this partial list of writers shows, is a vital part of the literary world.

*   *   *

Although there is general agreement that a flash is a work of fiction less than 1,000 words, there are many ways besides length of thinking about the genre. The indispensable *Field Guide to Writing Flash Fiction* (2009) offers a number of essays by flash fiction writers who provide definitions of and reflections on the form. Editor Tara L. Masih, who is also a flash writer, explains that "[a] flash is simply a story in miniature, a work of art carved on a grain of rice—something of import to the artist or writer that is confined and reduced, either by design or outcome, into a small square space using the structural devices of prose line and paragraph form with the purpose of creating an intense, emotional impact" (xi). Brief, intense, and almost miraculous, flash fiction is no literary novelty.

Nathan Leslie argues that "a great work of fiction in this form can . . . yield quite a bit more than the hundred thousand words of a mediocre novel" (7). According to Leslie, "the writing of flash fiction takes great care and attention to detail; it doesn't suffer fools. This is a slop-free zone" (7). Jennifer Pieroni emphasizes the idea of "smart surprise" (65)—using unexpected language and imagery throughout a work to compel readers to continue. This can include "odd words; uncommon pairings or de-packaging common phrases; invented words; and conscious crafting of the rhythm of words when brought together into a sentence" (66). Under extreme pressure, unusual and arresting things will happen to language. In short, because flashes are so short, the best of them dazzle at nearly every turn.

One of the more prolific contemporary flash fiction writers and theorists is Randall Brown, whose excellent *A Pocket Guide to Flash Fiction* (2012) provides numerous interesting ways of thinking about the genre. Brown (who has written two chapters for this volume) calls flash fiction "A machine of compression—a mindset—that desire to make the most minute of movements matter" (2). Flash is not the start or suggestion of something larger, more well-developed. According to Brown, "[f]lash is a very tiny thing that doesn't want to be anything else" (2). Writers of flash are concerned about "getting words to count more than they might in other less-compressed forms" (9). In "The Definitive Flash: Fifty Shades of (Very) Short Fiction," Brown provides several definitions to explain flash as a genre and solidify "flash" as the most fitting moniker for the form. A flash is "a brief, sudden burst of light" (188). It is "a very brief moment; an instant" (189). It is a verb that means "to burst suddenly into view or perception" (193). It is used to describe "the experience [of] the intense effects of a narcotic or stimulant drug" (195). At the same time, the word "flash" can be used to describe something "gaudy" or "pretentious," something "false" or "fake" (200). All of these definitions contribute to an understanding of the form. Readers might wish to judge a flash fiction after a mere glance, thinking that creative prose cannot possibly appear so brief. Its appearance might even seem, ironically, as unnecessarily showy. If readers get beyond this bias and read a flash, they might be rewarded only with a feeling of great disorientation. They might finish the piece and have no other response than, "This can't be for real!" But readers and critics must do away with the expectations brought to other prose forms. Flash does not build slowly, like a novel. And, unlike a conventional short story, it often does not have a series of escalating conflicts that lead to a climax. Often, because of its intensity—because of its compression—a flash fiction bursts all at once upon readers and is done, leaving them to gather themselves, to blink in the afterglow while trying to make some sense of what has just been witnessed.

*　*　*

The lines between flash fiction and prose poetry are often blurred. No one would object to the assertion that Raymond Carver's often-anthologized piece "Little Things" is a flash fiction. With no backstory and very little description of place, this spare, Hemingwayesque story about an argument between an unnamed man and woman is filled with tension. After a brief opening paragraph describing the dreariness of the world outside, the narrator takes us into an equally grim house, where a man is hurriedly packing a suitcase, determined to leave the house and his relationship. Things escalate when he expresses his desire to take their baby with him, and she refuses. A vocal and physical struggle ensues, which culminates with the chillingly vague final line: "In this manner, the issue was decided" (Carver 154). Although the piece is under a thousand words, it shares many similarities with longer, more conventional stories: an inciting incident, a clear conflict, a rising of tension, and a climax.

Unlike "Little Things," some extremely short prose pieces are driven less by narrative than by image or mood. Carolyn Forché's "The Colonel" and Robert Hass's "A Story of the Body" are both often labeled as prose poems, yet share many qualities with flash fiction. Forché's piece is a single scene depicting the narrator having an elegant dinner with a ruthless Central American despot. The sophisticated food and the mundane details of the family's day are juxtaposed with images of violence: the bars on the windows, the

Colonel's pistol, the dried human ears of victims that are spilled onto the table before the poet. The piece ends with the following lines: "[s]omething for your poetry, no? he [the colonel] said. Some of the ears on the floor caught this scrap of his voice. Some of the ears on the floor were pressed to the ground" (Forché 85). The powerful image of the ears suggests not only the horrible atrocities committed by ruthless leaders but also the power of victims to hear such stories and record them. "The Colonel" may not be a story, but it is most certainly a stunning work of literature.

Robert Hass's piece confuses the issue of genre even more. The title declares it is a "story," and indeed it has all of the attributes of one. Set at an artists' colony, the piece depicts a main character who yearns for an attractive Japanese artist. She stops him with her brutal honesty, saying that she's had a double mastectomy. This cools his ardor, and he quits his pursuit of her. The next morning, he finds at the doorstep to his cottage a bowl of rose petals, underneath of which lay a number of dead bees. The closing image is striking, symbolic of the contrast between the appearance and the reality of not only the woman, but of the man as well. There is nothing in this piece, however, that makes it different from a story. There are characters, a conflict, and a resolution of sorts.

Kim Chinquee, whose first book *Oh Baby* (2008) was subtitled "Flash Fictions & Prose Poems," attempts to draw a distinction between the two closely related genres. In "Flash Fiction, Prose Poetry, and Men Jumping Out of Windows: Searching for Plot and Finding Definitions," an essay in the *Field Guide to Writing Flash Fiction*, she writes that "I believe that a prose poem is more about language and poetics, whereas a flash carries more narrative and story" (Chinquee 112). In the end, however, she admits that, "all-in-all, they are simply interchangeable" (113). This blurry conclusion is not a failure on Chinquee's part. It is another way of saying that, as Charles Johnson explains, a flash fiction is "protean, assuming any shape" (233). Moreover, "it must be an innovative, attention-grabbing exploration of that perennial mystery that is the origin and end of expression itself: language" (233). The difficulty of distinguishing flash fiction from prose poetry is clear; however, this is cause not for despair but for celebration. This kind of ambiguity might frustrate a certain kind of literary critic for whom taxonomy is all-important, but for readers, it is one of the things that makes flash fiction so endlessly compelling.

* * *

Many respected literary journals publish flash fiction today and have been doing so for quite some time. *Smokelong Quarterly*, *Wigleaf*, *Vestal Review*, and *The Journal of Compressed Creative Arts*, for example. In addition, a significant number of fine anthologies of flash have been published in the last thirty years. The genre was given its most frequently used name with the publication of *Flash Fiction: 72 Very Short Stories* (1992), an anthology edited by Tom Hazuka, Denise Thomas, and James Thomas. In the preface, James Thomas writes that, in their original conception, they wanted to collect pieces that could be presented "on a two-page spread" (12). They took to calling these works "'flash' fictions because there would be no enforced pause in the reader's concentration, no break in the field of vision. They would be apprehended 'all at once'" (12).

Without question, flash is an international phenomenon. *Flash: The International Short-Short Story Magazine* has published the work of Ama Ata Aidoo, Margaret Atwood, Beryl Bainbridge, and Ana María Shua, among others. Shouhua Qi, editor and translator for the anthology *The Pearl Jacket and Other Stories: Flash Fiction from Contemporary China* (2008), traces the genre in China back to ancient times. More recently, James Thomas, Robert Shapard, and Christopher Merrill's *Flash Fiction International* (2015) features the work of writers from the US, Mexico, England, Germany, Sri Lanka, Taiwan, and other countries. Flash is everywhere—and more and more, with each passing year.

* * *

Along with a growing global reputation, flash fiction is also a genre that invites innovation. It is a genre that often—and with great joy—untethers itself from reality. Anything goes, especially when it only goes for a brief period of time. Israeli writer Etgar Keret has enjoyed world-wide renown for several collections of extremely brief fictions that oftentimes veer into the fantastical. Ben Loory attracted a major publisher for *Stories for Nighttime and Some for the Day* (2011), a collection of mostly flash pieces that, with their mixture of realism and fantasy, read much like fables. Often, Loory begins stories by presenting a relatively banal situation in crisp, matter-of-fact prose; soon, however, the flash spins out into a bizarre or fantastical direction. Other idiosyncratic flash writers of note include Gary Lutz, who burst on the scene with *Stories in the Worst Way* (1996), a collection remarkable for, among other things, the "strangulated ingenuity" of his sentences (Christman); and Amelia Gray, whose most recent collection, *Gutshot* (2015), is filled with "fables (a town is divided in half by a giant snake), horror stories (a woman is about to be killed in a stranger's house), absurd stories (two women get into an escalated battle of thank-you gifts, including a tube of mice that poop out a message) and more serious stories about love" (Ausubel). For these and other writers, risk-taking in style, content, and theme occur with exciting regularity.

There are several examples of flashes that take the form of dramatic monologues. Michael Martone's *Pensees: The Thoughts of Dan Quayle* (1994) is a collection of humorous short-short monologues told in the voice of George H. W. Bush's vice president. More recently, Robert Olen Butler published *Severance* (2006), a collection of internal monologues of famous and not so famous people who have suffered decapitation, and *Intercourse* (2008), which presents the thoughts of characters engaged in the act of sex. Michael Czyzniejewski's *Chicago Stories* (2012) takes a similar approach, focusing more narrowly, however, on famous Chicagoans past and present, including Oprah Winfrey, Roger Ebert, and Hillary Clinton.

Many flash writers push boundaries through the appropriation of forms. For example, G. A. Ingersoll's "Test" is told in a series of parts—"Word Problems," "Matching," "Short Answer," "Essay," and "Extra Credit"—one would find on an examination. Even more than other short-shorts, this piece invites readers to become an active participant in the creation of meaning. "Pledge Drive" by Patricia Marx employs the form of public radio fund drives to present the life and self-centered interests of Patty, who "is standing by to take your money" (154). In *Modern Manners for Your Inner Demons* (2012), Tara Laskowski appropriates the form of etiquette manuals to create a darkly comic guide to adultery, homicide, and discrimination, among others.

The limits of narrative are stretched even further by flashes that are comprised of lists. Amanda Holzer's "Love and Other Catastrophes: A Mix Tape" is nothing more than a list of popular songs from the last forty years that are arranged to tell the story of a speaker who endures a troubled relationship. Leslie Busler's "Memoir of a Bookshelf" does something similar, using the titles of books. An extended version of the list flash is a piece like Derrick Ableman's "Games My Father Played," which is comprised of a series of paragraph-length stories about each game—from Peek-a-Boo to Basketball to Monopoly to Hide and Go Seek—the father participated in over the years.

A number of flashes are "how to" stories, among them pieces such as Stace Budzko's "How to Set a House on Fire," Lee Harrington's "How to Become a Country-Western Singer," Latanya McQueen's "How to Cheat (On Your Wife)," Ander Monson's "To Reduce Your Likelihood of Murder," and Ron Carlson's "You Must Intercept the Blue Box Before It Gets to the City." Such experiments might be difficult to sustain over the course of a more traditional-sized story.

While individual flash stories provide discrete flights of fancy, in recent years, flash writers are seeing more possibilities for the form by connecting pieces to form a novelistic whole. Similar to short story cycles such as Sherwood Anderson's *Winesburg, Ohio* (1919), Jean Toomer's *Cane* (1923), and Ernest Hemingway's *In Our Time*, Sandra Cisneros's *The House on Mango Street* (1984) is an early—and excellent—example of what might be called a novella-in-flash. Taught in elementary schools, high schools, and colleges around the country, it is comprised of forty-four pieces, many well under 1,000 words, to dramatize the life of Esperanza Cordero, a young girl who comes of age in a tough Chicago neighborhood. Some of the pieces are narrative driven, but others focus more on character and imagery. If, as Robert Olen Butler argues, a flash fiction can be distinguished from a prose poem "because it has at its center a character who yearns" (102), then the title piece of Cisneros's book is most definitely a story. It is true that not much happens. Esperanza describes the deficiencies of her new house and reflects on the time that a nun humiliated her by making her point out her old house on Loomis Street. At the end of the piece, however, she explicitly announces her desire—her yearning: "I knew then I had to have a house. A real house. One I could point to. But this isn't it. The house on Mango Street isn't it. For the time being, Mama says. Temporary, says Papa. But I know how these things go" (Cisneros 5). On its own, the story is a powerful piece, one that presents with blunt realism the pain of a young girl who wishes for better circumstances at the same time she feels fated for nothing better. This flash fiction is enhanced, however, by its connection to the subsequent flashes, which show how she is able to navigate the difficult waters of childhood and adolescence.

More recently, such works have been given a name: the novella-in-flash. Rose Metal Press, a publisher devoted to flash writing, has put out a number of novellas-in-flash. *They Could No Longer Contain Themselves: A Collection of Five Flash Chapbooks* (2011) features collections of flash fiction by Elizabeth J. Colen, John Jodzio, Tim Jones-Yelvington, Sean Lovelace, and Mary Miller. Another title— *My Very End of the Universe: Five Novellas-in-Flash and a Study of the Form* (2014)—features longer works of interconnected flash fiction by Chris Bower, Margaret Patton Chapman, Tiff Holland, Meg Pokrass, and Aaron Teel. This collection is noteworthy not only for the quality of the fiction but also for the insightful craft essays that foster a clear understanding of this new and exciting genre. Pokrass describes the novella-in-flash by comparing it to a crazy quilt "made of many found scraps and pieces of cloth in different sizes" (47) Flash writers assemble "fragments and stories . . . to form a layered, narrative arc" (47). Teel says that "[i]f flash fetishizes the moment, the novella-in-flash provides a space for myriad moments to co-exist, rub up against, and reverberate off of one another" (102). Using a different metaphor than Pokrass, Teel says that "[i]f a single flash is a snapshot then the novella-in-flash is a slideshow" (102). Other notable book-length works of interconnected flash include Mary Robison's *Why Did I Ever* (2001), told in a number of vignettes, some of which are a mere handful of words, Matt Bell's *Cataclysm Baby* (2012), a post-apocalyptic novella presented in short chapters connected by theme and imagery, and Matthew Salesses's *I'm Not Saying, I'm Just Saying* (2012), an extended work about fatherhood told in a series of vignettes.

Despite the popularity of the flash—despite the numerous anthologies, despite the "how-to" books and articles, despite the ever-proliferating list of publications eagerly soliciting short short fiction—there is a dearth of scholarship on the genre. It is hoped that this volume will not only give readers a richer understanding of important flash fiction writers of the last one hundred plus years, but will also inspire further literary criticism on this compelling, shape-shifting genre.

As Philip Stevick explains, "Our dailiness, our aural/oral world is made up of short-short stories. But everything militates against translating that shortness into print. A writer who would write short does not merely choose; he strains, resists, contends against the compulsion to write long" (242). Flash fiction is an unflinching acknowledgment of reality, an attempt to capture the stuff of life that is always beginning and ending before our eyes. It is also an act of resistance. These works are not ephemeral—lightweight literature for the Internet Age. Flash fiction matters, as each moment of our lives matter, if we're willing to pay attention.

Works Cited

Ausubel, Ramona. "'Gutshot,' Stories by Amelia Gray." *The New York Times*, 22 May 2015, www.nytimes.com/2015/05/24/books/review/gutshot-stories-by-amelia-gray.html?_r=0/. Accessed 1 Nov. 2016.

Brown, Randall. *Pocket Guide to Flash Fiction*. Matter Press, 2012.

Butler, Robert Olen. "A Short Story Theory." *Field Guide to Writing Flash Fiction*, edited by Tara Masih, Rose Metal Press, 2008, pp. 102-104.

Carver, Raymond. "Little Things." *Where I'm Calling From.* Vintage, 1988, pp. 152-154.

Chinquee, Kim. "Flash Fiction, Prose Poetry, and Men Jumping Out of Windows: Searching for Plot and Finding Definitions." *Field Guide to Writing Flash Fiction,* edited by Tara Masih, Rose Metal Press, 2008, pp. 109-115.

Cisneros, Sandra. *The House on Mango Street.* Vintage, 1991.

Christman, Philip. "Gary Lutz's Stories in the Worst Way." *Identity Theory,* 28 Jul. 2009, www.identitytheory.com/gary-lutz-stories-worst-way/. Accessed 21 Nov. 2016.

Dunlop, Lane. Translators' Notes. *Palm-of-the-Hand Stories,* by Yasunari Kawabata. Translated by Lane Dunlop and J. Martin Holman, Farrar, Straus, and Giroux, 1988, pp. xi-xiv.

Forché, Carolyn. "The Colonel." *Flash Fiction.* Norton, 1992, pp. 84-85.

Hass, Robert. "A Story About the Body." *Human Wishes.* Ecco, 1989, p. 32.

Hemingway, Ernest. "A Very Short Story." *In Our Time.* 1925. Scribner, 2003, pp. 65-66.

Johnson, Charles. Afterwords. *Sudden Fiction: American Short-Short Stories,* edited by Robert Shapard and James Thomas, Gibbs-Smith, 1986, pp. 232-233.

James, Henry. "The Art of Fiction." *Essays on Literature, American Writers, English Writers,* edited by Leon Edel, Library of America, 1984, pp. 44-65.

Kawabata, Yasunari. "Love Suicides." *Palm-of-the-Hand Stories.* Translated by Lane Dunlop and J. Martin Holman, Farrar, Straus, and Giroux, 1988, pp. 56-57.

Leslie, Nathan. "That 'V' Word." *Field Guide to Writing Flash Fiction,* edited by Tara Masih, Rose Metal Press, 2008, pp. 7-14.

Marx, Patricia. "Pledge Drive." *Flash Fiction Forward,* edited by James Thomas and Robert Shapard, Norton, 2006, pp. 152-154.

Masih, Tara. Introduction. *Field Guide to Writing Flash Fiction,* edited by Tara Masih, Rose Metal Press, 2008, pp. xi-xxxviii.

Pieroni, Jennifer. "Smart Surprise in Flash Fiction." *Field Guide to Writing Flash Fiction,* edited by Tara Masih, Rose Metal Press, 2008, pp. 65-67.

Pokrass, Meg. "Breaking the Pattern to Make the Pattern: Conjuring a Whole Narrative from Scraps." *My Very End of the Universe: Five Novellas-in-Flash and a Study of the Form*, Rose Metal Press, 2014, pp. 47-53.

Silverman, Jacob. "Why Flash Fiction is an Overrated Genre, and Why Etgar Keret is a Master of It." *Politico*. 27 Mar. 2012. Accessed 21 June 2016.

Stevick, Philip. "Toward a New Form." *Sudden Fiction: American Short-Short Stories*, edited by Robert Shapard and James Thomas, Gibbs-Smith, 1986, p. 242.

Teel, Aaron. "A Brief Crack of Light: Mimicking Memory in the Novella-in-Flash." *My Very End of the Universe: Five Novellas-in-Flash and a Study of the Form*, Rose Metal Press, 2014, pp. 101-105.

Thomas, James. Introduction. *Flash Fiction: Very Short Stories*, edited by James Thomas, Denise Thomas, and Tom Hazuka, Norton, 1992, pp. 11-14.

CRITICAL
CONTEXTS

Flash Fiction: From Text to Audio to Music, Stage, and Film Adaptations

Pamelyn Casto

Then Came Flash Fiction

The history of literary flash fiction, especially as a world-wide phenomenon, is just now being pieced together. Brief stories can be found throughout the ages but they have flown just outside literary radar so have escaped most serious critical notice. But all the while, the stories have been metamorphosing, assuming different shapes, displaying different strategies. Then one day, brief literary stories acquired the name "flash fiction."

So where did flash fiction come from? Tzvetan Todorov explains in *Genres in Discourse* that "a new genre is always the transformation of an earlier one, or of several: by inversion, by displacement, by combination" (15). Flash fiction is no exception. It is related to and draws from several genres—short shorts, anecdotes, vignettes, prose poems, short stories, lyric poetry, narrative poetry, journalism, memoir, and more—but does not adhere to one single convention. However "flash fiction" was not a label used by writers, editors, critics, or readers until 1992. For years stories of such brief length were most often called "short shorts," but with the publication of the popular literary anthology *Flash Fiction: 72 Very Short Stories* edited by James Thomas, Denise Thomas, and Tom Hazuka, the new name gradually came into common use. The goal of the anthology was to determine how short an effective literary story could be, and a limit was generally drawn, with each story being no longer than 750 words. Out of many possible names, snappy and memorable "flash fiction" took the strongest hold, especially once it became the name of choice and habit on the Internet. Today, the designation "flash fiction" often includes stories up to 1,500 words, depending on a length determined by a publication's editor and/or individual writers. The label frequently serves as an umbrella term for short-

short fiction in general. Some other popular labels include sudden, skinny, micro, minute, smoke-long, nano, hint, and quick fiction.

Prose Poetry's Influence

A major influence for short-short work gaining critical notice was the publication of Charles Baudelaire's *Paris Spleen* in 1869. The collection of stand-alone pieces ranging from a half page to three pages in length was inspired by Aloysius Bertrand's *Gaspard de la Nuit* (ix), which was published in 1842 but not translated into English until 1994. Baudelaire wanted to use the same method Bertrand used but for "applying to the description of our more abstract modern life. . . " (ix). While Baudelaire called his work "prose poems," Alan Ziegler notes that not all the pieces are poetic and many are "closer to stories, fables, essays, memoirs, and anecdotes but by appropriating these modes of expression for his *petits poems en prose*, Baudelaire provided us with a mix of models that makes *Paris Spleen* an exemplar for the whole gamut of short prose forms" (xxvi).

The rise in interest in this highly experimental type of writing also contributed to the rising experimentation in literary flash fiction. Following Charles Baudelaire's work, more writers of prose poetry came into prominence. Stéphane Mallarmé (1842–1898), like Baudelaire, was inspired by Aloysius Bertrand's work. Mallarmé in turn inspired cubist, futurist, dadaist, and surrealist writers, and these styles of writing continue to inform and influence today's flash fiction and prose poetry. In the United States Michael Benedikt edited *The Prose Poem: An International Anthology* in 1976, and then in 2000, Peter Johnson edited *The Best of The Prose Poem: An Internal Journal.* Just as Baudelaire's collection spurred interest in both prose poems and flash fiction, so did Michael Benedikt and Peter Johnson's popular anthologies in modern times.

Sometimes there is a clear difference between prose poetry and flash fiction, but many times there is no reliable way to separate the two types of writing. The label used often depends on what the writer, the editor, or the reader wants to call a piece. Many pieces are also published as prose poetry and later republished as flash fiction (or as flash essays or flash memoir). They are clearly related and sometimes interchangeable. A few of the pieces that have been published under different labels are Jamaica Kincaid's "Girl," Carolyn Forché's "The Colonel," Margaret Atwood's "My Life As A Bat," W. S. Merwin's "The Reaper," and "Jayne Anne Phillips' "Happy." Anne Carson's prose poems from *Short Talks* have been published in Best American Essays.

Other writers of short pieces exerted strong influences on present-day literary flash fiction. Those writers include O. Henry (1862–1910), known for twist endings; Guy de Maupassant (1850–1910), known for stories that reveal the hidden in people; Anton Chekhov (1860–1904), known for stories that raise questions; Hector Hugh Munro (Saki) (1870–1916), praised for his short macabre stories; Ambrose Bierce (1842–1910), lauded for brief stories of the supernatural; and Franz Kafka (1883–1924), known for themes of alienation. All of these author characteristics are also characteristics of a lot of literary flash fiction.

Ernest Hemingway (1899–1961) is another major influence on modern day flash fiction writers. He is known for his deceptively simple and spare prose style and for his method of withholding information so readers can draw necessary conclusions. His style works especially well with literary flash fiction which is often a condensed form of fiction that suggests more than it states. Some of Hemingway's flash-length stories can be found in *Men Without Women* (1927) and *Winner Take Nothing* (1933). His prose poetry or prose vignettes can be found in *In Our Time* (1925).

Writers working in popular genres have also influenced the development of flash fiction. One example is Frederic Brown (1906–1972), who wrote mysteries and science fiction and was known for his humorous and macabre short shorts with twist endings. His popular collection of horror stories, *Nightmares and Geezenstacks* (1961), is composed of stories one to two pages in length.

With the advent and sharpening interest in the production of a more literary type of flash fiction, increased critical notice came more into play as well. Many early non-literary short-short stories were not particularly challenging or difficult to understand, but literary flash fiction, much less straightforward, required more effort from writers, readers, and critics alike. The literary types of flash fiction show moments in time that suggest much larger questions or meanings.

While there have been many influential present-era short-short stories published in collections by talented writers such as Yasunari Kawabata, W. S. Merwin, Donald Barthelme, Russell Edson, Raymond Carver, Margaret Atwood, and Lydia Davis (plus many others), what follows will focus on influential literary anthologies and publications that, in addition to flash collected by individual authors, furthered the writing and appreciation of short-short work worldwide.

Early Publications and Anthologies

From the mid-1920s through the early 1950s short-short stories, as they were usually called then, were published in newspapers and magazines and were usually done in a straightforward style that was more popular than stories with more challenging literary appeal.

In 1926, *Colliers Weekly* published one-page stories they called "short shorts" and claimed they were "the greatest innovation in short story publication since O. Henry" (Reid 13). In 1929, the first science fiction anthology of short-shorts was published, *The Best of Amazing Stories*, and it was edited by Hugo Gernsback (Masih xxv).

In the 1930s, three particularly influential anthologies were published. *Writing the Short, Short Story* was edited by Walter Alderman, who called the stories "tabloid tales" (Masih xxv). In 1934, *One-Smoke Stories* was edited by Mary Austin. The tales were published as told by peoples of the Southwest: various American Indian tribes, Spanish Colonials, Mexicans, and white Americans from several different European backgrounds (xxvii). They are called "one-smoke stories" because they were to be completed in the length of time it took to smoke a corn-husk ceremonial cigarette (xxv). Then in 1936, *365 Days* was edited by Kay Boyle, Laurence Vail, and Nina Conarain. Each story was one page in length.

The 1940s also saw the publication of anthologies that furthered the interest in short-short fiction. *Technique SELLS the Short-Short*

(1944) was Robert Oberfirst's first edited collection, which was composed of instructional articles he first published in *The Writer* from 1939 to 1944. The collection was used in universities and schools in the US, Canada, England, and Australia, and included examples by a variety of authors from several magazines (Masih xxvii). In 1947, *Writers: Try Short Shorts!*, edited by Mildred I. Reid and Delmar E. Bordeaux, included some early history along with various types of stories. From the "slicks to the pulps," over two hundred magazines and newspapers were publishing short-short stories as regular features. The stories were also being broadcast on radio (Reid and Bordeaux 25). In 1948, *The Best Short Short Stories from Colliers* was edited by Barthold Fles, who viewed short-shorts as an art form representative of America as much as "the subway, the tabloid, and the automat. It is capsule narrative, and it can be read and digested in a hurry" (Masih xxx).

In the 1950s, two influential anthologies appeared. *Short Short Stories* by William Ransom Wood (1951) was created for classroom use and included stories by renowned writers of short short stories. In 1952, the first annual short-short story series anthology was published. Edited by Robert Oberfirst, the series ran until 1960 (Masih xxx).

1960s and 1970s Collections and Anthologies
During this time period, the work of Jorge Luis Borges and Richard Brautigan had a strong influence on literary flash fiction writers. James E. Irby says of Borges' work, "Greater and more important than his intellectual ingenuity is Borges's consummate skill as a narrator, his magic in obtaining the most powerful effects with a strict economy of means" (xx). Irby also notes that approaching blindness caused Borges to concentrate on writing much shorter fictions that were, in part, easier to dictate (xxii). Some of his many stories are as short as a half page. In 1971, Richard Brautigan added to the experimentation and expansion of short-short work with the publication of his only story collection, *Revenge of the Lawn*. Many of the collected stories, which are less than a half page, inspired interest in short-short stories that blurred genre boundaries.

In 1973, Robert Coover and Kent Dixon edited *Stone Wall Book of Short Fictions*, which is likely the first anthology of literary short shorts published in the United States. In their introduction, the editors acknowledge the growing diversity and importance of this type of writing, and they collected a range of stories from the straightforward to the highly experimental. Later, in 1976, Robert Coover and Elliot Anderson coedited "Minute Stories" in *TriQuarterly*, which featured eighty-seven stories, some as short as an average paragraph and some two or three pages long.

1980s Anthologies

The 1980s saw the continued and increased publication of both literary flash fiction and genre flash fiction, offering a clearer indication that flash fiction can accommodate stories of all types. In 1980 *Microcosmic Tales: 100 Wondrous Science Fiction Short-Short Stories* was edited by Isaac Asimov, Martin H. Greenberg, and Joseph D. Olander. The stories are "quick dips in the ocean of the mind," and "a few refreshing minutes away from the ordinary and prosaic" (xxi). Four years later, *100 Great Fantasy Short Short Stories* was published, edited by Asimov, Terry Carr, and Greenberg. In both anthologies, some of the stories are 2,000 words or fewer with many as short as a half page.

Short-Shorts: Anthology of the Shortest Stories (1983), edited by Irving Howe and Ilana Wiener Howe, includes literary flash fiction pieces from around the world. The median length for included stories is 1,500 words (with some as short as only a couple of pages). The introduction includes a brief and informative discussion of the various types of short-short fiction. The editors claim that with this type of writing "everything depends on intensity, one sweeping blow of perception. In the short short the writer gets no second chance. Either he strikes through at once or he's lost" (xi).

In 1986, two anthologies appeared that also helped to define the genre and extend its readership. One, *Short Short Stories*, edited by Jack David and John Redfern, included stories by Canadian and international authors. Featuring pieces that are two to six pages long, the anthology was used in college classrooms (Stern 18). The second anthology, *Sudden Fiction: American Short-Shorts*, edited by Robert Shapard and James Thomas, features stories ranging from one to five pages and includes a good discussion of this type of writing. It also includes a search for a fitting name for literary short-short stories. The editors' preferred label is "sudden fiction" because, as Robert Shapard notes, the stories are "all suddenly just there" (xvi). Some other names considered include snappers, blasters, minute, quick, flash, micro, and skinny fictions.

In 1987, *Four-Minute Fictions: 50 Short-Short Stories from the North American Review* was edited by Robley Wilson Jr., who continues to examine flash fiction as its own genre. The anthology includes a brief introduction to fifty stories that range from 200 to 2,000 words. Wilson notes that each of the stories "works in its own way, on its own terms" (iii).

Sudden Fiction International: 60 Short-Short Stories (1989), edited by Robert Shapard and James Thomas, includes a section where writers, editors, and theorists comment on characteristics of very short stories. More attention is given to names, including names used in other cultures. Some names used in China are pocket-sized stories, palm-size stories, and smoke-long stories (Shapard and Thomas, *Sudden Fiction International* 299). Nearly thirty years later, all over the literary world, writers and editors continue to wrestle with what to call these brief stories.

1990s Anthologies

Flash Fiction: 72 Very Short Stories (1992), edited by James Thomas, Denise Thomas, and Tom Hazuka, explores how short can a story be and still be viewed as a story. The selected stories run between 250 and 750 words. The editors chose the name "flash" fiction "because the stories would be apprehended "all at once" (12). The snappy name caught on and became the term of choice and habit, especially on the Internet, for literary short-short stories in general.

Sudden Fiction (Continued) (1996) was edited by Robert Shapard and James Thomas who claim that "the spirit of experimentation continues to be most alive these days in the shorter forms. No longer relegated to special sections, they are scattered as regular fare throughout the pages of an even larger number of magazines, including the larger-circulation magazines" (12). The editors also point out that one thing remains constant, that "each story revels in its own elements of surprise; each, whether traditional or experimental, proves that a tale told quickly offers pleasure long past its telling" (12).

Helping to push the limits of flash fiction while further lessening the word count, in 1996 editor Jerome Stern published *Micro Fiction: An Anthology of Really Short Stories*. Stern featured winners and finalists from the annual World's Best Short Short Story Contest, which had been running since 1986. The length limit set by Stern was between 250 to 300 words, and he derived it "from the notion of an author's most familiar unit of measure, the single typewritten page" (19). Stern claims, "This is a strange little form, demanding fictional strategies that are both ancient and yet to be discovered" (16).

Another sign of the growing interest in flash fiction was the appearance in 1997 of Roberta Allen's *Fast Fiction: Creating Fiction in Five Minutes*, an instructional book on how to turn five-minute writings into short-short stories. Allen says, "A short short is a story that gets quickly to the core and reveals the essence of a situation or moment in very few words" (40). The book includes writing prompts along with many story examples by her students and by various renowned writers.

Twenty-First-Century Anthologies

The spread of flash fiction continues in the twenty-first century, and the spreading brings even more interest in and focus on protean flash fiction. Additional experimentation is ongoing. Essays on flash fiction appear in more books, magazines, and in more and more Internet publications. Several online courses arrive on the scene (in colleges, adult education, and online), more literary journals seek flash fiction to publish, and many new flash fiction anthologies and collections appear as well.

In 2003, *Sudden Stories: The MAMMOTH Book of Miniscule Fiction*, edited by Dinty W. Moore, includes stories that are mostly

350 words or fewer (with a few slightly over). In addition to the several stories in the anthology, various writers continue to grapple with an effective definition for this type of fiction. Also published in 2003 was *Crafting the Very Short Story: An Anthology of 100 Masterpieces*, edited by Mark Mills (2003), which contains 100 stories and twenty-six critical essays. The anthology, clearly meant for creative writing instruction, includes stories by renowned authors from various cultures, including Fyodor Dostoevsky, Nadine Gordimer, James Joyce, Clarice Lispector, Vladimir Nobokov, Lorrie Moore, and others. The book also includes text analyses by distinguished writers, critics, and scholars.

The matter of length continued to be an important issue in *Flash Fiction Forward: 80 Very Short Stories*, edited by James Thomas and Robert Shapard and published in 2006. The editors stuck to their original maximum length limitation—750 words— for two reasons: 1) because that is the length of Ernest Hemingway's classic, "A Very Short Story" and 2) because they feel a reader should not have to turn a page more than once (12). Genre definition continued to be debated in *PP/FF: An Anthology*, edited by Peter Connors, which was also published in 2006. Connors features both flash fiction and prose poetry, preferring not to separate the two and pointing out that "*PP/FF* is meant as a label that locates the territory of prose poetry and flash fiction by symbol rather than by language prejudiced by old genre baggage. *PP/FF* is prose poetry and flash fiction balanced on a makeshift teeter-totter that never lands" (9).

During 2006 and 2007, some prominent magazines also featured short-short work. In 2006, *Wired* magazine published "Very Short Stories," six-word science fiction pieces by thirty-three writers. Also in 2006, *Esquire* featured "napkin stories," which were written on five-inch-square cocktail napkins. The magazine solicited hundreds of stories and published nearly eighty pieces by many renowned writers ("Esquire's Cocktail Party"). Then in 2007, *O, The Oprah Magazine* ran several flash fiction pieces, all of three hundred words or fewer and all by writers known for their flash fiction.

While focusing on stories from the twenty-first century, in *New Sudden Fiction: Short Stories from America and Beyond* (2007), editors Robert Shapard and James Thomas sought a distinction within the genre of short-short fiction. "Stories of only a page or two seemed . . . different not only in length but in nature; they evoked a single moment, or an idea; whereas a five-page story, however experimental, was more akin to the traditional short story" (Shapard and Thomas, *New Sudden* 15). For the new anthology, they read nearly six years of magazine issues, web pages, and books (16) and discovered that "suddens," even more than "flashes," were "the regular contents of the literaries and the big slicks and in single-author book collections" (17). They found that "the turn of the page" took readers "more deeply into the realm of story" (18). The differences will continue to be explored.

You Have Time For This: Contemporary American Short-Short Stories, edited by Mark Budman and Tom Hazuka (2007), contains flash fiction of 500 words or fewer. The editors refine what they are seeking and in their view "Flash fiction rests on a tripod of plot, language and characters" (10). They also claim that "Rich, literary fiction can never be completely understood by writer, by editor, or by reader. Various possible interpretations are always possible." Readers, they say, "must cooperate in the process of making sense of a text" (Budman and Hazuka 10).

One of the more popular and influential anthologies of essays about flash fiction that includes many samples of flash fiction is *Field Guide to Writing Flash Fiction: Tips from Editors, Teachers, and Writers in the Field*, edited by Tara Masih (2009). Each essay in the anthology includes an example of the type of flash fiction under discussion. The essay writers are prominent in the field of flash fiction and the example stories are by writers of strong and established writing talent.

In the twenty-first century flash continues to gain international attention. *Sudden Fiction Latino: Short-Short Stories from the United States and Latin America*, edited by Robert Shapard, James Thomas, and Ray Gonzales (2010), features stories of 1,500 words or fewer and offers an excellent introduction by Luisa Valenzuela. In this historic gathering, the editors attempt to show "how the short-short form transcends borders and that Latin American literature's influence continues, even as Latinos create their own literary tradition" (Shapard, Thomas, and Gonzales 14). With international flash fiction, genre definition is also an issue. In 2014, for example, Alan Ziegler edited *Short: An International Anthology of Five Centuries of Short-Short Stories, Prose Poems, Brief Essays, And Other Short Prose Forms*. The anthology includes prose poems, short-short stories, brief essays, fragments as well as unclassified pieces, all under 1,250 words. Ziegler notes that "the concept of genre is slippery, shape-shifting, and sometimes nonexistent. One writer's prose poem may be another's flash fiction or brief essay" (xxv). The worldwide conversation on flash fiction continues in *Flash Fiction International: Very Short Stories from around the World* (2015) edited by James Thomas, Robert Shapard, and Christopher Merrill. The anthology includes a "flash theory" section with thoughts on the topic from various prominent writers. The flash fiction pieces included are by authors ancient to modern.

In the past ten years, online magazines have been increasingly publishing flash fiction. *Narrative*, an online publication, began publishing a segment in 2010 called "6 Word Stories" by writers who "demonstrate their mastery of the sword thrust form." In 2014, Tara Laskowski edited *SmokeLong Quarterly: The Best of the First Ten Years, 2003–2013*. That same year, *KYSO Flash Anthology: Volume 1* was published and edited by Clare MacQueen. The following year, MacQueen edited and published *Volume II*. Both KYSO anthologies include stories up to 1,000 words.

Collections of highly original flash stories previously published elsewhere are now quite common. A new series, and another indication that flash fiction is here to stay, began in 2015 when *The Best Small Fictions* was published. Tara L. Masih served as series editor, and the first volume is guest edited by Robert Olen Butler. The selections are considered the best stories received in "traditional flash form and in its subgenres: micro, Twitter fiction, iStories, fictional prose poetry and fictional haibun, and anything in between" (Masih and Butler x). All stories included are 1,000 words or fewer. A second volume was published in 2016, and that volume has Stuart Dybek serving as guest editor with Masih again as the series editor. According to Dybek, "this is . . . an anthology where writers locate their work along a continuum of infinite gradations that spans the poles of fiction and poetry, and of the narrative and lyric" (Masih and Dybek xvi). Also in 2016, *FLASHed: Sudden Stories in Comics and Prose*, edited by Josh Neufeld and Sari Wilson was published, and the work pushes boundaries and cross fertilizes creative communities. The stories in the anthology are arranged in triptychs, where each grouping creates a conversation between forty-five prose writers and cartoonists and between the forms of prose and the comics.

Flash fiction continues to attempt to rebel against various rules of literature and often tries to go against reader expectations. Flash fiction is various and protean. It is made up of straightforward stories that have a clear plot, and of stories that are plotless, such as mood or tone pieces. Stories using second person or dialogue only work well in short-short fiction as do monologues, which are often tedious in longer fiction. There are stories using only clichés, stories written in imperative mode, stories buried within acknowledgments pages, stories done in Q & A style, stories that are all telling and no showing, stories where the narrator is both "I" and "you," pieces with only one character name shared by several people, and stories where the protagonist and antagonist cannot be differentiated. There are stories two or three pages long using just one or sometimes two or three sentences, and stories done as stage presentations, stories that offer a choice of endings, metafictional stories, stories where the metaphor becomes literal, and so much more.

Technological Changes Bring Adaptations

Technological innovations have helped increase the range and form of flash fiction. During the 1930s and 1940s short-shorts were common features on radio broadcasts, and modern-day flash fiction continues to be presented on programs such as *National Public Radio* (NPR). Beginning in 2003, flash fiction also became a staple of online digital podcasts such as *Flash Fiction Online*, *No Extra Words*, and *Every Day Fiction*. The podcast *Pseudopod* specializes in flash fiction horror stories, *The Drabblecast* features weird stories,

Flash Pulp broadcasts pulp stories, and *Escape Pod* includes flash fiction along with longer pieces.

Flash Fiction Musical Interpretations

Musical adaptations of flash fictions demonstrate a considerable imaginative cross-fertilization. Maurice Ravel (1875–1937) a French composer, wanted to say with notes what a poet uses words to express so he adapted Aloysius Bertrand's *Gaspard de la nuit* to music. As noted earlier, Bertrand's work was inspiration to both Charles Baudelaire and Stephen Mallarmé. What Ravel did earlier with prose poetry, creative musicians of today are doing with flash fiction. In 2015, *NANO Fiction* paired flash fiction with music to create the blending of two artistic forms. There were two live performances with the fall issue of *NANO Fiction* featuring the music, stories, and sheet music as triptychs. The project was inspired by *sehr Rasch*, a "German tempo marking for very fast music," and Texas composers Russell Podgorsek and Hermes Camacho created "full—yet very short—arrangements" for each of the stories. Most recently, *Symphony Space* of New York City has joined with Experiments in Opera to create six short operas based on stories in the flash and sudden fiction anthologies. The "Flash Operas," ten to fifteen minutes in duration, will be fully staged and presented in May 2017.

Video and Film Adaptations

Professionals and amateurs have adapted many flash fiction pieces to video and film, whether authorized or unauthorized. Many are viewable on YouTube and Vimeo. Further, a number of film adaptations of flash stories have garnered praise at film festivals. Among these is Peter Markus's story, "Good Brother," from his collection of the same title and which is included in *New Sudden Fiction*. The film adaptation, produced and directed by Mathew Zacharias and Greg Fadell, premiered at Slamdance Film Festival in 2002. Lawrence C. Connolly's short-short "Echoes," published in over a dozen publications worldwide, was twice adapted to film. The first, a film festival production, was filmed in Hollywood by Steve

Muscarella. The second was directed by Rodney Altman and won Best Achievement in Cinematography at the Fusion Film Festival in New York City in March 2004. Gathering several film festival awards is an adaptation of Katharine Weber's "Sleeping." The story was originally published in *Vestal Review* and later republished in Thomas and Shapard's *Flash Fiction Forward: 80 Very Short Stories*. Another award winner at numerous film festivals is director Henry Zaballos' adaptation of Stace Budzko's story "How to Set a House on Fire," which was first published by *Southeast Review* and then in *Flash Fiction Forward: 80 Very Short Stories*.

Foreign language flash stories have also drawn interest from filmmakers. Lynda Sexson's story "Turning" was originally translated into Japanese by Haruki Murakami for inclusion in his anthology titled *Birthday Stories*, and the entire anthology was then translated into English. Later the story was adapted to film by Karni and Saul and shown at several film festivals, where it won a BAFTA award and was part of the BBC Film Network's BBC Drama Shorts 2009 in conjunction with Lighthouse Arts and Training and BBC Writersroom. Eduardo Galeano's classification-defying short-short "Los Nadies" ("The Nobodies"), from his collection *El libro de los abrazos* (*The Book of Embraces*) was adapted to film by Spanish director Carlos Salgado and by German animator Laura Saenger.

Two of Pamela Painter's flash fictions were also adapted to film. The first, "God," was originally published in *Story Quarterly*, and the second, "Office at Night," originally appeared in *SmokeLong Quarterly*; both stories are collected in the volume *Wouldn't You Like to Know*. The film versions for both, adapted and produced by Anthony Russo, were shown at the Marketplace Festival in 2013 and University at Redlands in 2012.

Flash Fiction into Feature-Length Films

Italo Calvino created his novel, *Invisible Cities*, using several stand-alone short-short stories. Alan Lightman did similar with his *Einstein's Dreams*. Likewise, some filmmakers have created longer, even feature-length films by combining and adapting several short-short stories to film.

In 1993, stories by Raymond Carver, renowned for writing short-short work, were made into a feature-length film directed by Robert Altman. The film, *Short Cuts*, is comprised of several of Carver's short stories and one of his poems. The film won the Golden Globe Award in 1994 and was nominated for other awards. While some of the short stories in the film are longer than the usual flash fiction length, the film likely inspired montage films that followed. In 1995, Barry Yourgrau's flash fiction collection, *The Sadness of Sex*, was made into a feature-length film of the same name. Created from fifteen flash fiction pieces, the romantic comedy montage, also starring Yourgrau, depicts many hilarious phases and types of love, and the stories are separated by different types of camera work and by various styles of music. More recently, *Exquisite Corpse*, filmed in 2006, is an experimental montage, a collaboration between independent and international film directors, multimedia artists, and animators. The film is a series of film adaptations from Michael Arnzen's poetry and from his award-winning flash fiction collection *100 Jolts: Shockingly Short Stories*.

Etgar Keret's flash fiction pieces have been adapted to individual short-short films, to feature-length films, and to the stage. Some of his short-short stories adapted to stand-alone mini films include "One Hundred Percent," "Monkey Say, Monkey Do," "Good-Looking Couple," "What Do We Have In Our Pockets," "Crazy Glue, and "A Buck's Worth." His "Lieland" premiered at the Cannes Film Festival in 2013 and did a festival circuit run in the United States and Europe. A 2008 collaboration with Tatia Rosenthal wove several of Keret's flash fiction stories together to create a feature-length film titled *$9.99*. In 2016 a play, *Suddenly a Knock on the Door*, also based on several Keret stories, was adapted for the stage by playwright Robin Goldfin. Directed by David Carson, the play ran for two weeks in June 2016 at the East Village in New York (Merwin).

Flash fiction refuses to stay still, refuses to remain in the shape of text alone. This world-wide protean form of writing thrives on experimentation. It is adaptable, makes leaps from text to audio, to music, to opera, to stage, to video, and to film. Flash fiction is a sign of our times and of our need for condensed and thought provoking shorter fiction that takes little time to read in a world overflowing with too much information. Flash fiction has also inspired the popularity of flash memoirs, flash creative nonfiction, American haibun, paragraph-length prose poetry, and short-short plays. All of these are being read by appreciative audiences all over the world. Gitte Mose sums it up well: ". . . writers of short shorts are able to show the world as fickle and immense, a world we cannot fathom but perhaps approach when it is captured at the "roots" of a kind of fiction that is probing and challenging the capabilities of language." These writers show, says Mose, that "the world is full of possibilities, that it can be examined and told by imposing their artistic form on some small corner of chaos" (93).

Works Cited

Allen, Roberta. *Creating Fiction in Five Minutes*. Story Press, 1997.

Anderson, Elliot, and Robert Coover, editors. "Minute Stories." *TriQuarterly*, vol. *35*, Winter 1976.

Arnzen, Michael. "Exquisite Corpse." *Gorelets*, n.d. Accessed 30 July 2016.

Asimov, Isaac, Martin H. Greenberg, Joseph D. Olander, editors. *Microcosmic Tales: 100 Wondrous Science Fiction Short-Short Stories*. Daw Books, 1992.

Asimov, Isaac, Terry Carr, Martin H. Greenberg, editors. *100 Great Fantasy Short Short Stories*. Doubleday, 1984.

Austin, Mary. *One-Smoke Stories*. Swallow Press/ Ohio UP 1934.

Baudelaire, Charles. *Paris Spleen* 1869. Translated by Louise Varese, New Directions, 1970.

Berenshtin, Nava, director. "Monkey Say, Monkey Do." *YouTube*, uploaded by The Brightside, 28 Feb. 2014. www.youtube.com/watch?v=5jrwBCJ7kz0/. Accessed 28 July 2016.

Borges, Jorge Luis. *Labyrinths: Selected Stories & Other Writings*. New Directions, 1964.

Boyle, Kay, Laurence Vail, and Nina Conarain, editors. *365 Days*. Harcourt, Brace and Co., 1936.

Brautigan, Richard. *Revenge of the Lawn/ The Abortion/ So the Wind Won't Blow It All Away.* Omnibus Edition, Houghton Mifflin, 1995.

Brown, Fredric. *Nightmares and Geezenstacks.* Bantam, 1961.

Budman, Mark, and Tom Hazuka, editors. *You Have Time for This: Contemporary American Short-Short Stories.* Ooligan Press, 2007.

Budzko, Stace. "How To Set a House on Fire." *YouTube*, uploaded by Bay Area Video Coalition, 6 Aug. 2009, www.youtube.com/watch?v=t2RiZYJaiFs/. Accessed 27 July 2016.

Calvino, Italo. *Invisible Cities.* Translated by William Weaver, Harcourt Brace & Co., 1974.

Short Cuts. Stories by Raymond Carver. Trailer. *YouTube*, uploaded by Video Detective, 29 Oct. 2014. www.youtube.com/watch?v=YK_PoMY0MOw/. Accessed 31 July 2016.

Connolly, Lawrence C. "Echoes." *YouTube*, uploaded by Rodney Altman, 19 July, 2011. www.youtube.com/watch?v=a5qYvUOuFwQ/. Accessed 27 July 2016.

Connors, Peter, editor. *PP/FF: An Anthology.* Starcherone Books, 2006.

Coover, Robert, and Kent Dixon, editors. *The Stone Wall Book of Short Fictions.* Stone Wall Press, 1973.

David, Jack, and John Redfern, editors. *Short Short Stories.* ECW Press, 1986.

Dukic, Goran, director. "What Do We Have In Our Pockets?" *YouTube*, 16 Jan 2013, www.youtube.com/watch?v=6qrwwM1Hgwk/. Accessed 28 July 2016.

"Esquire's Cocktail Party: Stories Written on Napkins." *Poets and Writers*, 29 Jan. 2007. Accessed 29 November 2016.

Feintuch, Danna, director. "Good-Looking Couple." *YouTube*, uploaded by aswingkido, 12 Mar. 2009, www.youtube.com/watch?v=WIFpHJILVTg/. Accessed 28 July 2016.

"Flash Operas." *Symphony Space*, n.d., www.symphonyspace.org/event/9401/Music/flash-operas/. Accessed 31 July 2016.

Galeano, Eduardo. *The Book of Embraces.* Translated by Cedric Belfrage, W.W. Norton., 1991.

_____. "Los Nadies" ("The Nobodies"), filmed by Carlos Salgado. *Moving Poems*, 23 Apr. 2015. Accessed 28 July 2016.

_____. "Los Nadies" ("the Nobodies"), filmed by Laura Saenger. *Moving Poems*, 23 Apr. 2015. Accessed 28 July 2016.

Grossman, Silvia, director. "Lieland." *YouTube*, uploaded by Shorts Showcase, 28 Aug. 2013, www.youtube.com/watch?v=JjCx5BkNv8Q/. Accessed 28 July 2016.

Hemingway, Ernest. *The Complete Short Stories of Ernest Hemingway (The Finca Vigia Edition)*. Simon & Shuster, 1998.

Howe, Irving, and Ilana Wiener Howe, editors. *Short Shorts: An Anthology of the Shortest Stories* Bantam Books, 1983.

Johnson, Peter, editor. *The Best of the Prose Poem: An International Journal*. White Pine Press, 2000.

Keret, Etgar, and Tatia Rosenthal, directors. *$9.99*. Trailer. *YouTube*, 3 Dec. 2008. www.youtube.com/watch?v=TO2_hr_y3mA. Accessed 27 July 2016.

_____, and Shira Geffen, directors. "What About Me?" *YouTube*, uploaded by artfortheworld001, 11 Mar. 2009. www.youtube.com/watch?v=baUG5er7s7A/. Accessed 28 July 2016.

Laskowski, Tara, editor. *SmokeLong Quarterly: The Best of the First Ten Years, 2003–2013*. Matter Press, 2013.

Lightman, Alan. *Einstein's Dreams*. Bloomsbury, 1993.

MacQueen, Clare, editor. *KYSO Flash Anthology,Volume 1: Knock Your Socks Off Art and Literature*. KYSO Flash, 2014.

_____, editor. *KYSO Flash Anthology Volume 2. Knock Your Socks Off Art and Literature.* KYSO Flash, 2015.

Marcus, Peter. "Good Brother" by Peter Markus. Produced by Matt Zacharias and Greg Fadell. *Vimeo*, 30 Oct. 2014. Accessed 27 July 2016.

Masih, Tara L., series editor, and Robert Olen Butler, guest editor. *The Best Small Fictions 2015*. Queen's Ferry Press, 2015.

_____, series editor, and Stuart Dybek, guest editor. *The Best Small Fictions 2015*. Queens Ferry Press, 2016.

Masih, Tara L, editor. *Field Guide to Writing Flash Fiction: Tips from Editors, Teachers, and Writers in the Field*. Rose Metal Press, 2009.

Merwin, Ted. "Keret Comes to the Stage." *The Jewish Week*, 31 May 2016, www.thejewishweek.com/arts/theater/jew-vs-jew-onstage%20

%22post%20a%20comment%22%20~taciturn?page=0%2C1/. Accessed 31 July 2016.

"Micr-O Fiction: 8 Provocative Writers Tell Us a Story in 300 Words or Less." *O, The Oprah Magazine*, July 2006, www.oprah.com/ omagazine/Micro-Fiction-Short-Stories-from-Famous-Writers/. Accessed 31 July 2016.

Mills, Mark, editor. *Crafting the Very Short Story: An Anthology of 100 Masterpieces*. Prentice Hall, 2003.

Moore, Dinty W., editor. *Sudden Stories: The Mammoth Book of Miniscule Fiction*. Mammoth Press, 2003.

Mose, Gitte. "Danish Short Shorts in the 1990s and the Jena-Romantic Fragments." *The Art of Brevity: Excursions in Short Fiction Theory and Analysis*, edited by Per Winther, Jakob Lothe, and Hans H. Skei. U of South Carolina P, 2004.

Neufeld, Josh, and Sari Wilson, editors. *FLASHed: Sudden Stories in Comics and Prose*: Pressgang, 2016.

Painter, Pamela. "God." *YouTube*, uploaded by cronogeo, 20 Dec. 2011, www.youtube.com/watch?v=7uPjnhFzE78/. Accessed 27 July 2016.

_____. "A View: Office at Night." *YouTube*, uploaded by cronogeo, 15 Nov. 2010, www.youtube.com/watch?v=M4DN36j8p88/. Accessed 27 July 2016.

Reid, Mildred I., and Delmar E. Bordeaux, editors. *Writers Try Short Shorts: All Known Types With Examples*. Bellevue Books, 1947.

"Sehr Flash: Fiction Becomes Music." *NANO Fiction*, vol. 9, no.1, 7 Sept. 2015, nanofiction.org/events/2015/09/sehr-flash-fiction-becomes-music/. Accessed 11 Nov. 2016.

Rosenthal, Tatia, director. "Crazy Glue." *YouTube*, 23 May 2006, www. youtube.com/watch?v=6UyzD-GxNYU/. Accessed 28 July 2016.

Sexson, Lynda. "Turning" by Lynda Sexson, directed by Karni and Saul. *Vimeo*, 17 June 2013. Accessed 27 July 2016.

Shapard, Robert, and James Thomas, editors. *New Sudden Fiction: Short-Short Stories from America and Beyond*. W. W. Norton, 2007.

_____, editors. *Sudden Fiction: American Short-Short Stories*. Peregrine Smith Books, 1986.

_____, editors. *Sudden Fiction (Continued): 60 New Short-Short Stories*. W. W. Norton, 1996.

_____, editors. *Sudden Fiction International: 60 Short Short Stories.* W. W. Norton, 1989.

Shapard, Robert, James Thomas, and Ray Gonzales, editors. *Sudden Fiction Latino: Short-Short Stories from the United States and Latin America.* W. W. Norton, 2010.

"Six-Word Stories | Narrative Magazine." *Narrative Magazine*, 05 Oct. 2014. Accessed 31 July 2016.

Stern, Jerome, editor. *Micro Fiction: An Anthology of Really Short Stories.* W. W. Norton, 1996.

Thomas, James, Denise Thomas, and Tom Hazuka, editors. *Flash Fiction: 72 Very Short Stories.* W. W. Norton, 1992.

_____. *Flash Fiction Forward: 80 Very Short Stories.* W. W. Norton, 2006.

Thomas, James, Robert Shapard, Christopher Merrill, editors. *Flash Fiction International: Very Short Stories From Around the World.* W. W. Norton, 2015.

Todorov, Tzvetan. *Genres in Discourse.* Translated by Catherine Porter, Cambridge UP, 1990.

"Very Short Stories." *Wired*, 1 Nov. 2006, www.wired.com/2006/11/very-short-stories/. Accessed 11 Nov. 2016.

Weber, Katharine. "Sleeping" by Katharine Weber, directed by Doug Conant. *YouTube*, 30 Mar. 2008. Accessed 27 July 2016.

Wilson, Robley, Jr., editor. *Four Minute Fictions: 50 Short-Short Stories from the North American Review.* Word Beat Press, 1987.

Yourgrau, Barry. *The Sadness of Sex* by Barry Yourgrau, directed by Rupert Wainwright. *YouTube*, 17 Feb. 2011. Accessed 28 July, 2016.

Ziegler, Alan, editor. Short: *An International Anthology of Five Centuries of Short-Short Stories, Prose Poems, Brief Essays, and Other Short Prose Forms.* Persea Books, 2014.

Flash Fiction and the Critical Scholarship: A Search for Independence

Randall Brown

At a conference's dinner reception for workshop presenters, a well-known poet asked me what I wrote, and when I said flash fiction, he replied, "Is that so you don't have to write middles and endings?" This sense that flash fiction pieces are failed longer pieces—that they desire to be something other than what they are—is reflected in a view of flash "as hack work, exercises, or preliminary studies for works on a larger scale, using generic designations like 'drafts,' 'reflections,' and 'experiments'" (Mose 82). As this opening anecdote illustrates, flash fiction has had its challenges finding its place at the literary dinner table—not quite a short story, not quite a poem, never sure of its word count borders, something that seems to have failed to reach its full potential of being a full-blown something. Also, flash fiction's accessibility makes flash prone to dismissal. As M. Kaspar and M. Kasper write, "Short-prose and photography are both democratic. Shucks, anyone can do them well. Shallow critics dismiss them for this" (162). It's easy to react to flash's small size with small regard. For example, the translator of Yasunari Kawabata's palm-of-hand stories confesses that he "mistook their subtlety for slightness, their lack of emphasis for pointlessness" (Dunlop xi). In his study of ktsartsarim ("short shorts") in Israeli literature, Adam Rovner found that such fiction "has been subject to a battery of opposing and muddled claims by scholars and practitioners, in much the same way the short story has suffered from haphazard attention from critics." He continues, "The lack of rigorous theorization . . . indicates its hierarchically inferior position vis-à-vis the novel, and even the short story, in contemporary critical discourse" (Rovner 113).

Set against that bias is a growing number of critical theories and scholarship devoted to very short stories. As W. Nelles argues, "The popularity of the [flash fiction] genre (and the increasing number of college courses devoted to it), combined with the number of distinguished writers who have increasingly come to practice it, justifies further attention" (88). What follows is a look at what that "further attention"—the critical scholarship and theoretical articles—has revealed about the nature, literary value, origins, and cultural significance of flash fiction.

When scholars and literary critics begin their explorations of this genre, it makes sense that they have to think about the nature of their chosen topic, and thus they might begin with a genre study of flash fiction. *What is a flash fiction piece? What makes it flash fiction and not something else? What exactly is it that is being studied?* Length might be a good starting place to begin such genre studies, but most critics don't consider flash's length to be a defining factor, taking their cue from short story theorists, such as Norman Friedman and his seminal article "What Makes a Short Story Short?" in which he argued "to haggle over the borderlines [of length] is almost always fruitless" (103). In looking at the real-word guidelines for flash fiction, however, those interested in flash might see length as *the* defining factor. If length is indeed a reader's concern, well-known flash fiction editor Robert Shapard provides some guidance in "The Remarkable Reinvention of Very Short Fiction": "On average, a very short fiction is ten times shorter than a traditional story, but numbers don't tell us everything" (46). Because word-count does not provide the full picture about very short fiction, critical discussion steps into that space beyond the quantitative to act as a guide for readers and writers to the qualitative.

Taking Friedman's advice to focus on more qualitative traits, for example, Austin Wright developed these characteristics for the short story, which he argues "tends to be between five hundred words long and the length of Joyce's 'The Dead'" (51). His characteristics include the following: (1) it deals with character and action; (2) this action tends to be externally simple; (3) the short story tends to be more strongly unified than other short prose narrative forms; (4) it has a preference for plots of small magnitude, plots of discovery, static or disclosure plots, Joycean epiphanies, and the like; and (5) a short story tends to leave significant things to inference (Wright 51–52).

In doing the same for the smallest of fictions—the microfiction—W. Nelles writes, "Specifically, I propose that a generic distinction may be drawn between short stories and microstories on the basis of six key narrative elements: action, character, setting, temporality (especially duration and order), intertextuality, and closure" (88). To detail such attributes through critical analysis of a genre is partly the focus of this kind of scholarship, and these discussions and debates not only focus on defining characteristics but also upon their overall effect on the reading, something this essay will discuss later.

However, if a brief definition is what you're after, then Allan H. Pasco's pithy entry for short story is an interesting starting point. He writes, "[A] short story is a short, literary prose fiction" (411). It might follow, then, that flash fiction is a very short, literary prose fiction. Tara L. Masih's "In Pursuit of the Short Short Story" defines flash:

> as a story in miniature, a work of art carved on a grain of rice—something of import to the artist or writer that is confined and reduced, either by design or outcome, into a small square using the structural devices of prose line and paragraph form with the purpose of creating an intense, emotional impact. (Masih xi)

John Gerlach defines flash fiction by this genre's ability "to extend our imagination along the lines of characters, and conflict, space and time" (82). For Mark Mills, flash can be defined by its end result—"evocative structural design, extremely pure sentences, and radiant distillations of light upon the soul" (xiv). A number of factors—e.g., structure, artistic intent, language, and, reader response—arise in these definitions, with the notion that what is created is "something of import." Short-shorts flash something brilliant and radiant beyond their confined borders. A closer look inside reveals those additional defining characteristics that make such pieces bedazzle, both for writers and readers.

Attention. In her critical essay "What is Flash Fiction," Katey Schultz, author of *Flashes of War*, does make a case for length as a defining feature: "Flash fiction stories are 250-750 words, but this length has more to do with quality of attention than duration of attention" (par. 5). Notice how she moves from the quantitative to the qualitative, with length being more of a preference than an important defining trait. The attention demanded by flash, though, becomes primary for Schultz. Federico Paccchioni similarly points to attention in his study of Italian very short fiction: "This narrative compression channels the attention of the reader right to the core of the story and onto what we might call the emotional highway of its dramatic dynamics" (84). Credited with giving these very tiny stories the name *flash fiction*, James Thomas also argues that their "success depends not on their length but on their depth, their clarity of vision, their human significance—the extent to which the reader is able to recognize in them the real stuff of real life" (12). He believes flash fiction views "the meaningful glance as more consequential than the long (but less intense, less informed) look or stare" (12). These "fixations of the moment" with their "focus on the singular" (Mose 83) zoom in upon the world and its particulars, revealing through their sharp lens the world's fine points, its hidden recesses and depths, bringing to light the essential nitty-gritty, the beating heart, the big-league bottom line.

Brevity. Writing about Italian very short fiction, Pacchioni finds brevity—defined as "conciseness" (84)—to be a key characteristic of flash, one that allows readers "to tap into the story's meaning shortly after the reading has begun" (84). This "microscopic concision" (Dunlop xii) creates the sense that readers "experience everything at the same level and at the same time as the characters and narrator" (Mose 84). Rovner also sees brevity as a key component within flash, but views its effect somewhat differently. He writes, "Some narratives enact a poetics of amplification (*amplificatio*), which tends to increase reader anticipation. Other narratives enact a poetics of contraction (*brevitas*), which tends to decrease reader anticipation" (Rovner 116). Flash desires its ending almost right from the outset, something that contracts rather than draws out, giving birth to a new way of looking at "time, and therefore, of causality and human agency" (116). In his look at the Moroccan short-short, Abdellatif Akib also focuses on brevity, in particular the use of "omission and implication," "terse" language, and "concentrated meaning" that "suggests through symbols and hints through signs" (83). These techniques introduce a new challenge to reading, as signifiers now imply, hint at, or suggest the signified. A single word might represent a character's backstory, for example. And thus each word carries with it the need for close attention. Robert Shapard and James Thomas in the editors' note to *Flash Fiction Forward* posit, "[Readers] may allow an entire page in a novel to be forgettable, but [they] approach a flash fiction as if it all may be memorable" (13).

Subtraction. The story's reliance on subtraction is something John Barth recognized in short story writers also: "That the genre of the novel tends toward inclusion, that of the short story toward exclusion, goes without saying . . . exceptions granted, we may safely generalize that short-story writers as a class, from Poe to Paley, incline to see how much they can leave out" (26). Ibrahim Taha's study of the Arabic very short story led him to "three main techniques employed in the structure of the text: paralipsis, summary, and ellipsis." Summary and ellipsis will figure into later conversations about flash, but here *paralipsis* is the focus, defined as "subtraction of data concerning the characters, their identities, their social status, their professions, their ages, etc." (Taha 63) This technique of brevity, Taha asserts, "turns the story into a more general and non-local entity . . . so that every reader, at any time or place, can treat it as if were written especially for him or her and dealt with his or her personal problems" (63). "Characters," Gitte Mose believes, "are reduced in almost every respect" (84), and "characters of a flash fiction . . . are endowed with certain ethical, intellectual and sentimental traits and are momentous in the plot of the story" (Mousavi and Mousavi 55). The subtraction of idiosyncratic, individualistic traits might be privileged in some short fictions for those that carry cultural, critical, and thematic characteristics. Lydia Davis, a well-known writer of very short fiction, explains the process and reasons for such subtractions:

> I work by instinct, so sometimes I start by naming and then take the name out. I try to name because I think, Why not? and end up taking it out again. By now, I think I understand why I would rather say 'a large city in the East' than 'New York.' You can see this large city

whatever way you want. If you say 'New York,' then you not only have to see New York in your mind's eye, but you also have all these associations with New York—you think of the Big Apple, Sartre's essay about New York, Radio City Music Hall. It often doesn't matter whether it's New York City or San Diego or any other place—and then I'd rather leave it open like that. (Knight 549)

This purposeful subtraction creates space that readers fill with their own imaginations and experiences, thus placing themselves into the flash piece while also expanding the "contracted" flash beyond its confines.

Actions and Conflicts. Summary—"the occurrences themselves as they are actually reported in the text"—works with paralipsis to create "the impression that the entire fabula [the events of the story] is a matter of one instant" (Taha 64). Flash can feel like "very short, momentary 'snapshots' wherein the point of departure usually is a concrete sense impression being elevated to a universal level" (Mose 82). The actions within flash also undergo a contraction, and as the space between and among each tiny occurrence is compressed, the separate actions within the flash begin to feel like a singular event. Like the singularity that may have begun the universe, the flash can feel as if it begins out of nothing, bursts into existence "each narrative start[ing] with the scene most critical to understanding the piece" (Mills xiv). "Reading them," Lisa Nold writes, "is like being yanked into a world of vivid detail and suddenly confronted with an immediate and palpable conflict" (174). Flash doesn't have the time to create reader identification, so the conflicts that arise from these opening scenes may "depict interpersonal disputes, especially between close friends, married couples, and children, and it is precisely this use of recognizable circumstances that make the stories accessible in so few words" (174). Conventional stories might cover this same ground, but flash relies more on the representative relationship, one readers can readily recognize and bring to it their own deeply felt emotions. Because characters take on universal archetypal meanings and cultural representations, S. Habib Mousavi and S. Mohammad Ali Mousavi argue that "conflict is a clash of actions, beliefs, desires or intentions, and is the basis of the plot of the story" (55). Flash's "characteristic instantaneousness" (Mose 88) continues to open up from that original scene, the conflicts creating insights, so that "space is expanded through one or more epiphanic moments" (84). Those final insights carry the reader beyond the borders of the story into the larger and more expansive world of enlightenment, of following those last implications to all their possible meanings.

Time. "Ellipsis," that quality Taha saw in flash, "is interpreted as skipping whole periods of time" (64). Rovner focuses on this specific element of time in his critical look at the very short story:

> [A] symmetry exists between microfiction's compressed spatialization, and the compression—and hence violation—of temporal norms of the reader's anticipation. The violation of conventional reading anticipation makes microfiction seem not only to be new but also transgressive. Much microfiction is indeed transgressive of prevailing ideologies of time that are premised on the existence of contingency and the efficacy of human agency. (112)

In other words, time is often thought of as flowing, from past to present to future, and humanity, like something on its surface, is along for the ride. But microfiction treats time differently, as if the past, present, and future existed all it once, crammed into the same space, something disconnected and scattered. Rovner explains further: "Time is familiarly depicted by the metaphor of a flowing river. Microfiction, by contrast, treats time as an intermittently leaky tap" (116). Instant drips into instant, the boundaries between past, present, and future flowing into one another yet seeming unconnected, like detached bubbles. Flash's tendency to "synthesize a chain of events may result in complex temporal structures that cause the present . . . to merge with and become indistinguishable from that of the past and future" (Mose 84). As that chain of cause and effect gets unlinked, readers begin to question the very idea of a character's actions causing other actions leading to change. Some other dynamic appears to be at work, something more fragmented, something less driven by desires and human actions.

Other more specific characteristics abound in the scholarship. For example, Nold observes "that many of them [flash fictions] start with tight and active first sentences" (174). Mose notices, within the Danish short-short that "classic rhetoric and mannerisms (e.g., paradoxes, absurd and grotesque effects, parallels, and emphatic anaphoras) become part of the style" (84). And Pacchioni writes, "In narrative, rhythm is essentially the result of repetition in the plot; in other words, the interplay between a set of narrative constants and narrative variable" (85). One exciting aspect of such scholarship, of course, is the space allowed for more continued studies of the genre's defining traits—additions and subtractions and qualifications to this ever-expanding and deepening list.

Studies also focus on the literary and cultural origins of flash fiction. Critically, flash fiction can be found as sitting somewhere between the short story and poetry. In discussing the modern Arabic very short story, Taha argues that "the blurring of borders between the short story and poetry has led to the birth of the very short story" (60). Mousavi and Mousavi argue that flash is a "newly born genre developed from the heart of short story" (52). Critics and scholars connect flash to other miniature forms as well. As Nelles argues, "there have always been artists willing to risk the miniature. Such short verbal forms as the parable, exemplum, fabliau, and fable have been widely and more or less continuously practiced for millennia" (87). Pacchioni evokes the folktale: "Italian fiction writer Italo Calvino addressed the idea of 'rapidita' or 'economia d' espressione' as a characteristic of folktales (and as one that he proposed as a narrative value for the fiction writers of the new millennium)" (84). In a study of brief Korean stories, Bruce Fulton came to this conclusion:

Aesop's fables would qualify, as well as several of the stories in Boccaccio's *Decameron*, several of the Grimm Brothers' tales, and certain works by such writers as Chekhov, Mérimee, Saroyan, Steinbeck, Hemingway, Cheever, and Zamiatin. In East Asia perhaps the best-known practitioner is Kawabata Yasunari, with almost 150 'palm-of-the-hand' stories to his credit. Murakami Haruki has also produced very short pieces, as has the Hong Kong writer Liu Yichang. (251)

Mose's Danish short-short study led her to antecedents such as "the anecdote, the joke, the fable, and the sketch" (84). As scholars and critics attempt to figure out when and out of what flash has originated, they might be uncovering a truth about flash—that artists in each time and culture have worked in "miniature," with every historical and cultural period creating their own labels to affix to it.

This article started with the criticism that flash has failed at becoming something real, complete, and worthy. Maybe, though, it isn't flash that has failed, but the short story that has failed to live up to its billing. Taha sees very short fiction's rise as linked to "the failure of the short story, as an institutionalized genre, to constantly innovate and explore new possibilities" (60). Shapard observes: "The traditional story (retold ten thousand times) suffers from repetitive strain injury. Television and the Internet have responded to this crisis without losing their audience. Literary fiction has not" (46). The "About this Issue" for a flash fiction-centered edition of *North American Review* links flash to print stories in the '30s and '40s:

> Do please indulge us (even as we indulge ourselves) in a small disquisition on the so-called short-short story. A few of our Constant Readers will recall that in the 1930s and '40s, a number of domestic magazines published fiction 'complete on these pages'—usually a pair of facing pages . . . whose length ran between a thousand and three thousand words. ("About" 2)

Mose connects the short-short to "the fairy tale, the legend, the fable, the myth, the exemplum, the chronicle, the anecdote, the aphorism, and so on" (90); and Rovner, to "parables and myths, Old English enigmata, jokes, fabliaux, anecdotes and sketches, literary fragments, and even examples of journalistic miscellany (e. g., the faits-divers of Félix Fénéon)" (115).

Besides previous iterations of the flash, critics look for historical and cultural reasons for flash's rising popularity and ubiquity in contemporary society. Writing of the Danish short-short, Mose connects them to "literary manifestations of the changes in the history of mentality," of a 'new' and 'nervous' subject enter[ing] the staged and insist[ing] on the privileged position of the individual in pursuit of an adequate ontology" (81). Worldwide, a new generation of writers sought "to break away from the Aristotelian conception of plot in the short story to meet the demands of rapid changes on the level of the social, intellectual, and political scene [as] in Morocco" (Akib 74). The form of flash fiction matched the desire of writers "no longer content with telling stories in the conventional manner of the older generation . . . [but rather] anxious to explore narrative possibilities discussed and practiced in modern writing" (Riemenschneider 409). It wasn't only this desire of writers to the turn from the more traditional story-form to the new one that led to flash's rise, but also, critics argue, the nature of contemporary society and culture.

Writing of his self-titled creation "quick fictions"—a name he gave to a "brief work [300 words or fewer] composed, revised, sharpened, and tightened, in order to be enduring and memorable, something to carry with you everyday"—Nicholas Royle views them as answering "the question of how to write—inventively, thoughtfully, memorably—in the age of the short attention span" (27). Dinty W. Moore writes about his experience with this question of attention spans in "The Moment of Truth: An Introduction":

> Since I also edit an online journal of sudden nonfiction, BREVITY . . . I am often asked to defend the brief prose form. I use the word 'defend' very deliberately. Some people become truly huffy about the matter, as if the choice to use a mere two or three hundred words was an affront of some sort to those writers who choose to use ten- or twenty-thousand. Is it the gradual deterioration of our intellect, I'm asked, or is it that the pervasive use of email, beepers, and text pagers, has left us with incredibly abbreviated attention spans. (15-6)

His answers is that, yes, "we consume information at a much-accelerated rate," but some of that information—such as that contained in flash fiction—"is incredibly sophisticated" (Moore 16). The Japanese phenomenon of cell phone novels, "keitai shosetsu," which also includes microstories, seems to be a response to the long daily commutes of many young Japanese workers, especially women (Nelles 88). As Fulton analyzed tchalbŭn sosŏl, "brief fiction" (252) in South Korean culture, he concluded that "dissemination offered by online media" created the opportunity for "experimentation with the parameters of the fictional form" (253). Aili Mu and Julie Chue connect flash to "a passion for speed—easy consumption and instant gratification—and a desire for greater diversity." They also see it as a reaction to contemporary "excess" (Mu and Chue xiv). Short-shorts, they argue, "readily participate in the change toward commercialization of social, cultural, and political discourse" (xiv). Similarly, Lee Rourke asserts that "flash fiction [has] found its small place amongst the rising tide of technological innovations" (164), and Rovner writes, "While modern Hebrew literature contains scattered feuilletonist short-shorts and other ktsartsarim variants that predate the appearance of [Hanan] Hever and [Moshe] Ron's collection, the form can only properly be said to have emerged in the last two decades of the twentieth century" (111). Although rooted in far-off forms that have been around for ages, flash has connected to the needs and technologies of modern culture to find a place in the twenty-first-century literary scene.

This connection to our specific historical present also leads critics and scholars to explore its place in contemporary literary theories and techniques. For example, Rourke argues in *A Brief History of Fables: From Aesop to Flash Fiction* that the "term 'flash fiction' . . . spans numerous theoretical and highly experimental techniques such as postmodernism, surrealism, fabulism, postfabulism, realism, and magic realism" (163). Similarly, a critical look at the brevity in Margret Atwood's work led Gilbert to conclude that the writer "employs the subversive methods commonly identified with the discourses of postmodernism, particularly metafiction, self-conscious narration, intertextuality, magical realism, the mixing of literary genres, parody, and irony" (222). Just as a poem announces itself as a poem, flash does the same thing, its small size announcing itself as a constructed thing. In postmodern story writing, Charles May argues, "the reader is made uncomfortably aware that the only reality is the depiction itself—the language act of the fiction making process" (84). Such a focus on language-making often works to blur boundaries, especially those that exist between genres. Lydia Davis, for instance, tells her interviewer, "Sometimes the stories are taken as prose poems for the sake of an anthology. . . . I haven't written or published stories with line breaks that look like poems" (Knight 546). Thus, flash fiction has been connected with the postmodern removal of genre markers, making contemporary readers and writers question the need for such labels. For example, Rourke views flash fiction as "exist[ing] in the space between the parameters of the more established and well-worn forms of expression set by poetry and prose; slipping in and out of view; often seeming both askew and remarkable in its brevity and conciseness of expression" (163-4). Citing Charles Baxter, David Shields asks in *Life is Short—Art is Shorter*, "What if length is a feature of writing that is as artificial as an individual prose style?" (22). And Mose sees in the Danish short-shorts "blurred distinctions between subject and object, characters and things [that] may result in changes, such as power relations" (84). As these boundaries begin to fade, the world itself begins to transform. If indeed borders create power, then it would make sense that blurring these not only changes readers' perspectives but also reveals the hidden agendas behind such boundaries. That idea of flash fiction's being "askew"—with its implication of aloofness or even hostility—links it to a subversive form, something that eludes its efforts to be grasped by traditional terms and techniques. And the idea of "slipping" connects flash fiction to the postmodern idea of slippage, that gap between signs and signifiers, between language and subtext.

Of such gaps, Etgar Keret says in an interview that a donut "is a wonderful metaphor" for the short-short story:

> "Because that hole, in its nonmaterialistic existence, is what makes the Donut a donut. The hole has to be just the right size. A story without gaps in it can never work, and a story that is made of too many gaps is just a hole and not a donut. It is the choice of not saying something that many times creates a story's brilliance and originality" (18).

Similarly, Nikole Brown's "Introduction" to an anthology of flash sequences argues, "With a close look at what happens *between* the segments, the white space often crackles with its own energy, acting sometimes as connective tissue, sometimes as the gravity between two discrete but related planets of prose." She continues, "Much like the gutter between panels in a comic book, the gap . . . is where the reader does the good work of imagination and juxtaposition, exploring the transitions, filling in what's left unsaid" (Brown 12). Interestingly, a recent anthology *Flashed: Sudden Stories in Comics and Prose* combines flash and comics. In that "Introduction," Josh Neufeld and Sari Wilson explain, "Why flash fiction? It's the perfect form for a project that's all about pushing boundaries and cross-fertilization" (x). To explore the space between things—words and images, prose and comics—the editors turned to flash fiction for its postmodern qualities of blurring and mixing.

Critics assign other postmodern qualities to flash fiction. Rovner, for example, connects "microfiction's peculiar shape of time" with the postmodern refutation of "the Western 'argument of progress,' which maintains that as human reason and science improve there is a concomitant increase in human enlightenment and a greater access to 'truth'" (128). Furthermore, he argues that forms such as flash fiction highlight "the impotence of individual action," a theme that is "consonant with a prevailing postmodern skepticism in the industrialized world" (128). Writing of Chinese short-shorts, Dao writes, "The line between fact and fiction, after all, is blurred—history has been read as fiction and fiction regarded as an extension of history" (xi). The short-short's accessibility matches, for Dao, that postmodern quality of contemporary times: "Calling upon little imagination, [Chinese writers] can tear any page from this book and turn it into a work of art" (xi). Flash reflects "a belief in the possibility of creating various kinds of relations between the elements . . . an urge to rebuild the world" (Mose 88, 89).

This blurring of genre, boundaries, time-held truths has led critics to question how much "story" does flash fiction have to tell. As Shapard, for example, recognizes, "very short fictions in Latin America are, on the whole, shorter than in the United States, and questions about them are often concerned less with how short stories can be than with whether very short fictions need to be stories at all" ("Remarkable Reinvention" 48). Gerlach touches upon similar issues, asking, "When do we finally reach the minimum unity of story, that is, a free-standing complete, and satisfying prose fiction? Might a story even become something else—a poem for instance? If that is possible, do such discriminations ultimately matter? Are we likely to look at a work differently if it is, or is not, a story?" (74). Does the very short story have to be a story? As might be expected, some say it should and some argue against it. On the one hand, Mousavi and Mousavi argue, "Flash fiction with its extreme brevity incorporates all of the structural elements that we run across in a short story, and this critical factor imposes an enormous difficulty on the author since he should be fairly careful about taking in all the structural components of a short story in an epigrammatic span" (59). On the other hand, Matt Hlinak contends, "Flash fiction in general lends itself well to experimentation because it allows the author to try out new ideas without the time commitment of a longer work" (23). Rather than viewing it as a traditional narrative, some view flash as more like a fragment—to "mirror a world consisting of bits and pieces, but implicitly a world that may be woven into a sequence of events, however 'tiny'" (Mose 92). Such a view supports the anti-narrative thread within postmodernism.

In short, flash fiction has a growing number of scholarly and critical articles devoted to discovering its nature, its defining characteristics, and its cultural, historical, and theoretical significance, perhaps a result of flash's becoming more popular throughout the world. As Aili Mu and Julie Chue assert in their introduction to an anthology of Chinese flash fiction, "the consumption of short-short stories has become a global phenomenon" (xv). The very thing that might make flash get overlooked—its small size—might also be exactly why it attracts attention, especially as the world seems to get busier and bulkier. In a "Gallery Note" for an exhibition of miniature watercolors, the poet Elizabeth Bishop writes, "It is a great relief to see a small work of art these days. . . . Why shouldn't we, so generally addicted to the gigantic, at last have some small works of art, some short poems, short pieces of music [. . .] some intimate, low-voiced, and delicate things in our mostly huge and roaring, glaring world?" (qtd. in Rosenbaum 61). Keret likewise says, "I never felt about any of my stories that they were too short. I do, however, often find stories too long" (18). Such artistic sentiments—combined with flash's popularity in both magazines and college courses—also have worked to focus the attentions of scholars and critics upon flash fiction's growing cultural significance.

And what of that poet from the opening who dismissed me? He turned to the person next to him, and so he didn't hear my reply to his question on why I write flash fiction: "It's so I don't have to write short stories or poems." Perhaps, then flash can be defined simply by its desire to be recognized for what it is—rather than for all the things it is not.

Works Cited

"About This Issue." *The North American Review*, vol. 282, no. 6, 1997, p. 2. *JSTOR*, www.jstor.org/stable/25126172/. Accessed 7 May 2016.

Akbib, Abdellatif. "Birth and Development of the Moroccan Short Story." *Rocky Mountain Review of Language and Literature*, vol. 54, no. 1, 2000, pp. 67-87. *JSTOR*, *doi:* 10.2307/1348420. Accessed 7 June 2016.

Barth, John. "It's a Short Story." *Mississippi Review*, vol. 21, no. 1/2, 1993, pp. 25-40. *JSTOR*, www.jstor.org/stable/20134554/. Accessed 7 June 2016.

Brown, Nikole. "A Note from the Series Editor." *Nothing to Declare: A Guide to the Flash Sequence*, edited by Robert Alexander, Eric Braun, and Debra Marquart, White Pine Press, 2016, p. 11.

Dao, Bei. "Foreword." *Loud Sparrows: Contemporary Chinese Short-Shorts*, edited and translated by Aili Mu, Julie Chu, and Howard Goldblatt, Columbia UP, 2006, pp. xi-xii.

Dawson, W. J. "The Modern Short Story." *The North American Review*, vol. 190, no. 649, 1909, pp. 799-810. *JSTOR*, www.jstor.org/stable/25106524/. Accessed 6 June 2016.

Dunlop, Lane. "Translators' Notes." *Palm of the Hand Stories* by Yasunari Kawabata. Translated by Lane Dunlop and J. Martin Holman. Farrar, Straus, Giroux, 1988, pp. xi-xii.

Friedman, Norman. "What Makes a Short Story Short?" *Modern Fiction Studies*, vol. 4, no. 2 1958, p. 103. *Proquest.* Accessed 21 June 2016.

Fulton, Bruce. Introduction. *Azalea: Journal of Korean Literature & Culture*, vol. 7, no.1 2014, pp. 251-53. *Project MUSE*, doi:10.1353/ aza.2014.0026. Accessed 21 July 2016.

Gerlach, John. "The Margins of Narrative: The Very Short Story, the Prose Poem, and the Lyric." *Short Story Theory at Crossroads*, edited by Susan Lohafer and Jo Ellyn Clarey. Louisiana State UP, 1989, pp.74-84.

Gilbert, Teresa. "Margaret Atwood's Art of Brevity." *Short Story Theories: A Twenty-First-Century Perspective*, edited by Viorica Patea, Rodopi, 2012, pp. 205-23.

Hlinak, Matt. "Hemingway's Very Short Experiment: From 'A Very Short Story' to 'A Farewell to Arms'" *The Journal of the Midwest Modern Language Association*, vol. 43, no. 1, 2010, pp.17-26. *JSTOR*, http:// www.jstor.org/stable/41756570. Accessed 7 June 2016.

Kaspar, M., and Kasper M. "Short-Prose." *Social Text*, vol. 23, 1989, pp. 161-64. *JSTOR*, www.jstor.org/stable/466426/. Accessed 6 June 2016.

Keret, Etgar, and Johnson Michelle. "A Conversation with Etgar Keret." *World Literature Today*, vol. 82, no. 6, 2008, pp.16-18. *JSTOR*, www. jstor.org/stable/20621396/. Accessed 7 June 2016.

Knight, Christopher J., and Davis Lydia. "An Interview with Lydia Davis." *Contemporary Literature*, vol. 40, no. 4, 1999, pp. 525-51. *JSTOR*, www.jstor.org/stable/1208791/. Accessed 22 July 2016.

Masih, Tara L. "In Pursuit of the Short Short Story: An Introduction." *The Rose Metal Press Field Guide to Flash Fiction: Tips from Editors, Teachers, and Writers in the Field*, edited by Tara L. Masih, Rose Metal Press, 2009, pp. xi-xxxviii.

May, Charles. *The Short Story: The Reality of Artifice*. Routledge, 2002.

Mills, Mark. Introduction. *Crafting the Very Short Story: An Anthology of 100 Masterpieces*, edited by Mark Mills, Prentice Hall, 2003, pp. xiv-xvi.

Moore, Dinty. "The Moment of Truth: An Introduction." *Sudden Stories: The Mammoth Book of Miniscule Fiction*, edited by Dinty Moore, Mammoth Press, 2003, pp. 15-18.

Mose, Gitte. "Danish Short Shorts in the 1990s and the Jena Romantic Fragments." *The Art of Brevity: Excursions in Short Fiction Theory and Analysis*, edited by Per Winther, Jakob Lothe, and Hans H. Skei. U of South Carolina P, 2004, pp. 81-95.

Mousavi, S. Habib, and S. Mohammad Ali Mousavi. "Flash Fiction, Defamiliarization and Cultural Criticism: A Case Study of Salahshoor's 'Please Smile.'" *International Journal of Humanities and Social Science*, vol. 4, no. 7, May 2014, pp. 52-60. www.ijhssnet. com/journal/index/2535/. Accessed 6 June 2016.

Mu, Aili. and Julie Chue. Introduction. *Loud Sparrows: Contemporary Chinese Short-Shorts*, edited and translated by Aili Mu, Julie Chu, and Howard Goldblatt. Columbia UP, 2006, pp. xiii-xxii.

Nelles, W. "Microfiction: What Makes a Very Short Story Very Short?" *Narrative*, vol. 20, no. 1, 2012, pp. 87-104. *Project MUSE*, muse.jhu. edu/article/464009/. Accessed 6 June, 2016.

Neufeld, Josh, and Sari Wilson. Introduction. *Flashed: Sudden Stories in Comics and Prose*, edited by Josh Neufeld and Sari Wilson, Pressgang, 2016. ix-xii.

Nold, Lisa. "Review." *Harvard Review*, vol. 32, 2007, pp. 174-75. *JSTOR*, www.jstor.org/stable/40346790/. Accessed 6 June, 2016.

Pacchioni, Federico. "Integrating Philosophical Inquiry into the Italian Language Classroom through the Use of Very Short Fiction." *Italica*, vol. 84, no. 1, 2007, pp. 79-95. *JSTOR*, www.jstor.org/ stable/27669127/. Accessed 6 June 2016.

Pasco, Allan H. "On Defining Short Stories." *New Literary History*, vol. 22, no. 2, 1991, pp. 407-22. *JSTOR*, www.jstor.org/stable/469046/. Accessed 7 June 2016.

Riemenschneider, Dieter. "Short Fiction from Zimbabwe." *Research in African Literatures*, vol. 20, no. 3, 1989, pp. 401-11. *JSTOR*, www. jstor.org/stable/3819173/. Accessed 7 June 2016.

Rourke, Lee. *A Brief History of Fables: From Aesop to Flash Fiction.* Hesperus Press, 2011.

Rosenbaum, Susan. "Elizabeth Bishop and the Miniature Museum." *Journal of Modern Literature*, vol. 28, no. 2, 2005, pp. 61-99. *JSTOR*, www.jstor.org/stable/3831716/. Accessed 22 July 2016.

Rovner, Adam. "The Shape of Time in Microfiction: Alex Epstein and the Search for Lost Time." *Shofar: An Interdisciplinary Journal of Jewish Studies*, vol. 33, no. 4, 2015, pp. 111-133. *Project MUSE*, muse.jhu.edu/article/583960. Accessed 6 July 2016.

Royle, Nicholas. "Quick Fiction: Some Remarks on Writing Today." *Mosaic: A Journal for the Interdisciplinary Study of Literature*, vol. 47, no. 1, 2014, pp. 23-39. *Project MUSE*, doi: 10.1353/mos.2014.0002. Accessed 6 July 2016.

Schultz, Katey. "What is Flash Fiction." *Fiction Southeast*, n.d. fictionsoutheast.org/what-is-flash-fiction/. Accessed 6 Jul. 2016.

Shapard, Robert. "The Remarkable Reinvention of Very Short Fiction." *World Literature Today*, vol. 86, no. 5, September/October 2012, pp. 46-49. www.worldliteraturetoday.org/2012/september/remarkable-reinvention-very-short-fiction-robert-shapard. Accessed 7 May 2016.

_____, and James Thomas. Editors' Note. *Flash Fiction Forward*, edited by Robert Shapard and James Thomas, W.W. Norton & Company, 2006, pp. 11-14.

_____, and James Thomas. Introduction. *Sudden Fiction (Continued)*, edited by Robert Shapard and James Thomas, W.W. Norton & Company, 1996, pp. 11-13.

Shields, David, and Elizabeth Cooperman. Introduction. *Life is Short—Art is Shorter: In Praise of Brevity*, edited by David Shields and Elizabeth Cooperman, Hawthorne Books & Literary Arts, 2016, pp. 21-29.

Taha, Ibrahim. "The Modern Arabic Very Short Story: A Generic Approach." *Journal of Arabic Literature*, vol. 31, no. 1, 2000, pp. 59-84. *JSTOR*, www.jstor.org/stable/4183407/. Accessed 6 June 2016.

Thomas, James. Introduction. *Flash Fiction: Very Short Stories*, edited by James Thomas, Denise Thomas, and Tom Hazuka, W.W. Norton & Company, 1992, pp. 11-14.

Wright, Austin M. "On Defining the Short Story." *Short Story Theory at Crossroads*, edited by Susan Lohafer and Jo Ellyn Clarey, Louisiana State UP, 1989, pp. 46-53.

Flash and Fabulism: A New Marriage of Old Forms

Kristen Figgins

When you talk to someone about very short fiction, Ernest Hemingway's name often comes up. He's sometimes credited with writing the famous six-word story, "For sale: baby shoes, never worn," which is frequently held up as the epitome of how to tell a whole lot of story with very few words. It's a fascinating display of brevity and emotion, but what this story does for most students of writing is ask them to consider the purpose of storytelling as an art. In this instance, the purpose is not so much to entertain or teach, but rather to affect a reader emotionally, to hold up a mirror to their lives and experiences, which resonates meaningfully. Since Hemingway began publishing in the 1920s, and especially in the last thirty to forty years, our culture has lent itself to brevity as the best way to impart information. In 2010, at a technology conference in Austin, Texas, called South by Southwest, a now-ubiquitous social media platform debuted the premise of its now-familiar guidelines for posting: 140 characters or less. Today, comedy; politics; news; and, yes, even literature, are shared on Twitter, in 140 characters or less, to enormous fanfare and acclaim. It's not surprising that flash fiction, that dynamic genre that has gained so much popularity since the 1980s, perhaps more than any other contemporary form, forces both reader and writer to focus on emotional impact within the confines of economy of language. However, what Hemingway and what modern flash fiction authors achieve within the constraints of limited word counts is not new. Rather, contemporary flash fiction has a great deal in common with a much older genre of flash, the fable, from which it borrows many techniques and tricks in order to affect readers.

For the most part, although there have been many traditional fabulists over centuries of writing, the word fable has been historically associated with one author: Aesop. Like Mother Goose or the Brothers Grimm, he is often introduced, even today, in early childhood. V. M. Perez Perozo says of fablists that:

> Aesop's work was so perfect that all the fable-makers since his time have followed slavishly in his footsteps. More than this: Almost all the fabulists who have followed him have merely appropriated his original themes. Some have done no more than versify the same themes, as Babrius, Phaedrus, and La Fontaine. Others have varied them slightly and added some interpretation of them. But a considerable fraction of the fables which are reckoned the patrimony of other writers still bear the unmistakable trade-mark of the old master. (364)

Indeed this is true. On my bookshelf, I have collected dozens of books of fables, including a 1744 Latin translation of Aesop's fables by Perrault, Tom McNeal's *Fables*, and *Fables by the Late John Gay*. Nearly all of these are blatant retellings of Aesop's collection or variations on his style and themes.

What makes Aesop's style and theme so remarkable is how simple they are: they deeply resonate with us in such an original way that it is difficult to conceive of altering them too greatly, even for effect. Aesop presented brief fables that featured flat characters (often talking animals) who had some sort of implicit lesson to impart to the reader. It is not a stretch of the imagination to assume that these tales would have been told, like other fairy and folk tales, over and over again at firesides or bedsides to generations of listeners. Pack Carnes asserts that fables have remained so popular because of their modern sensibilities: "Many of these early fables have modern reflexes and therefore have been in continuous use for at least four millennia in both written and oral forms, something that cannot be said for any other type of folk narrative" (2). The form of the fable has always been popular, and sometimes even the content of particular fables has endured over time, but it has not been until recently that many fabulists began to stray from Aesop's themes and style.

Although its short-form style was never quite as celebrated as the short story, novel, or play, the fable pops up throughout literary history, perhaps most notably in the works of Marie de France and La Fontaine. In addition to often dealing with animal characters, the fable during the medieval period and Renaissance, like flash fiction, was "one of the smallest of 'small' literary forms. The longest item in Marie de France's collection—*"De lupo regnante"* ("The Wolf as King")—has 124 lines, and the typical length of fables in her collection and in other medieval Aesops is from fifteen to thirty-five verses" (Needlers 428). In this way, the fable is one of the oldest and most consistent expressions of flash fiction in literary history.

However, brevity is not the only characteristic common to fables. Aesop's works, like Marie de France's, La Fontaine's, and other traditional fabulists, have a few other defining attributes. First, because they are all limited in word count, they require the reader and writer to eschew other traditional elements of storytelling. As Howard Needlers puts it, "[F]able lacks many characteristics of the larger forms and established genres: characterization, motivation, distinctions of foreground and background, circumstantial detail, narrative amplitude, and so on" (428). In other words, those five elements of literature—theme, character, setting, conflict, and plot—are often whittled down to essentials.

Secondly, traditional fables tend to blend genres; that is, while the typical fable might take place in a world that seems 'real'— devoid of spaceships, perhaps, or of wizards—it also distorts the real. Typically, this distortion is seen in the use of talking animals. For example, in de France's "The Woman and Her Hen," the two characters have a verbal exchange quite unlike what most of readers would expect to encounter on a typical farm. The woman says to her hen that she will provide her with an overabundance of food and the hen replies, ostensibly in human speech, that it would prefer to hunt and peck, as is in the nature of hens everywhere (de France 68). This encounter is given no explanation or context, and this is typical in the form of fable, which does not yield nor necessarily require world-building in order to impart its emotional impact.

Finally, the traditional fable typically ends with an epiphany. I phrase it thus because the common misconception that Aesop's fables ended with a moral, (as in, "The early bird catches the worm") is not accurate; the didacticism of fables is implicit and these easy-to-digest taglines were often tacked on in later renditions of the tales that "transformed the Aesopic fables into a collection of unified stories, each with a certain moral point or literary interpretation" (Lerer 41). This is important to note because fables, in their brevity, speak for themselves, and they speak loudly. Fables, like parables, are meant to resonate with readers in a visceral and emotional way. In the example of Marie de France's woman and hen, it is not necessary to tell us the moral of the story; rather, most readers will easily walk away with their own epiphany: that I, like the hen, will often follow my nature, even when better and smarter options lie in front of me. These three characteristics of the traditional fable resonate in flash fiction today. Because flash fiction is so concise, it is not surprising that, perhaps entirely unconsciously, writers of flash have borrowed so heavily from the form of the fable in their own works.

If you visit the submission page of any print or online literary journal, you will see length requirements based on word count (I've met the rare editor who takes a more laissez faire approach to submission length, but this tends to be the norm). Novellas are often 25,000-50,000 words. Novels are 60,000+, although many publishers prefer novels to be under 125,000 words. Short stories are usually 2,000-5,000 words, although sometimes they may extend as long as 10,000 words. For a long time, poetry was the trickiest of genres to divine: poets like T.S. Eliot proved that a singular poem could be nearly a book unto itself, while other poets, like William Carlos Williams, could affect their readers with fifteen words or less.

In the 1980s, a genre that seemed new began to gain public notice. At first, this genre was called by many names: micro fiction, quick fiction, nano fiction, hint fiction, quiction, the four-minute story, the short short story, and more. Eventually, one moniker established itself as sovereign: flash fiction.

Even the number of words by which a piece of writing may be considered flash fiction is inconsistent, without consensus in the literary community. Some, like *concīs*, a journal that specializes in short poetry and prose, ask for flash fiction of 250 words or less, although this is, they assure submitters, more a feeling than a rule.

Other journals, like *Cleaver,* ask for micro fiction under 900 words. For its Very Short Fiction Award, meanwhile, *Glimmer Train,* asks for submissions to be between 300 and 3,000 words.

Although the very term flash fiction impresses upon its readers and writers that the most salient characteristic of the genre is in its length, there is an undeniable personality to flash. Luisa Valenzuela says, "I usually compare the novel to a mammal, be it wild as a tiger or tame as a cow; the short story to a bird or a fish; the micro story to an insect (iridescent in the best cases)" (qtd. in Shapard 46). This quote encapsulates the sense of sudden impact that flash fiction demands, the quick-sparkling beauty that the form inspires. If the novel is a slow-burning fire, then flash is an illuminating firework, maybe best characterized by the smoky tendrils that it leaves behind in the sky (or the echoing impact that it imparts in the reader).

Many writers of flash fiction have argued that the genre itself should not be conflated with earlier genres: that it is something unique to the modern world. In "The Remarkable Reinvention of Very Short Fiction," Robert Shapard notes that "These stories weren't a *renaissance* of ancient forms. They were attempts to *reinvent* fiction" (47). It's not hard to imagine the reasoning behind this thinking. The modern form of flash fiction is a friendly and forgiving model of writing. Just like the novel and the short story, any writer, regardless of style or subject matter, can use the form of flash to tell an effective story. In addition, it is easy to chart the recent popularity of flash fiction as coinciding with Twitter, the internet, news delivered in sound-bytes, and other forms that are meant to appeal to consumers with short attention spans.

However, Shapard ignores the undeniable similarities between both the short form of the fable and of flash fiction. Although it is easy to draw the connection between fable and flash in their relative conciseness, the implications of that brevity in both forms reveal a deeper connection. Interestingly enough, both flash fiction and fable make sacrifices in traditional storytelling techniques in order to quickly resolve a satisfying story. For example, the entirety of Aesop's story "The Ass and the Grasshopper" in *Aesop's Fables* plays out thus:

> An ass having heard some Grasshoppers chirping, was highly enchanted; and, desiring to possess the same charms of melody, demanded what sort of food they lived on to give them such beautiful voices. They replied, "The dew." The Ass resolved that he would live only upon dew, and in a short time died of hunger.

In this story, we see little detail that is not strictly necessary to the telling of the story. There is no discussion of the donkey's ancestral lineage, the Grasshoppers' society, the donkey's emotional state, the setting of the story, or anything else. The story eschews many of these things in order to quickly and efficiently affect the reader.

The masterful quality of Aesop's animal characters is that they are often very obvious stand-ins for human characters; we attribute human characteristics to animals as a convenient shorthand for the follies and foibles inherent in humankind. Flat characters, which fairy tales often present in the forms of the ubiquitous Wolf or Witch or Evil Stepmother, are archetypes that are easily recognizable by the reader and often require no explanation or development. These are characters the reader has often encountered before. In fact, some flat characters, especially for a modern audience, are so moved by hundreds of years of reworking and rebuilding that they have nuances that other characters can only achieve across hundreds of pages of exposition and development. Kate Bernheimer discusses flatness in her essay, "Fairy Tale is Form, Form is Fairy Tale": "This absence of depth, this flatness, violates a technical rule writers are often taught in beginning writing classes: that a character's psychological depth is crucial to the story. In a fairy tale, however, this flatness functions beautifully; it allows depth of response in the reader" (67). In the story of the ant and the grasshopper by Aesop, those two characters are not given names or psychological depth; instead, they are identified by their most salient quality: their species and the attributes associated with their species.

One of Stephen Crane's stories, "A Man by the Name of Mud," is a piece of lovely, early flash fiction that exemplifies the use of flat characters, a common attribute of the form of fairy tale and fable. In the story, the protagonist is named simply Kid. He has a love interest named Girl, a device that quickly allows the reader to focus less on exposition and more upon the character's emotional state. Psychological depth is achieved through the plot of the story rather than through exposition. First and foremost, the moniker "Kid" is a diminutive and dismissive one for this character. In contrast to "Man" in the title, Kid implies an immediate atmosphere of a character at odds with his name (and thus defined by that contradiction). It also heavily implies an immaturity that plays out in the development of the character.

Other writers may not even bother to name the main character. Robert Coover, in his story "Going for a Beer," does not give the protagonist a name, which ties very well into that "depth of response in the reader" that Bernheimer discusses. The third-person narration follows a nameless protagonist, whom the reader may envision as any male. In fact, this is one of the central premises of the story— that the main character, who floats dreamily through life on the hazy wings of a solitary beer, is something of a stand-in for any reader who might find themselves, especially at a certain age, understanding the fabulist quality of reaching that age without quite understanding how quickly time must have passed. Both Crane's Kid and Coover's protagonist are mirrors held up to the experiences of the reader.

Another consequence of the brevity of fable and flash fiction is that the paring down of the story to essentials results in a sense of the unreal in an otherwise real world (a characteristic common to contemporary fabulism, as well). While realism demands a certain agreed-upon structure of reality within the boundaries of its stories—nothing should happen in the story that could not happen in real life—the fable is free of such constraints. Instead, it insists upon a reality that reflects the way that the world feels rather than looks. In this insistence, the felt reality of fables often feels more real than the limiting constraints of realism. In Aesop's "The Ant and the Grasshopper," the creatures talk to one another and communicate. They judge and offer advice and criticism. While insects do not have the power of human speech as we know it, it is easy to imagine that they might look at their neighbors in the insect kingdom and relate and interact with them. This is the felt reality, a reality that makes sense emotionally if not physically. When the grasshopper says,

"Why bother about winter? We've got plenty of food at present," he is reflecting an emotional reality of both the animal world as well as the human world circa 620 BCE. This is an excellent example of the unreal in an otherwise real world.

Likewise, flash fiction often demands a sense of the unreal. Because of word-limit constraints, character development, setting, and traditional plot structure are often rushed or ignored entirely. In order to create a brief story that nonetheless feels complete, the author must drop the reader into the world of the story without providing much exposition. For example, "Determining the Gull Bone Index" by James R. Gapinski, opens with three characters free-falling through the sky, always approaching the earth but never quite reaching it. This phenomenon is not explained in the story. Instead, Gapinski uses this unreal spectacle as a method of exploring the characters' felt realities: snapshots of their relationship with one another, the desperate problem-solving that occurs when confronted with a problem out of one's control, and the moments of levity in between. It is a beautiful piece of flash fiction precisely because it does not concern itself with reality.

Coover's contemporary fabulist flash, "Going for a Beer," is also incredibly dreamy, lending itself to an acute sense of unreality. The reader is meant to identify with the felt reality of growing older, which happens so gradually, as most readers might understand, that sometimes a person might feel themselves looking around at their lives in astonishment. In the story, this sense of unreality is exaggerated: the main character is drawn from important life event to important life event, often without even understanding what is happening to him, as though he is fast-forwarding between moments: "The child she bears him, his or another's, reminds him, as if he needed reminding, that time is fast moving on. He has responsibilities now and he decides to check whether he still has the job that he had when he first met her. He does" (Coover). This quintessential quality of "time fast moving on" is an important element of the unreality. It is, of course, unusual to not know whether you have a job or not (assuming that at least nine months have passed since the protagonist met his wife), yet this lends itself nicely to the felt reality of quietly and monotonously growing older.

Felt reality can also be achieved through language, such as in Stephen Crane's "A Man by the Name of Mud." The language in this story of flat characters is terse, lending itself to a sense of fragmentation which reflects the mental state of the Kid:

> Later, Kid asks girl to supper. Not wildly anxious, but very evident that he asks her because he likes her. Girl accepts; goes to supper. Kid very good comrade and kind. Girl begins to think that here at last is a man who understands her. Details ambitions—long, wonderful ambitions. Explains her points of superiority over the other girls of stage. Says their lives disgust her. (Crane 1220)

This passage is more than a snapshot of their relationship, but, like the description of the protagonist in Coover's "Going for a Beer," it is almost a fragmented montage of the beginning of a relationship, all expressed in short, choppy sentences. This is not the real world of a typical Crane story, in which the girl's ambitions may be explained in detail, but rather a real world distorted through the lens of brevity.

Finally, in the traditional fable, readers are led to a moment of epiphany upon the ending of the tale. Although Aesop's fables were not originally given morals (those were added later by editors as the tales became more popular for children), it is clear that in the original tales, the reader is encouraged by the language of the tale to infer a moral or deeper purpose or conclusion to the text. For example, in the traditional tale of the ant and the grasshopper, the two insects disagree with one another about their respective work ethics. The ant believes that it must prepare for the winter, while the grasshopper prefers to live in the moment. During the following winter, of course, the grasshopper finds itself starving and wishes that it had spent its time preparing. The moral of the story is clear: one must not live in the moment but instead prepare for the future.

In "A Man by the Name of Mud," we see an abrupt ending to the story of Kid and the girl, which allows the reader to extrapolate. After quickly detailing the development of the Kid's obsession with the girl of the story, the story ends thus:

Time goes on. Kid grows less noble. Perhaps decides not to be noble at all, or as little as he can. Still inveighs against the men who prey upon the girls of the stage. Thinks the girl stunning. Wants to be dead sure there are no others. Once suspects it, and immediately makes the colossal mistake of his life. Takes the girl to task. Girl won't stand it for a minute. Harangues him. Kid surrenders and pleads with her— pleads with her. Kid's name is mud. (Crane 1221)

The epiphany offered here is as clear as in one of Aesop's fables: the Kid, who obsessed over his object of desire, is his own worst enemy. Colloquially, one's name is usually dragged through the mud by others, by gossip or misfortune, but the Kid muddies his own name with his polluted attitude and infatuation with the girl. This contrast with the Kid's childish behavior and his adult feelings for the girl makes his description as a man in the title feel particularly ironic.

Coover's "Going for a Beer" ends with an extended musing on the monotonous futility of life:

So he has another beer, wondering where he's supposed to live now, and realizing—it's the bartender who so remarks while offering him another on the house—that life is short and brutal and before he knows it he'll be dead. He's right. After a few more beers and orgasms, some vaguely remembered, most not, one of his sons, now a racecar driver and the president of the company he used to work for, comes to visit him on his deathbed and, apologizing for arriving so late (I went for a beer, Dad, things happened), says he's going to miss him but it's probably for the best. For the best what? he asks, but his son is gone, if he was ever there in the first place. Well . . . you know . . . life, he says to the nurse who has come to pull the sheet over his face and wheel him away.

Coover's story, even more so than Crane's, offers an easy epiphany. The last musing of the protagonist ("Well . . . you know . . . life") is as pointless and dull as the endless montage of beers and bars of the rest of the story. Its comparisons to modern life, with its endless rotations of after-work drinks (or Netflix queues or drive-thru meals) are easy to imagine and resonate well with a contemporary reader.

Because the most salient characteristic of flash fiction is its length, it is easy and even appropriate to draw comparisons between it and other genres, which have also been traditionally characterized by their brevity, namely fairy tale and fable. As contemporary fabulism and flash fiction maintain their place in literary conversation, it becomes more and more important to note echoes between them. Our society's current interest in flash fiction and its brevity is likely to be as lasting and meaningful as our appreciation of the fables of old. Flash fiction is not a fad. If it's an iridescent insect, as Luisa Valenzuela supposes, then it is one that, like the locust, surrounds us now, in a thrumming and powerful swarm.

Works Cited

Aesop. *Aesop's Fables.* Translated by George Fyler Townsend, Project Gutenberg, 2013.

Bernheimer, Kate. "Fairy Tale Is Form, Form Is Fairy Tale." *The Writer's Notebook: Tin House Essays.* Tin House Books: 2009.

Carnes, Pack. "The Japanese Face of Aesop: Hoshi Shin'ichi and Modern Fable Tradition." *Journal of Folklore Research*, vol. 29, no. 1, 1992, pp. 1-22.

Coover, Robert. "Going for a Beer." *The New Yorker*, 14 Mar. 2011, www.newyorker.com/ magazine/ 2011/03/14/going-for-a-beer/. Accessed 5 Nov. 2016.

Crane, Stephen. "A Man by the Name of Mud." *The Complete Short Stories & Sketches of Stephen Crane*, edited by Thomas A. Gullason, Doubleday, 1963, pp. 1220-1221.

de France, Marie. "The Woman and her Hen." *Die Fabeln der Marie de France*, edited by Karl Warnke, Max Niemeyer Publishing, 1898, p. 68.

Gapinski, James R. "Determining the Gull Bone Index." *SmokeLong Quarterly*, 15 Feb. 2016. www.smokelong.com/determining-the-gull-bone-index/. Accessed 5 Nov. 2016.

Lerer, Seth. *Children's Literature: A Reader's History from Aesop to Harry Potter.* U of Chicago P, 2008.

Needler, Howard. "The Animal Fable among Other Medieval Literary Genres." *New Literary History*, vol. 22, no. 2, 1991, pp. 423-439.

Perez Perozo, V. M. "Fables and Fable-Writers." *Books Abroad*, vol. 20, no. 4, 1946, pp. 363-367.

Shapard, Robert. "The Remarkable Reinvention of Very Short Fiction." *World Literature Today*, vol. 86, no. 5, 2012, pp. 46-49.

The Destroyer and the Rotten Heart: Comparing and Contrasting Donald Barthelme's "The Baby" and Amelia Gray's "The Heart."

Megan Giddings

A way to distinguish between the writing of a traditional short story and flash is to think about how time works. In most traditional short stories—over one thousand words, written usually in the third or first person, where the plot follows the distinguishable pattern of situation, rising action, climax, falling action—most of the narrative time works as if readers are following characters directly over their shoulders or from within their own brain. Settings are clearly defined, people can have extended conversations, moments can be slowed down and examined.

Flash fiction in the first-person point of view, such as "The Baby" by Donald Barthelme and "The Heart" by Amelia Gray, tends to work more in memory time. The average person, with a fallible memory, will struggle to give concise, clear information about days from even a week before the present. Weeks in a person's life easily become blobs of memory: I went to work, sometime Monday, Tuesday? I had chicken for dinner, I went to the gym. But there are moments when memories that shape a person can be quickly, sharply recalled: a first kiss with someone deeply longed for, a first time eating a favorite food. In flash, there's less room for build-up or the monotony of the everyday. In this form the most important details are saved up. Writers have to move quickly from the grounding points—the who, what, when, where—to make it clear why the event or moment is important. They have to show quickly in a character-driven story how the character has been influenced or changed. In a thousand words or less, writers have to remain focused on what they feel are the most important details.

Especially in fiction that deals with the extraordinary and strange, more weight is put upon grounding a reader immediately in a new world. In literary fiction, this is usually filtered through characters' responses—both physical and emotional—to the events of the story. Karen Russell writes:

> No matter how foreign or strange your imaginary world may initially appear, if your characters move through it in ways that feel 'realistic'—if your characters' speech and behavior and moods and terrors ring true to what we know about their personalities and basic human behavior—then your readers are far more likely to accept the place on its own terms. (211)

Donald Barthelme, author of "The Baby," and Amelia Gray, author of "The Heart," show the different ways the first person point of view can shape a flash fiction story.

In "The Baby," the story has the initial shape of a typical parent's anecdote about raising a child: "The first thing the baby did wrong was to tear pages out of her books" (Barthelme 234). However, the story quickly escalates when the narrator says, "So we made a rule that each time she tore a page out of a book she had to stay alone in her room for four hours, behind closed doors" (234). The conversational "So," can make the harshness of the rule that follows, "alone in her room for four hours, behind closed doors" slip past; however, especially if the reader is familiar with how to take care of an infant or toddler, the story's tone has shifted. It's become darker, with a character admitting his negligence, his rigidity, and his tendency to take punishments too far.

One of the benefits of writing any story—especially one that's flash—in the first person, is that the character telling the story gets to shape reality. Readers look at how this character speaks, his reactions, and what he chooses to share to shape how we understand this world. If the unnamed narrator of "The Baby" had then written in the next line, "I knew I was doing things very poorly. I was not ready to raise a child," readers might be able to anticipate the main character learning a valuable lesson about child-rearing and becoming a better parent. But there's no reaction from the main character, no clues to tell readers that this world is exactly like or very similar to your own in how children are raised. The story simply continues. Within the long first paragraph, potentially months of this cycle are covered: the baby tears pages, spends more and more time locked in her room, the baby tears pages. The baby's mother is concerned about the rigidity of this cycle, but the narrator is forthright about their view of this situation: "But I felt that if you made a rule you had to stick to it, had to be consistent, otherwise they get the wrong idea" (Barthelme 234). By paragraph three, the baby has been locked up for eighty-eight consecutive hours in the room (three-and-a-half days).

I colloquially call this kind of narrator, one who is admitting all their faults and telling about a story that happened in the past, "That Weirdo at the Party"—an uninhibited someone who is able to corner multiple people and tell story after story because this character loves attention and is willing to tell a listener/reader everything. This is the kind of person one dreads being cornered by because there's never a clear sense of where the conversation is going or what they are going to say. On some level, however, it's possible to enjoy a person who, due to a seeming lack of inhibitions, can say anything. For one thing, there's always a potential for stories and anecdotes related to other people that arise from an encounter with this kind of character. In a more traditional craft-sense, this is a retrospective narrator trying to make some sense of the past. They're actively looking at and shaping their memories to tell the reader/listener, something about who they are. Even if they're exaggerating the details or being an obviously unreliable narrator, characters like this are attempting to communicate something essential about themselves. Even the attempt is important in fiction. The voice and the character behind it drive the story.

Remember, in flash fiction, there's little space for grounding details, such as setting and world-building-style exposition. In "The Baby" a first-person point of view, especially one that uses the past tense, can make the world feel quickly, vividly real. Everything is filtered through the unnamed narrator: we understand the world via their diction, the moments or explanations that they give to strengthen characters, and even through the details left out of the story. A strong narrator such as this one creates a sense of intimacy.

They've become real enough that a willing reader wants to believe everything they say.

By paragraph two, this story's reality has completely changed. The baby's name is given as "Born Dancin'." The parents have sat her down for glasses of wine, "red, white, and blue" and spoken seriously to her about the consequences of tearing pages out of books (Barthelme 235). Consider the juxtaposition: the parents are having a discussion with a baby about their arbitrary rules they have set, and the baby is given a glass of wine. They are both the authority and, by giving the baby wine and trying to reason with her, acting as if they are equals, as if the baby, despite being a baby, has absolute control over her actions. In *Story Logic and The Craft of Fiction*, Catherine Brady has this noteworthy observation about point of view and characterization: "Rather than helpfully clarifying at every moment the exact nature of a character's blind spots, we [writers] want to use point of view to coax the reader to question at least some of the character's judgments and some of her own, at least for a little longer" (94).

Because of flash's inherent brevity, Barthelme has to quickly show his narrator's blind spots: rigidity, an out-of-control need for order, and a sense that the baby must be treated as an adult. The space for consideration Brady feels is necessary to create an engaging and realistic character comes from the way the story is told. The protagonist feels as if they're directly speaking to the readers and relating moments from their life. The topic of the story—parenting—is one to which many people can relate. There's an emphasis on being charming and reasonable in these pages as the narrator continues telling and explaining things from the strange, along with hilarious details like sitting down to a glass of wine with the baby or even the fact that the titular baby is named Born Dancin'.

In paragraphs three and four, things have escalated to the point of absurdity. The baby is in solitary confinement for more than three days after innovating even sneakier ways to harm pages. The narrator tells us: "and you'd find a page that had one little corner torn, could easily pass for ordinary wear-and-tear, but I knew what she'd done, she'd torn off this little corner and swallowed it" (Barthelme

235). The narrator again asserts the necessity of obeying the rules in paragraph four: "the baby has a long life to live and had to live in the world with others, had to live in a world with many, many rules, and if you couldn't learn to play by the rules you were going to be left out in the cold with no character, shunned and ostracized by everyone" (235). Although the narrating parent offers useful wisdom about the importance of rules, the punishment has gone too far for the mother. She rescues Born Dancin' after seventy-six hours of her eighty-eight hour sentence. The narrator responds by making it so only they can access the baby's door by installing a magnetized keycard entrance with only one corresponding keycard (Barthelme 235).

The next paragraph details Born Dancin's continued refusal to improve or bow down to the rules her parents have created. The last line of this paragraph explicitly states one of the main concerns of this story, one of the reasons why the main character has even chosen to tell this story: "We had more or less of an ethical crisis on our hands" (Barthelme 235).

And here is another advantage of using the first person: often when a character is using a conversational style, he can say a truth and make it feel like a natural revelation that has come from the very process of telling this story. It's a way to get a reader to refocus and connect with this character, no matter how strange and absurd he is.

Consider the third person. The way many stories are written utilizes a style called the third person close. It's a way of telling a story where there isn't a narrator who's a separate character explaining the story. This point of view acts more like a camera crew following a protagonist. The shape of the story doesn't come directly from the voice of the main character as it regularly does in a first person narrative; instead, the story is organized around the main character's actions.

If, in the third person, the text directly says: "This is an ethical dilemma," a lot of readers might perceive that as the author asserting himself in the text or as breaking the fourth wall, a term first regularly used in television, where the majority of the scene would stop, a character would look directly into the camera and comment upon something that has happened. Especially if the story has been traditionally told without using meta elements of an author explaining the story and why it's being told, having what feels like a sudden interjection of this style can feel like a stylistic mistake to some readers.

"The Baby" ends with the main character declaring that they are the decider who changes the rules to bring their family back into harmony. The narrator and their daughter are united in violence perpetrated on the objects around them: "The baby and I sit happily on the floor, side by side, tearing pages out of books, and sometimes, just for fun, we go out on the street and smash a windshield together" (Barthelme 236). Beyond the hilarity and strangeness of a toddler smashing a windshield, the image is one last twist for this story. While the main character is using very positive words and phrasing—"happily" and "just for fun"—the reader is left to consider why this character felt this story needed to be told. What have readers learned about this narrator? The events are humorous, but they also reveal how the narrator was changed. If they hadn't overreacted to the baby's perceived misdeeds or hadn't been so initially rigid about how things were supposed to be, they might not have become more baby-like and engaged in destruction.

There are differences and variations in how the first-person point of view works. Reading Amelia Gray's "The Heart," reveals definite aesthetic similarities between Gray and Barthelme. In these selected stories, neither author is interested in writing a realistic story. They write imagery-heavy sentences. Moments are quickly built through description and the main character's voice. Both writers enjoy utilizing off-kilter names that can strengthen the sense that this is not ordinary life being represented. There's Born Dancin'—a name that feels more appropriate for a children's dance studio than a person— and Applebee, a name reminiscent of the chain restaurant that also has an inherent childishness because of its portmanteau of an early learner's words.

An important difference is that while "The Baby" is written in the first-person past tense, "The Heart" is written in the first-person present tense. In the present tense, everything that happens in the story's narrative is an immediate action, i.e., the main character is feeling and thinking and doing in the story's space. Often when a story is in first-person past tense, it allows the main character space to relate what has happened and to be able to contextualize the story's moments and memories. The power of the present tense is its swiftness: when done well, readers can feel as if they're carried away and directly into the story. There can be a feeling akin to being directly inside the narrator's brain.

An often-anthologized story that plays with the layers of directly being in someone's brain is Charles Yu's "Standard Loneliness Package." In this story, using a vaguely described technology to feel the pain of others, a character is paid to feel all the difficult emotions that the wealthy people in the story would prefer not to feel. The story is written in the first-person past tense. The main character is the narrator, thinking, and feeling from inside someone else's brain, while also being a character with whom readers are reading and feeling, thinking, and feeling. The narrator tells us, for example: "Heartbreak. When I first started this job, I thought physical pain would be hardest. But it's not. This is the hardest. To be inside here, looking at this man's face, at the lowest moment of his life, watching him try to keep it together. To be inside here, feeling what this woman is feeling, having done this to him" (Yu 590). When done well, the first-person present tense makes it feel as if the reader is sitting in a similar venue. The reader still has a sense of distance, but she can still see, hear, and potentially even feel everything that the narrator does. If the story is extraordinary, the reader feels all of those emotions.

Beginner writers are often encouraged to use the first-person style that Barthelme used in "The Baby" because it's a style of storytelling that most people naturally do. In ordinary life, people do not narrate their actions, walking around saying things like, "I open the window because I am hot. I look out and there's my former best friend walking down the street." We discuss what has happened after the fact. The first-person past tense, in which a character clearly reflects upon their life, forces the writer to consider why the story is being told, helps to mold a strong character who is telling the story, and to make sure things actually happen in the story.

In the first-person present, it can be harder to make the story feel like something that needs to be told and to make it clear why all the things that are happening are important. It can be easy for beginner writers to focus more on the feeling of immediacy that comes with the first-person present tense. The main character telling the story can end up just thinking and seeing rather than doing what realistic characters who can successfully anchor a story do: thinking, seeing, acting, feeling and reacting (Townsend). Karen Russell, again in "Engineering Impossible Architectures," emphasizes the need for strong character reactions to ground an unrealistic world: "But equally vital, I think, is the convincing emotional detail. Characters must have convincingly human reactions to their world for it to feel real" (208).

Amelia Gray begins "The Heart" with this line: "I think it's a whale heart." This opening gives the story its shape: in a thousand words or less, the reader will explore the mystery of this heart. The reader can consider several possibilities as to where the narrator might be—where is this character seeing this heart, how are they seeing it, what has happened? The next lines bring in more context for the heart and the main characters. The narrator mentions being in science class with Miss Pritchard where they saw a blue whale's heart. Then they move to these lines to give readers a sense of their age and deepen the mystery of the heart: ". . . so I figure that's what it is, a blue whale's heart, here in the living room, as wide as a car. One of the kids at school says You would be cool if you weren't so stupid, and I think like Yeah, this heart is the same way" (Gray 119).

Barthelme and Gray's approaches to building a world that is realistic, but with strange elements, are very different in these stories. In "The Baby," Barthelme builds toward his point, first making readers think they're reading an ordinary story about a toddler before the continued escalations. By the end of paragraph one of "The Heart," the reader is immediately confronted with a mysterious giant whale heart that has somehow appeared in the main character's living room.

In *How Fiction Works*, a key concept is thisness, which is defined as "any detail that draws abstraction toward itself and seems to kill that abstraction with a puff of palpability, any detail that centers our attention with its concretion" (Woods 67). To put this in simpler terms, it means to take something that could feel too strange or like an obvious metaphor and make it feel real enough that it can become a focal point for a reader's understanding of a character or situation. In the case of flash fiction, thisness can guide a reader toward understanding the story and its complexity. There's rarely enough space in a complete flash story for more than one large metaphor that fits into this term. In "The Heart," the thisness is the whale's heart.

Gray links the heart with emotional moments while still making it feel real. The majority of paragraph four focuses on establishing it as real, with details about its changing textures ("like cutting into a milk jug") and its scent ("like the trash behind the grocery store") (120). But the final line of that paragraph reestablishes it as a metaphor: "He [the narrator's father] says it's there because of Mom and I figure when we get it cut down enough she'll be inside" (120). There are few images as closely tied to emotions, especially love, as a heart. Gray takes something that could feel like cliché—a giant heart appearing in a family's living room after a family member's unexplained disappearance—and uses descriptions (as well as a slight tweaking of the usual image by making it a whale's heart) to turn the heart from an abstraction to an image that is both metaphor and a driving plot device. The family has to get this whale heart out of their living room to make their home livable again, but also, as becomes clear by the end of the story, to begin healing after the mother's disappearance.

It's harder in "The Baby" to point toward an image that embodies that concept of thisness. Barthelme doesn't linger on descriptions of the room Born Dancin' is locked into. The readers aren't given vivid descriptions of the books that were damaged, the home where this is all happening, or the main character and the wife. The story doesn't even take the time to clearly describe what Born Dancin' looks like throughout the process (the only mention of what she looks like beyond being a toddler is the disclosure that she has grown much thinner from her confinement). Everything is filtered through the narrator whose primary focus is the damage the baby has done and relating those initial events of early parenting. The way the story is told makes it clear that everything in it has already happened to the narrator.

"The Heart," in contrast, continues with the process of making the whale's heart more and more tangible in the next four paragraphs by describing the way the main character slices through the heart; the tools the younger brother, Applebee, uses; and their process of dumping parts of it so the neighbors don't become suspicious. The narrator's descriptions of the whale heart make it clear how important this image is to the story. The descriptions make it less and less abstract and also give a sense of how this mysterious object has become the new center of the family's life.

Paragraph eight feels like more of the same with its continued emphasis on the whale's heart: "The heart is cold and dry on the outside but grows warmer the more we cut into it" (Gray 121). However, things turn in the paragraph, when Applebee makes a mess and cries. The dad and the narrator seem to freeze at the sight of the tracked blood and the tears. And the narrator relates, "I say that I miss my mom and Dad says, 'Sure'" (Gray 122). It's a reminder that the heart is indeed a metaphor for all the things they're feeling about the missing mother. The main character—because we don't know enough about this person to know if it's due to age or personality—can't express their grief most of the time. It's only when things feel briefly insurmountable, something disgusting to clean up and a younger brother crying and not being soothed, that the main character makes the story's subtext clear by saying, "I miss my mom."

In "The Heart," the use of a child narrator, as well as the present tense, leaves more room for the reader to consider the story's layers. The main character doesn't know enough about the situation on either level (where the mother is, what happened to the mother to make her leave, what the heart is, or why it has appeared) to tell the readers exactly what this all is about. The child narrator doesn't have the benefit of being older and wiser and looking back to explain how these moments changed them and their family. They are stuck thinking and feeling in the present. This kind of story where an image or object is in the forefront can require more work from readers who rarely read poetry or aren't well-versed in the techniques for reading and drawing meaning from poetry.

If a reader approaches "The Heart" looking for something definite—a character has changed, a problem has been resolved—the story can appear to be a failure.

Sometimes, especially with first-person present tense flash fiction pieces that utilize thisness, the story needs to be also considered and read as if it were lyric poetry. Readers need to read not just for narrative or character development, but for how the combination of style and images contributes to a feeling, mood, and/or tone. The success of stories like this lies less in a resolution than in how evocatively they communicate a feeling.

In "The Baby," Barthelme has created a retrospective narrator who can directly say what has happened, how his life has changed due to becoming a parent. Because of time, the use of the past tense, and the character, there's room for an articulation of what the story is truly about. The story, especially because of the way the first-person, past-tense point of view is used, can be read with the expectations of character change and growth.

"The Heart" is the type of story that shows how flash fiction as a genre is more than just very short stories. There is room for thisness, an image that can take a first-person, present-tense flash story from feeling like a blog post that articulates everything in someone's day to feeling full and complete because of the layers of image, character, and events. The story's meaning is transmitted via metaphor and its descriptions.

In the essay "Smart Surprise in Flash Fiction," Jennifer Pieroni discusses the similarities between good flash fiction and poetry, "As in a sonnet, every word in every line matters in the mathematical sense." (66) The reader has to look not just at the characters and the events, but at the mood, tone, word choice and the particular order and rhythm of sentences. In other words, the reader needs to consider

---

the unspoken things beneath the story's surface. Readers who can approach image-driven flash as they would a poem, often have an easier time connecting and understanding these kinds of stories. This isn't to say "The Baby" can't be read this way as well. The images and diction in that story, as in the majority of Barthelme's stories, are lyric and well-chosen. The key difference is it still follows in a narrative path that could be graphed using the traditional Freytag's Pyramid model: a situation is defined, rising action occurs, the story has a climax, and then there's falling action/a potential resolution. "The Heart," however, doesn't really follow that narrative mode. There's a lot of narrative tension, but there isn't a moment that leads to a (perceived or real) change. At the end, the characters are still stuck in the middle of their situation.

In "The Heart's" last paragraph, the narrator has taken over the mother's role in this family. The father ignores Applebee and leaves the protagonist to clean, soothe, and put him to bed. In the middle of those activities, the narrator notes: "My hands smell like a dead whale basically" (Gray 122). Earlier in the story, the main character hoped to find their mother within the heart, to find a clue, but the reality is the main character's mother is really and truly gone. The narrator doesn't entirely know this, but the reader can infer the loss from the line: "all there is, is a dead whale heart" (122). The story ends with the main character still unsure with how to act and be in this strange, new motherless life. The narrator decides, echoing what the mother may have done: "I'll leave him alone" (122). The word "alone" is a reiteration of the meaning and mood of "The Heart." Think again of how to read a poem; in poetry, the placement of the words can be just as important as which words are chosen.

There are, of course, different ways to use the first-person point of view than described in this essay. One of the wonderful things about fiction is how elements such as the character narrating the story and the tense the author chooses can make the story being told feel unique and new. "The Baby" is only three pages, but through compression and strong details takes what could feel like an everyday anecdote about the difficulties of parenting a baby and turns it into something extraordinary. Because of Barthelme's use of the first-person past tense with the narrator reflecting on the events, "The Baby" can still be read and considered through the traditional methods of reading a story. A problem has been solved. A character is relating something about themself.

"The Heart" is an image-driven story that demonstrates how flexible the genre of flash fiction is. The thisness of this story strengthens the first-person present tense. So while the actions of the story don't evoke many changes or developments, considerations of the metaphoric meanings of the whale's heart add to the story's resonance.

Flash fiction encompasses both of these ways of telling a story in its name. The word flash adds an abstraction; it can signify the length of time the story takes, the feeling a reader might have after being in a character's life for a very short amount of time, or even act as a reminder that this kind of fiction can utilize abstractions. And fiction is a reminder—even if the story is a thousand words or less, even if it doesn't follow traditional plot structures—that the writer is still creating a new world that can possibly inform her own understanding of living.

Works Cited

Barthelme, Donald. "The Baby." *Forty Stories*. Putnam, 1987, pp. 234-36.

Brady, Catherine. *Story Logic and the Craft of Fiction*. Palgrave Macmillan, 2010.

Gray, Amelia. "The Heart." *Gutshot*. Farrar, Straus and Giroux, 2015, pp. 119-22.

Pieroni, Jennifer. "Smart Surprise in Flash Fiction." *Field Guide to Writing Flash Fiction: Tips from Editors, Teachers, and Writers in the Field*, edited by Tara L. Masih, RoseMetal Press, 2009, p. 66.

Russell, Karen. "Engineering Impossible Architectures." *In The Writer's Notebook II*. Tin House Books, 2012.

Townsend, Jacinda. "Creating Strong Characters in Fiction." Craft Lecture. Ballantine Hall, Bloomington, Indiana. 27 Jan. 2015.

Wood, James. "Details." *How Fiction Works*. Farrar, Straus and Giroux, 2008, p. 67.

Yu, Charles. "Standard Loneliness Package." *New American Stories*, edited by Ben Marcus, Vintage Books, 2015, p. 590.

CRITICAL READINGS

Kate Chopin's Flash Fiction and Flash Fiction Theory

Robert C. Evans

Kate Chopin is arguably one of the most important American writers of flash fiction (often defined as texts of roughly a thousand words or less). It is hard to think of another important American author (until, perhaps, very recently) who wrote more very short-short stories than she did. At least two examples of stories by Chopin that could now be called flash fiction—"The Story of an Hour" and "Ripe Figs"—are frequently anthologized and routinely taught. Her earliest surviving piece of fiction, "Emancipation. A Life Fable," was also one of her shortest, and she continued to write flash fiction throughout her career.

My purposes here are several. First, I will examine how Chopin's flash fiction helps illuminate—and can be illuminated by—certain ideas about flash fiction proposed by various authors and literary theorists. My essay is as much an introduction to (and survey of) flash fiction theory as it is a discussion of Chopin's own brief tales. Secondly, the essay examines several Chopin stories more specifically, focusing particularly on the traits that make some effective and some less effective. Finally, the essay explores various themes and methods that run throughout Chopin's career as a flash fiction writer. As this exploration will reveal, Chopin's very short stories are among her most artistically and morally complex works of fiction.

A conservative listing of Chopin's flash fiction (with word counts in parentheses) would include "A Reflection" (251), "Ripe Figs" (288), "The Night Came Slowly" (295), "Old Aunt Peggy" (317), "Emancipation. A Life Fable" (342), "An Idle Fellow" (374), "Doctor Chevalier's Lie" (385), "A Little Free-Mulatto" (390), "A Harbinger" (401), "Boulôt and Boulotte" (438), "Croque-Mitaine" (524), "A Very Fine Fiddle" (557), "Two Summers and Two Souls" (620), "A Turkey Hunt" (636), "The Bênitous' Slave"

(647), "Vagabonds" (718), "The Blind Man" (755), "Juanita" (799), "Caline" (890), "The White Eagle" (900), "The Story of an Hour" (1009), "The Kiss" (1028), and "Fedora" (1036). In addition, Chopin wrote many other stories that might be considered "flash" (or perhaps "sudden") fiction if the requisite word count is limited to roughly 2000 words or less. Such stories include "Madame Celestin's Divorce" (1293), "The Recovery" (1298), "A Visit to Avoyelles" (1329), "A Respectable Woman" (1462), "La Belle Zoraide" (1477), "Regret" (1479), "Odalie Misses Mass" (1848), "The Lilies" (1890), "A Pair of Silk Stockings" (1897), and "Desiree's Baby" (2160), to mention just a few. However, although Chopin was often invested in the idea of writing short stories that were *truly* short, this aspect of her writing has not been much explored.

Chopin's Flash Fiction and Flash Fiction Theory

Despite the recent interest in flash fiction and in longer works often called sudden fiction, surprisingly little criticism has been published about it. One fine but brief guide to the genre appears in various "Afterwords" published in *Sudden Fiction: American Short-Short Stories*, edited by Robert Shapard and James Thomas (227-58). This book, an early and influential anthology, first appeared in 1986. In the thirty years since then, no comparable survey of commentary has been issued. Flash fiction itself has been published in abundance, but no one has yet succeeded in collecting comments on the form as well as Shapard and Thomas did (hereafter abbreviated "S&T").[1]

Many comments they collected (usually only a paragraph long) can provide helpful insights into the nature and effectiveness of Kate Chopin's flash fiction. The writer Fred Chappell, for instance, argues that the "short-short story can take as many shapes and moods as the longer short story can manage." Flash fiction, he continues, is "not necessarily limited to reminiscence, it is not constrained to cover a very brief period of time, [and] it can be voiced in almost any known mode: realism, naturalism, fantasy, allegory, parable, anecdote" (S&T 227). Certainly these comments apply to Chopin's flash texts. Although many of the stories listed above are realistic, some (such as "Doctor Chevalier's Lie") veer toward naturalism, while others—

70

such as "Emancipation" and "An Idle Fellow"—are either openly or implicitly symbolic, allegorical, or parabolic. Many of Chopin's smallest fictions (such as "Ripe Figs") emphasize the anecdotal, while other relevant categories include meditative essays, character studies, local color stories, and tales ending with a final ironic twist (or, as in "The Kiss" and "Two Summers and Two Souls," double twists).

The tone of Chopin's shortest stories is often slyly whimsical and subtly humorous. If her shortest tales reveal a common thread, it is a keen, sympathetic, amused, and often amusing sense of human foibles and complexities. Challenging the mistaken criticism that flash fiction lacks nuanced characterization, Chopin's briefest works often grant insight into the lives of real, complicated human beings, not manikins stuck together to fill out a short episode. Her best short-short stories thus satisfy another of Chappell's criteria: they *imply* a larger world the story only briefly (but effectively) suggests (S&T 227). Sometimes, in fact, Chopin's shorter works have *more* power than her longer, more elaborate stories. The sheer concentration of "The Story of an Hour," for instance, has made it a classroom and popular favorite. Few people who have read it ever forget it. The same might be said of "Desirée's Baby" and numerous other brief works by Chopin.

Yet Chappell, although claiming that flash fiction can adopt many different styles and tones, seems less convincing when arguing that a good short-short story has to be "troubling." "*Unease,*" he claims, "whether humorous or sad," is the intended effect. "Even if the story achieves resolution, it cannot be a simple resolution and it should not give the impression of permanence" (S&T 227). In this case, Chappell's attempt to limit successful flash fiction seems strained. It fits such well-known Chopin tales as "The Story of an Hour" or "Doctor Chevalier's Lie," and it also fits such similarly disturbing or unsettling tales as "The Blind Man," "Caline," "Juanita," and "A Very Fine Fiddle," to mention just a few. It seems less applicable, however, to some of Chopin's more obviously whimsical or humorous works, such as "Boulôt and Boulotte" (with its amusing twelve-year-old twins who head off to buy their very first pairs of shoes), or "Ripe Figs" (with its wise old woman and impatient young girl), or "Croque-Mitaine" (with its credulous youngster afraid of the boogey-man). If Chopin's shortest fiction is any indication, it seems best to avoid demanding inflexible, single effects from every short-short tale.

Paul Theroux's double claim that a good brief tale should "not be mistaken for an anecdote" but should be "highly calculated" in "effects" and "timing" certainly seems applicable to the best examples of Chopin's flash fiction. So, too, does his assertion that an effective short-short story "contains a novel" (S&T 228). "Caline," about a young rural girl's disillusioning visit to a city, could easily have been expanded both into the past and into the future. Caline could well be the central figure in an intriguing novel. So could the title character of "Doctor Chevalier's Lie." A compassionate physician in a rough part of town, he risks his own social standing to aid the downtrodden. The episode Chopin recounts could easily be just one chapter in a much longer book. And it goes without saying that the "backstory" to the marriage of Louise and Brentley Mallard in "The Story of an Hour" would make an absorbing novel. All the works just mentioned also satisfy another of Theroux's criteria: like most of Chopin's best brief works, they are exceptionally well designed. They may be short, but they are not simple.

John L'Heureux's statements in the Shapard and Thomas anthology also fit many of Chopin's briefest tales. Works such as "The Bênitous' Slave" and "Old Aunt Peggy" (both about former slaves living nostalgically after 1865) definitely and memorably "anatomize a character" (S&T 228), as do such stories as "Juanita" (about a mysteriously attractive unattractive woman), "The Kiss" (about a woman finally less clever than she assumes), and "The White Eagle" (about an imaginative young girl who becomes a lonely old woman). Practically all of Chopin's briefest tales are the kind of stories that, according to L'Heureux, "we can't help reading fast, and then re-reading, again," even though "no matter how many times we read [them], we're not quite through" (S&T 228). Chopin's most obviously comic tales, such as "Boulôt and Boulotte" and "Croque-Mitaine," can perhaps be fully digested at one sitting.

But most of her other very short works both stimulate and repay repeated re-reading.

The frequent effectiveness of Chopin's flash fiction is all the more impressive in light of Gordon Weaver's claim that "the shorter the fiction, the greater become the odds against success" (S&T 229). Anyone who has read hundreds of short-short stories might agree with Weaver. He argues, in fact, that "most short-shorts fail" (S&T 229). Perhaps it is better to say that few achieve their full potential. But this is true of practically all writing, and flash fiction is no exception. Even Chopin occasionally falls flat. "Emancipation" seems too obviously simple and too relentlessly didactic. (It was, after all, a very early work.) "A Reflection" seems more a hyped-up romantic essay than an exercise in the subtle irony Chopin so often elsewhere employs. Aside from these two works, however—and perhaps I am being too hard even on *them*—I would willingly read and re-read any of Chopin's other shortest tales. As the enthusiastic responses of my students suggest, Chopin truly mastered the form.[2]

One especially effective aspect of her very brief fiction is her use of sudden concluding twists. These were often formulaic in her day, especially in writing influenced by Guy de Maupassant. But Chopin frequently manages to surprise us even when we *anticipate* a surprise. In some stories, in fact, she piles one surprise on top of another. In "The Kiss," for instance, a woman tries to manipulate a man into marrying her even though she only wants his money, not him. When, before their marriage, he accidentally witnesses another man enthusiastically kiss her, we assume that her matrimonial schemes will collapse. She manages to convince him, however, that the other man is just an overly familiar friend of her brother. So the duped target not only forgives her but even encourages the brother's friend to kiss her at their wedding. Apparently, then, the woman has doubly triumphed, winning both a rich husband and a continuing sexual affair. Chopin thus creates two surprises: the wedding itself and the kiss the groom not only allows but proposes. Yet Chopin saves the biggest surprise for the very end: the brother's friend resolutely refuses to kiss her, apparently tired of her games. Here is a story that could easily have been inflated into a novel by Henry

James. By being so concise, Chopin gains immediacy of impact, effective emphasis on startling irony, and appeal to a broad range of possible readers.

Chopin's best flash fiction exemplifies many other traits of the flash fiction genre mentioned in the Shapard and Thomas volume. Good flash fiction (says Lydia Davis) has a literal presence: "You don't have time to get used to it (forget it) as you read" (S&T 230). Certainly this is true of many of Chopin's best short-short tales. Her characters, like many people in flash fiction, tend to be (in Davis's words) "unheroic"—that is, common, realistic, everyday persons (S&T 230). Davis suggests that flash fiction is especially appropriate for dealing with such characters, and Chopin's briefest tales confirm this claim.

But Chopin's best works contradict negative assertions about flash fiction made by H. E. Francis. Francis argues that in very brief works, "characters approach anonymity, setting nears irrelevance, situation (however flimsy) almost invariably presides, or tone. Tone and situation are the prima donnas" (S&T 231). Francis continues: "The form matches the instant's perception. The brevity is the joy, the Roman candle thrust, burst,—*Ahhh!*—and darkness. As a too-frequent experience, they bore. I seldom find one which bears re-reading" (S&T 232).

Why Francis should feel this way is hard to understand. After all, some of the greatest, most resonant, most thought-provoking literary works are brief poems. Why should a few words arranged in one form be innately more (or less) interesting than a few words arranged in another? Few people tire of reading good, brief lyrics in succession; why should they tire of reading successive short-short stories? The problem is not with any *form itself* but with specific examples. Reading a series of fine poems can be exceptionally satisfying; reading a series of fine short-short stories can be, too.

Chopin's Flash Fiction: Individual Examples

Chopin, of course, wrote some less-than-fully-impressive, short-short tales. Here, however, I want to concentrate on the varied successes she achieved in some of her briefest works. "Ripe

Figs," for instance, despite being only 288 words long, is one of her most frequently anthologized stories. It is reprinted so widely precisely because it *is* brief. However, unlike other stories such as "A Reflection" (which is rarely read though it is even briefer), "Ripe Figs" is an extraordinarily rich "flash" work that repays frequent re-reading.

Precisely because this story *is* so short, perhaps it is worth reprinting in full:

> Maman-Nainaine said that when the figs were ripe Babette might go to visit her cousins down on the Bayou-Boeuf where the sugar cane grows. Not that the ripening of figs had the least thing to do with it, but that is the way Maman-Nainaine was.
>
> It seemed to Babette a very long time to wait; for the leaves upon the trees were tender yet, and the figs were like little hard, green marbles.
>
> But warm rains came along and plenty of strong sunshine, and though Maman-Nainaine was as patient as the statue of la Madone, and Babette as restless as a humming-bird, the first thing they both knew it was hot summer-time. Every day Babette danced out to where the fig-trees were in a long line against the fence. She walked slowly beneath them, carefully peering between the gnarled, spreading branches. But each time she came disconsolate away again. What she saw there finally was something that made her sing and dance the whole day long.
>
> When Maman-Nainaine sat down in her stately way to breakfast, the following morning, her muslin cap standing like an aureole about her white, placid face, Babette approached. She bore a dainty porcelain platter, which she set down before her godmother. It contained a dozen purple figs, fringed around with their rich, green leaves.
>
> "Ah," said Maman-Nainaine, arching her eyebrows, "how early the figs have ripened this year!"
>
> "Oh," said Babette, "I think they have ripened very late."
>
> "Babette," continued Maman-Nainaine, as she peeled the very plumpest figs with her pointed silver fruit-knife, "you will carry my love to them all down on Bayou-Boeuf. And tell your Tante Frosine I shall look for her at Toussaint—when the chrysanthemums are in bloom." (Chopin, "Ripe Figs" 90)

This work is brief in length but rich in themes, meanings, phrasing, and design. It begins and ends symmetrically (with references to a planned journey associated with ripening of various sorts). One theme concerns the metaphorical ripening of young Babette, who herself grows in maturity as she waits for the figs to develop. The story also contrasts the ways time is experienced by the old and young. Time's passing seems rapid to the elderly but slow to the youthful. Family connections are emphasized at the beginning and end of the tale as well as throughout. Also throughout, references to natural growth (including the growth of sugar cane, fig trees, figs, and chrysanthemums) emphasize the theme of maturation. Babette's very name suggests her youth, while the fact that "Maman-Nainaine" is identified by her title (which means "grandmother" and/or "godmother") makes her seem almost archetypal—almost more important as a symbol than as a particular person. She is an old woman set in her ways who feels no need to explain her thinking; her authority cannot be challenged. She is both imposing and amusing, while Babette's impatience is both charming and funny. Despite the work's brevity, its characters seem real and convincing; although they are archetypes, they are also nicely individualized. They are not allegorical stick figures.

Archetypal themes, characters, settings, and processes, in fact, seem strongly emphasized in this brief tale, and perhaps flash fiction is especially well-suited to dealing with archetypal issues. Very brief tales can draw on readers' wide acquaintance with familiar situations, personalities, and relationships. In this story, Maman-Nainaine is the kind of quirky, eccentric old person most of us of us have either encountered (or have or will become), while Babette is the kind of innocent, inquisitive, energetic youngster we all have met or perhaps once were. Successful flash fiction can often take much for granted if the writer knows how to tap into archetypes, as Chopin often does.

But the specifics of this story also win admiration. It uses vivid imagery (such as the reference to "little hard, green marbles"), striking contrasts (the grandmother as a statue; Babette as a humming-bird), evocative verbs (Babette "danced" out to the trees), effective shifts (having first "danced," Babette then "walked slowly," "carefully peering"), and still more vivid imagery (as in the reference to the "gnarled, spreading branches"). The contrast between the gnarled branches and the hard, green marble-like figs replicates, symbolically, the contrast between the old woman and the young girl. In fact, hardly a detail seems out of place. Symbolic contrasts abound. They include the characters' contrasting, concluding comments; the association of Babette with movement and Maman-Nainaine with stasis; the association of Babette with outdoors and nature and Maman-Nainaine with indoors and with civilized surroundings (note the "dainty" platter and the "silver" fruit-knife); the association of Babette with nature and the old woman with religion, and so on. No brief discussion can do real justice to this tale's artistry and resonance. Like a skillful lyric, this story can be re-read repeatedly without exhausting its rich significances. It shows, as Chopin often shows, just how many meanings and implications she can pack into a brief space.

Much the same might be said of a very different short tale—"Doctor Chevalier's Lie." Like much flash fiction, it immediately plunges us into the midst of things, opening with the "quick report of a pistol" in "the quiet autumn night" (Chopin, "Doctor Chevalier's" 728). Both details foreshadow the darkness and death that soon predominate. Doctor Chevalier (whose very name suggests his later chivalry) hears the gunshot from his office in an "unsavory quarter" (728) of the city. This location suggests either that he is not especially talented or, as we later discover, that he is a good man who both figuratively and literally cares for the less fortunate. He has been up late reading, a fact suggesting his intelligence, which we will soon see balanced by real practical knowledge. He is summoned to examine another dead body—that, it turns out, is yet another prostitute. At first the story's depiction of prostitutes might seem demeaning (they are variously described as "tawdry," "hysterical," and "morbidly curious" [728]). If the story initially invites judgment of these women, ultimately we will be invited, instead, to put aside our stereotypes. We will finally see things, as Chevalier does, with more sensitive, discriminating eyes. Chopin's flash stories may be unusually short, but they often involve real moral complexity.

They also often involve fairly blunt realism. Here, for instance, she does not hesitate to mention the "hole in the temple" that the prostitute "had sent the bullet through" (Chopin, "Doctor Chevalier" 728). The girl's death, then, was not a murder but a suicide, making her seem less a victim of someone else than a victim of her own depression and despair. Already she seems more sympathetic than we might initially have expected: once again, Chopin is packing genuine ethical complexity into little more than three hundred words, thereby challenging, once more, simple moral stereotypes. This prostitute seems less the generically evil, reprehensible woman some of Chopin's readers may have anticipated than a woman in genuine pain. And eventually we learn that Chevalier himself *knows* this woman: he had met her years before, when she was still an innocent, beautiful girl. He and a friend had happened to stay in her family's rural Arkansas cabin while hunting. Ultimately, Chevalier writes to her family, telling them that their child and sibling died of sickness. He never mentions suicide. Intelligent, practical, and compassionate, Chevalier is everything one might hope a doctor would be. Yet Chopin, of course, has another final twist in store. The story's last lines are these: "Of course it was noised about that Doctor Chevalier had cared for the remains of a woman of doubtful repute. Shoulders were shrugged. Society thought of cutting him. Society did not, for some reason or other, so the affair blew over" (729).

Chopin often ends her briefest tales not only with twists but with double or even triple twists. These add to her texts' complexity, and they are often delivered, as in "Doctor Chevalier's Lie," in understated, ambiguous, highly resonant language. Thus the phrase "noised about" implies stupid gossip rather than intelligent commentary or real concern. The reference to "cutting him" implies social violence committed by well-to-do "Society" (the capitalized word suggests a single-minded corporate entity). But they do *not* cut him. This fact suggests multiple possibilities: compassion, indifference, and/or lack of any real interest in the woman and/or the doctor himself. Rather than ending by moralizing, Chopin here (as so often) lets us puzzle things out for ourselves. Her flash fiction, at its best, does not so much settle questions as raise them.

Stories like "Doctor Chevalier's Lie" undercut the claims of anyone who would easily disparage flash fiction as either artistically or morally simple. Compare and contrast the skill of this story (for instance) with the assertions of James B. Hall:

> Because its roots were in popular culture, the intention of the short-short was to entertain. Because its language was largely journalistic, the early short-short presented a characteristic weakness. The combination of brief scope and truncated language precluded complex comment on the nature of human life, and yet this order of comment is of central value in prose fiction. (S&T 234)

However accurate an assessment this may seem of much flash fiction, it does very little justice to many short works by Chopin. Her best flash fiction often develops and ends in ways that give readers real pause (and cause) for thought. Her final sentences, far from being predictable twists, are often the most subtle and suggestive sentences in the entire work.

Consider, for example, the conclusion of "A Very Fine Fiddle," which describes how a desperately hungry child, acting on behalf of her equally hungry younger brothers and sisters, manages to sell her father's old, beloved violin for a much newer, much better instrument. She makes a fine profit from the sale, ensuring that she and her siblings will no longer have to worry about food, and she even manages to provide her fiddle-loving and constantly fiddle-playing father with a brand new violin. The story, then, should end with everyone happy; however, it does not. Instead, it ends with these words by the father: "It's one fine fiddle; an' like you say, it shine' like satin. But some way or udder, 't ain' de same. Yair, Fifine, take it—put it 'side. I b'lieve, me, I ain' goin' play de fiddle no mo'" (Chopin, "Very Fine" 215). Instead of being delighted with his daughter's gift, the father is broken-hearted. The loss of the old fiddle, which for him had real sentimental value, has broken his heart. If that were the story's *only* point, the tale might seem mawkishly sentimental. But Chopin, as usual, manages to make her ending morally complex. The father did, after all, neglect his family's real need and even hunger; the daughter's decision to sell the old violin can thus be easily justified. Yet the story still ends with the father in real pain, perhaps mainly at the loss of the violin, but perhaps also because of the implied rebuke from his own daughter that its sale implies.

Similarly complex is the ending of "The Blind Man," which describes how the title character—poor, ignored, hungry, and desperate to earn some money—wanders aimlessly through the streets of a large city whose residents often treat him either with indifference or even hostility. The story implicitly satirizes the values of the city's residents, but the effectiveness of the satire depends largely on Chopin's understatement. She never openly condemns the townspeople's callous behavior; instead, she merely lets the facts speak for themselves. When a rich businessman is the person accidentally struck and killed by a streetcar (rather than the poor blind man, as Chopin had led us to expect), the "point" seems not some cheap notion of poetic justice but rather a more disturbing suggestion about the sheer randomness of fate. Rather than concluding with some overt bit of easy moralizing, Chopin instead finishes the story this way: "The blind man did not know what the commotion was all about. He had crossed the street, and there he was, stumbling on in the sun, trailing his foot along the coping" (Chopin, "Blind Man" 829). The story ends as it began, thus typifying the skillful design of so many of Chopin's briefest tales. Instead of drawing some obvious, simple conclusion, Chopin here, as so often elsewhere, leaves us thinking for ourselves. She does the same thing at the end of many of her other briefest tales, including "Caline," "The White Eagle," "The Story of an Hour," "Vagabonds," and especially the mysterious "Fedora," which ends with a shocking kiss that takes everyone—readers as well as the astonished recipient—by surprise.

Chopin's flash fictions, however, are often impressively complex, both morally and otherwise, from start to finish, not just in their conclusions. Once again, "A Very Fine Fiddle" is a good case in point. When the young girl takes her father's old fiddle up to a nearby plantation to sell it, three men at a fancy party there are very eager to look it over. They not only give her a brand-new violin in its place but also a big roll of cash as well. Their apparent generosity, however, immediately seems suspect. Obviously, her father's old fiddle is in fact very valuable. It may even be a Stradivarius, although he appears not to know this. The three men, therefore, far from being selflessly kind-hearted, have in fact exploited an impoverished, ignorant young girl. Rather than selling the immensely valuable violin *for* her and letting her, her siblings, and her father profit from the sale, they have cheated her and will keep the immense profit— or the immensely valuable violin—for themselves. Anyone who considers this story merely a bit of sentimental, local-color scene-painting with whimsical characterizations has missed its moral complexity.

Even more disturbing is a series of intriguing passages from the middle of "The Blind Man." The narrator reports that earlier one "morning some one who had finally grown tired of having [the title character] hanging around had equipped him with this box of pencils, and sent him out to make his living" (Chopin, "Blind Man" 828). What might otherwise have seemed a generous act seems instead merely the result of annoyance. Later, a "kind-hearted woman who saw [the blind man] from an upper window felt sorry for him." Just when we think that she may take some positive action to help him, the narrator instead reports that she merely "wished that he would cross over into the shade" (828). Later still, the blind man encounters a group of children. Attracted by his colorful box of pencils, "they wanted to know what was in it." This seems innocent enough, until one "of them attempted to take it away from him." When he resists, a policeman approaches, apparently to help him. Instead, the narrator reports that the policeman "jerked him violently around by the collar; but upon perceiving that he was blind, considerately refrained from clubbing him and sent him on his way" (829). In all these instances, the story subtly suggests that the blind man is hardly the only person whose perceptions are limited. Others in the tale are far blinder than he. Here, as so often elsewhere, Chopin's brief tales give us plenty to think about when the story concludes.

This may even be true of a "flash fiction" that has often been described as one of Chopin's least complex: "A Little Free-Mulatto." This story, one of Chopin's shortest, describes a little girl of mixed race. Although her father is so light-skinned that he could easily pass for white, he is too proud of his mixed status to let his infant daughter play either with white children or with young blacks. Eventually, though, when her parents notice her becoming depressed because she is isolated, they move to an all-mulatto community, where she has many friends. The story's final two sentences are these: "Well, there is no question about it. The happiest little Free-Mulatto in all Louisiana is Aurélia, since her father has moved to 'L'Isle des Mulâtres'" (Chopin, "Little Free" 745).

One way to read this tale is as a simple-minded endorsement of racial segregation. This interpretation, however, does scant justice to the potential irony and complexity of the work. The very sentence "Well, there is no question about it" raises all sorts of questions. Should we admire or condemn the father's pride? Should we accept or reject the racial segregation to which he feels compelled to respond? Is the little girl happy only because she *is* a little girl, as yet ignorant of the ways racism will affect her later life? Is it fortunate or actually sad that mulattoes have their own segregated community? Is Chopin really endorsing the story's final sentence, or is she, with her characteristic irony, giving us a typical final twist?

However one chooses to answer these questions, the mere fact that they can be asked suggests one of the great virtues of Kate Chopin's flash fiction. Rarely do her brief works end unambiguously, and rarely do the works themselves fail to display impressive moral and artistic complexity. Chopin set a high standard for later writers of American flash fiction, and perhaps it is best to end with a comment by one of her most talented successors. In the words of Joyce Carol Oates, describing flash fiction in general, "We who love prose fiction love these miniature tales both to read and to write because they are so finite; so highly compressed and highly charged. The tension is that of . . . an epic writ so small that one can hardly bear to watch it"

(S&T 246). As Chopin's best flash fictions demonstrate, we can also hardly bear to look away.

Notes

1. Because the selections included by Shapard and Thomas have no titles, I have cited them by referring to authors' names and location in the Shapard and Thomas volume.

2. I wish to thank the students in my summer 2016 flash fiction course for sharing their splendid insights into the form in general and into Chopin's stories in particular. I am especially grateful to Caitlin Celka, Amos Davidson, Patsy Head, Elizabeth Huggins, Andrew Mitchell, Joshua Parrish, Jennifer Scott, and particularly Benjie Thomas.

Works Cited

Chopin, Kate. "The Blind Man." *Kate Chopin: Complete Novels and Stories*, edited by Sandra M. Gilbert. Library of America, 2002, pp. 828-29.

_____. "Doctor Chevalier's Lie." *Kate Chopin: Complete Novels and Stories*, edited by Sandra M. Gilbert. Library of America, 2002, pp. 728-29.

_____. "The Kiss." *Kate Chopin: Complete Novels and Stories*, edited by Sandra M. Gilbert, Library of America, 2002, pp. 775-77.

_____. "A Little Free-Mulatto." *Kate Chopin: Complete Novels and Stories*, edited by Sandra M. Gilbert, Library of America, 2002, pp. 744-45.

_____. "Ripe Figs." *Vogue*, 19 Aug. 1893, p. 90.

_____. "A Very Fine Fiddle." *Kate Chopin: Complete Novels and Stories*, edited by Sandra M. Gilbert, Library of America, 2002, pp. 214-15.

Shapard, Robert, and James Thomas, editors. *Sudden Fiction: American Short-Short Stories*. Gibbs-Smith, 1986.

Against Short Attention Spans: "Fragmentary" Fiction for "Fragmentary" Lives_____

Santino Prinzi

Alongside its undeniable increase in popularity, two common claims haunt criticism about flash fiction and other short forms of fiction: they are incomplete and somewhat lacking in comparison to the novel, and they are increasing in popularity in our contemporary age because the form caters to our shorted attention spans. I say "haunt" because these arguments are continually asserted; however, while these claims are attempts to discredit very short fiction, they actually highlight its strengths. For example, although short fiction by Robert Walser and Franz Kafka has been considered incomplete or fragmentary, an analysis of their prose reveals only the appearance of lack in flash fiction as a literary form. It is precisely this awareness of something missing or fragmentary that draws the reader's attention to Walser's and Kafka's work and that intensifies its meaning. The stories of these writers were considered fragmentary or incomplete because they appeared to "lack the development and closure we normally attribute to the short story" (Thiher 23), but flash fictions suggest more than the language alone states; this apparent absence is intentional. The rationale for looking at Kafka's short fiction should be obvious; he is well established in the canon of European short story writers—one whose "greatest talent" lies in "shorter works rather than the novel" (Ryan 63). Walser, a contemporary of Kafka and from whom Kafka "learned decisively" (Adorno 253), is often overlooked; however, "when Kafka's first stories appeared, many thought the name was a pseudonym adopted by [. . .] Walser" (Ryan 61), so "it was more likely to be Kafka who was seen through the prism of Walser" (Sontag vii) rather than the other way around. Therefore, an examination of the flash fiction by these two particular authors establishes the presence of absence in fiction and its power to steer one's attention to a specific point. The second part of this chapter proposes that our attention spans have become fragmented instead of shortened in order to adapt to our increasingly divided modern lifestyles; in other words, we have adapted the way we think and, as a result, the way we read. With these two strands of thought in mind, it is possible to assert that the rise in the popularity of flash fiction is not due to shortened attention spans. Instead, flash fiction is popular because it serves a contemporary need to engage with literature in a way that complements current lifestyles. Flash can be read quickly, but it can keep a reader thinking for a long time thereafter. There is nothing reductive about the form or our engagement with it.

The Presence of Absence

The issue that always arises in discussions that use "the novel as a point of comparison, or rather of contrast" (Pratt 94) with flash fiction and other short forms is the notion of length, with the assumption that, because they are comprised of fewer words, flash fictions cannot achieve the same level of intensity as longer fiction. Critics disagree with the importance of length, such as Mary Louise Pratt describing it as "too material a feature to be given top billing" (95) and Ian Reid claiming that "it would be unsatisfactory to make a word-count the sole criterion" (10) for judging the quality of a piece of short fiction because "only a naive reader would confuse significance with bulk" (2). Of course, the fact that flash is short means that the theory that it suits a shortened attention span is an attractive one, but there are other features of flash fiction more deserving of our attention. These features "can move us by an intensity which the novel cannot sustain" (Reid 2); in other words, the form uses devices in a way that longer forms of fiction may use but cannot rely on. This does not mean that flash is reliant on these features either, only that the form lends itself, because of its length, to the most effective use of these devices. After all, if "nothing about the novel is really needed to explain" shorter fiction (Pratt 96) and, "in the unfinished stories of Kafka's notebooks, some fragments a page long can carry us over a whole abyss of events" (Jarrell 12), then there must be something about these fictions besides length that compels the attention of readers.

The words "unfinished" and "fragments" from Jarrell's above statement implies there is something incomplete and lacking about Kafka's stories. Maurice Blanchot argues in his essay "Reading Kafka" that the idea of something lacking in Kafka's short prose "is not accidental" on the writer's part because "the pages we read are utterly full" and "nothing is lacking in them, not even the lack that is their purpose" (6). Paradoxically, this purposeful absence calls attention to precisely the point of the text. Similar claims are made about Walser's fiction, too, as Samuel Frederick and Nilima Rabl state that "Walser's texts trace multiple noughts" and they "dance around an absent center" (76), and Walter Benjamin identifies in Walser "a neglect of style that is quite extraordinary" ("Robert Walser"137). Like Kafka, the absences in Walser's fiction are deliberate; the stories "only *appear* to have no aim," and they are "never without the gravitational pull from *that which is most important*" (Frederick and Rabl 77). This idea of the gravitational pull suggests flash draws its reader to what appears to be lacking in order to intensify its point; in other words, flash uses the implicit rather than the explicit to emphasise its purpose. This is obviously not a device exclusive to the form as much literature employs implication and subtext; however, the continual use of such a device would be difficult to maintain over longer narratives. The short prose by Walser and Kafka has more to say between the lines, as well as the words themselves.

Kafka's first book-length publication, *Betrachtung* (Mediation), published in December 1912, contains prose pieces that were originally mistaken for Walser's. Allen Thiher claims that it is "difficult to call most of these pieces [in the collection] fully developed stories, since as open-ended expressions of rupture and flight they are often poetic texts that lack the development and closure we normally attribute to the short story" (23). Judith Ryan has described Walser's style as "seemingly unmistakable," consisting of "playful" writing that notices "the small details in the world around the narrator, as he wanders through natural landscapes" or engages "with flights of fancy," and she distinguishes this style from Kafka's because it does not sound like the Kafka we know (61). However, though flash fiction "should not be void or without form," the form in which the story appears "may be whatever the author pleases" (Matthews 77), and there are similarities between these two authors. This does not mean that flash writers have a free pass to write what they will and define it as such. Brander Matthews distinguishes the difference between a story and a sketch, claiming that in a story "there must be an action," whereas a sketch "may be an outline of character, or even a picture or a mood of mind" (77). Although Walser's and Kafka's flash fiction is poetic and although their flash works may not possess the qualities we may "normally" associate with fiction, defined here as development and closure, they can still be considered stories.

Walser's "A Little Ramble" is one of many stories in which the narrator takes us through a description of a natural landscape and the events, or non-events, which occur. The man walks through the mountains, encounters another man searching for his two companions, and later crosses paths with the other two men. The narrator does not see many other people during this excursion, and there seems to be no real story here as nothing appears to happen. However, Reid states "there is usually in the sketch some movement towards a narrative dimension" (32); therefore, to claim there is a "nothingness [to] Walser's content" is to "understand at once nothing and everything" about Walser's writing (Plug 655). By appearing to present nothing, Walser brings the reader's attention back to the very purpose of the text, when the narrator in the final two lines of the story says, "We don't need to see anything out of the ordinary. We already see too much" ("A Little Ramble" 31). This statement is both the "withdrawal of what [Walser] has to say" (Plug 655) and its inclusion. This story, in which nothing out of the ordinary happens, is about a world in which so many shocking things commonly happen that a series of non-events is in itself an event.

A similar situation occurs in Kafka's story "Rejection" in which the narrator walks past a pretty girl, asks her to come with him, and she ignores him. Afterwards, the narrator fabricates a dialogue in his mind and offers an interpretation of what the girl's rejection means. In this imagined exchange, each character highlights the shortcomings of the other, and, in the acknowledgement that they are both correct in their opinions, the girl suggests they both continue on their way (Kafka, "Rejection" 383-384), with the girl stating that the narrator is "no Duke with a famous name" (383) and the man suggesting her smile is "inviting mortal danger" after commenting further on her dress. Like in Walser's "A Little Ramble," nothing has actually happened beyond a girl ignoring a man yet, through this imagined dialogue, we have a story concerned about the way men and women are supposed to publicly behave and how people regard others in terms of their social status rather than as individuals. This theme of the non-event appears too in Kafka's "Clothes" in which the narrator comments on how we wear "the same fancy dress" (383) in order to maintain public appearances; here, mere thoughts about clothes reveal more about societal conventions. The narrator brings the reader to this point at the end of the story when he comments on how the clothes are "puffy, dusty, already seen by too many people, and hardly wearable any longer" (383) to suggest that we have become exhausted by how we are expected to behave according to society's stipulations. These stories appear to be about nothing important, but actually they suggest more through their non-events, stretching the very definition of what we conventionally call a story.

Kafka and Walser's theme of the non-event plays with the reader's perception through these absences and the withholding of information. Another example of suggestive omission can be found in Walser's "The Boat." The opening line distances the reader from the rest of the narrative: "I think I've written this scene before, but I'll write it once again" (Walser, "The Boat" 28). This technique of making the reader conscious that the narrator is both telling and recording the story is not uncommon in Walser's work. This story is about the observations of a writer, brought to life through the various rhetorical questions he asks himself about the man and the woman he observes sitting in a boat. He does not know why they are there, and, though they share a "long kiss" (28), the context remains unknown. As the onlooker, the narrator cannot possibly know precisely what is going on inside the mind of another human being, a fact that conflicts with our desire for a cohesive explanation of what the story is about; is this story about two people sitting in a boat or something more? The same sense of not knowing emerges in Kafka's "Passers-by" in which the narrator watches a man chasing another and entertains the various reasons why the man could be being chased. Then the narrator addresses the reader at the end, stating, "You're thankful that the second man is now long out of sight" (Kafka, "Passers-by" 388). The story of one man chasing another becomes one about an onlooker's relief at not having to take any action about a witnessed event and embracing the relief over not having to work out what is happening. Both stories, like the others already discussed, have more going on than the physical space on the page permits, encouraging readers to think for themselves rather than being told explicitly what to believe.

In Walser and Kafka's writing, the presence of absence is deliberate and, though this creates the impression that flash fiction is somehow fragmentary, these are complete pieces, which do have a story to tell. Moreover, these stories are relevant to our contemporary culture despite the charge that the rise of flash fiction is due to our shortened attention spans. Though the increase in the popularity of flash fiction is indisputable, the fact that the form has existed long before the internet or many other media suggests that flash was "not created to satisfy the small attention spans sadly synonymous with the twenty-first century, or to benefit readers who would prefer to peruse online material rather than paperbacks" (Howitt-Dring 49). The nature of the form encourages readers to engage with the text and think for themselves, and this is why flash is rising in popularity; the form requires greater attention and engagement from its reader, not less. Fewer words do not equate to less depth, content, or attention required from readers. However, this contradicts assertions about attention spans and the way readers engage with text in our digital culture, so the next section will explore these charges and their validity.

Your Attention, Please?

Length was dismissed as the sole factor in the rise in the popularity of flash because, though a quick read, flash fiction is not always

---

quickly grasped. The form cannot simply cater to readers who have short attention spans, those in need of instant gratification because flash demands the reader's attention both during the act of reading and afterwards. At the same time, one cannot deny how the digital revolution has affected our ability to think in our culture, and some critics, such as Sven Birkerts, believe "concentration is no longer a given," that it has to be "strategized, fought for" (155), although some of his evidence for "the repeated fragmentation of focus" (85) is very anecdotal. However, critics like William Nelles claim those who discuss the shortcomings of short forms are often "too dependent on" (88) anecdotal evidence. Despite this, Birkerts does make a strong case about the nature of our contemporary culture, which is "saturated with vivid competing stimuli" (146). He observes that, when online, "psychologically [he is] fragmented" (168). In some respects, Martyn Lyons agrees when he acknowledges that "the internet encourages a kind of fragmented reading in which the reader rushes distractedly from one short item to another" (196). What is key about these debates, and their relevance to flash fiction, is that discussions about attention and distraction within culture are not new, just like flash fiction itself.

Walter Benjamin acknowledged in the 1930s that "distraction and concentration form an antithesis," which, though distinguishable from one another, are related ("Work of Art" 119). One might assume that, through this antithesis, there is a positive and negative relationship between concentration and distraction (presumably, the assumption being that distraction is negative and concentration is positive), but Benjamin suggests distraction and concentration, rather than being good or bad, are simply different. Both distraction and concentration manipulate our attention in different ways, meaning there is a difference in how an individual engages with a work of art (in our case, literature). He states that "a person who concentrates before a work of art is absorbed by it," and they enter "into the work," whereas, "by contrast, the distracted masses absorb the work of art into themselves" (119); someone concentrating on a text perceives the text differently from someone who absorbs it into themselves. This means that "distraction [is] a spur to new ways of perceiving" (Eiland 9), and, if there can be a new way of perceiving in which the individual is distracted as Benjamin implies, then there must be a new way of perceiving in which the individual is, to use Birkerts' term, "psychologically fragmented" (168). In other words, there must be a new way of perceiving and engaging with literature, and this would require a new way of thinking, one in which our attention span is fragmented in order to adapt to the way the internet promotes fragmented reading (Lyons 196). Fragmented reading requires fragmented thinking, and this complements, rather than resists, our contemporary lifestyles.

This is not uniquely our challenge; like our own lives, Kafka's life was fragmented between the various responsibilities vying for his attention. Adorno believes the "crucial moment [. . .] towards which everything in Kafka's work is directed, is that which men become aware that they are not themselves—that they themselves are things" (255), and this is true for Kafka himself. In his diaries and letters, Kafka often refers to how life gets in the way of his writing, stating "I finish nothing because I have no time" (*Diaries* 80) and lamenting that "everything has combined to keep [him] away from writing and from [his] pleasure in it" (*Letters* 96). The "thing" that Kafka has become is not the writer he wants to be but the roles he plays within his professional and family lives, the responsibilities that act as obstacles that keep him from concentrating on what he describes to Max Brod as his "happy distraction" (*Letters* 88). Kafka's own attention is fragmented between what he has to do and what he would rather be doing. Are we not the same in our preference to be "distracted" from what we do not wish to do in favor of the things we do? Before his committal to a psychiatric institution for the last twenty-three years of his life, Walser too had various jobs and so shared many of Kafka's concerns around having to balance his writing and supporting himself financially. For Kafka, in particular, "the world provides time, but takes it up" (Blanchot, "Work's Demand" 60), a recurrent theme throughout his diaries and letters; as a result, "some job-fiction connections are apparent" (Greenberg 356) in his prose, illustrating the way in which Kafka's attention itself is divided between his writing and his employment.

In other words, these "job-fictions" can be defined as narratives in which their central characters are concerned with their jobs and other such responsibilities, as we see with Gregor Samsa in *The Metamorphosis*. This demonstrates how Kafka, in his ambition to be nothing but a writer, "was driven to despair each time he thought he was being prevented from being one" (Blanchot, "Literature" 13) and how these themes of despair and employment filter through into Kafka's fiction.

Kafka's "Poseidon" is a flash fiction that perfectly demonstrates the way in which he lamented how employment prevented him from writing. The story is not only an example of "a job-fiction connection" but also the way flash fiction can take myths and legends and, rather than merely retelling them, playfully subvert them into extended metaphors (Howitt-Dring 49). Kafka successfully subverts our perception of Poseidon to tell a story in which nothing is lacking, returning to this idea about the presence of absence. The opening line of the story immediately defamiliarizes Poseidon: "Poseidon sat at his desk, going over the accounts" (Kafka, "Poseidon" 434). A sentence like this grabs the reader's attention, and, though this is not uncommon in any form of prose, it fulfils the idea that flash fiction "must overcome the restraints of limited length and communicate not a segment, a tattered fragment, but a world" (Pasco 127). This sentence establishes the world Kafka explores: a world in which Poseidon is confined to his desk by his workload. When reading the rest of "Poseidon," we see how this world is a parallel to Kafka's own, demonstrating Jack Greenberg's "job-fiction" observation and how none of us are immune from the mundane drudgery of the everyday that distracts us from our desires. Other than "an occasional visit to Jupiter being the only interruption of the monotony" and his fleeting ascent to Olympus, Poseidon remains stationary behind his desk throughout the story, having "hardly seen the oceans" (Kafka, "Poseidon" 435). This is due not only to the amount of work he has to do but also to his anxiety about his work. Although he has assistants to help him, Poseidon takes "his job very seriously" and insists "on going through all the accounts again himself" (435). What makes the situation worse for Poseidon are the rumors circulating that he spends his time "cruising through the waves with his trident" (435) when this is far from reality. Instead, Poseidon "used to say he was postponing this until the end of the world, for then there might come a quiet moment when, just before the end and having gone through the last account, he could still make a quick little tour" (435), but he does not say this anymore because his work is unrelenting and continuous; Poseidon will not have a quiet moment, even before the world's end. His work and responsibilities prevent Poseidon from doing what he would like to do—visiting the oceans he is in charge of—as much as Kafka's work and responsibilities prevent him from doing what he would rather be doing—writing.

Walser does something similar to Kafka in his story "Hercules" when he reinvents the story of Hercules and withholds a lot of detail about the myth as we know it in order to draw emphasis to Hercules' domestication and loss of identity. Subverting the myth, Walser presents a Hercules who has become a "gentle-hearted and well mannered" man who "knitted socks, shook out pillows, peeled potatoes" and takes "a fancy to washing dishes" ("Hercules" 22). The final line of the story states "May worse not befall us!" (22), and though it may seem Walser thinks that there is worse that could happen, the story does not read as such. This is not the same as Kafka's "job-fiction," but it does present a similar theme of our responsibilities getting in the way of our desires; Walser's Hercules loses his legendary strongman identity that we associate with Hercules because of his newfound responsibilities.

Like the other stories discussed in this chapter, "Poseidon" and "Hercules" contradict what critics claim about flash fiction requiring "an action" (Matthews 77) or a "purpose" (Howitt-Dring 49) because it appears again as if nothing is happening. However, the purpose of these stories is demonstrated where their "instant of perception" (Reid 28) occurs. In particular, "Poseidon" is reminiscent of Kafka's following aphorism: "'And then he went back to his job, as though nothing had happened.' A sentence that strikes one as familiar from any number of old stories—though it might not have appeared in any of them" (*Aphorisms* 107). Poseidon returns from his daydreaming to his job much like Kafka has to break from his writing to fulfill his obligations. With this aphorism in mind, Thiher is correct in his observation that Kafka's work is "a mixture of parody and near-parody that suddenly seems to open up a world of authentic anguish" (20) because there is something tragically comic about the lack of action in the story. The real tragedy is that, though Poseidon's torment is fictional, Kafka's is very real. Poseidon remains at his desk waiting for a future that never comes, as Kafka, too, waits for the time he can return to his writing. Both of their attentions are fragmented; they concentrate on their responsibilities but are distracted by the possibility of escaping them. As acknowledged at the end of Kafka's aphorism, this ending is never stated because this escape never materializes, but the act of it never occurring is implied and becomes an event in itself.

In spite of this, Kafka does not claim that it is only his responsibilities that divide his attention; the act of writing itself distracts him from his writing. Blanchot remarks how "many considerations restrain[ed] Kafka from finishing almost any of his 'stories' and cause[ed] him, when he [had] scarcely begun one, to leave it in search of peace in another," and this could be due to the fact that Kafka "cannot, or will not, consent to write 'in little bits'" ("Work's Demand" 81). Kafka wants nothing more than to either be able to write continuously or to discover a means of "solder[ing] fragments together into a story that will sweep one along" (Kafka, *Diaries* 360) because he "cannot prevent himself from writing, but writing prevents him from writing: he interrupts himself, he begins again" (Blanchot, "Literature" 23). Kafka is not alone in this experience: he has the desire to write without distraction from the responsibilities of life—whatever they may be—and yet, when time permitted, he could not put pen to paper or, as may be a more appropriate image for us, populate the on-screen Word document. Like the majority of us, Kafka had to snatch whatever time he could from a world filled with competing stimuli in order to pursue what he wanted most, and even then, attention and concentration was not guaranteed just because he desired it.

Flash: Time and Space

This analysis of the work of Robert Walser and Franz Kafka has attempted to establish why flash fiction is so popular today by responding to criticism that disparages short fiction and our attention spans. Firstly, there is nothing lacking about flash fiction, be it the content, the style, or the language. We find that "there is so much going on inside a [flash fiction] that it feels bigger than its small space on the page allows" (Howitt-Dring 57), and it is this paradoxical presence of absence that creates a false impression of lack, thereby emphasizing the implicit elements of fiction. Length as a factor has been identified as unimportant; however, it is an attractive theory because flash fiction does not take long to read. Yet flash fiction is "not as recent a form as some may imagine, as it has historical precedents [all over the world], where it has been used for many centuries," and, therefore, despite "their ties to our contemporary culture," they are not a product "created to satisfy the small attention spans" associated with contemporary society (Howitt-Dring 49). Although not a product of our modern lifestyles, the form fits seamlessly into it. This does not mean that the contention that our attention spans have become shorter because of our digital culture, or that "purposeful doing is now shadowed at every step with the possibilities of distraction" (Birkerts 170), should be outright rejected. To a certain extent, there is truth in these types of claims; however, it is not necessarily the idea that our attention spans are shorter, but that, like our lifestyles, our attention spans have become fragmented. Perhaps our attention spans are the same, except they have been compartmentalized so we can divide ourselves between the various aspects of modern life that demand our time. Birkerts argues this has happened because there is "too much information," and so we "graze it lightly, applying focus only where it is most needed"; therefore, we "orient ourselves with a necessarily fractured attention" (Birkerts 147). More accurately, Lyons observes the shift in our lifestyles and acknowledges that "the regulated working day allows only short fragments of reading time, which must be seized in the interstices between home and work and sleep, in lunchbreaks, on commuter trains" (Lyons 185). We must take advantage in today's world of any moment that does not remove us from our pursuing what Kafka would have called our happy distractions, whatever they may be.

At the same time, we do experience instant gratification when reading flash fiction because it takes so little time to consume. It is for this reason it could be claimed that flash fiction has become more popular because it seems to pander to a shortened attention span. This is because the digital world, fully integrated with our physical existence, means "more and more people are being persuaded to access their culture through screen portals, ordering up what they need for their Kindle, their iPod, their nightly watching streams" (Birkerts 72). This sense of immediacy is something readers may expect from their fiction, too, but readers and writers of flash know this is not always true. It is true that an entire flash can be read in moments; however, instant gratification is not always attainable— nor should it be. Flash fiction demands the reader's attention and does not accommodate distraction. Without concentration, one might assume flash fictions have nothing to say, which is not the case. The internet has provided an appropriate space, a seemingly unlimited one, for the publication of flash fiction; the text is of a length we can quickly consume in between the moments of our fragmented lives and is accessible wherever we are able to attain a connection. When Walser and Kafka first began publishing stories, they "appeared in magazines and newspapers," which was "typical of the literary scene at the time" (Ryan 62), and nothing has changed; there are a vast array of online magazines and journals publishing flash fiction, among other forms of literature. Even though flash fiction and other variants have been around for centuries, flash fiction has found its right time and space within our modern, digital, fragmented lives. It will only continue to increase in popularity.

Works Cited

Adorno, Theodor W. "Notes on Kafka." *Prisms*. Translated by Samuel and Shierry Weber, First MIT Press, 1983, pp. 245-271.

Benjamin, Walter. "Robert Walser." *Microscripts* by Robert Walser. Translated by Susan Bernofsky. New Direction Books/Christine Burgin, 2012, pp. 137-141.

_____. "The Work of Art in the Age of Its Technological Reproducibility: Second Version." *Walter Benjamin: Selected Writings Volume 3, 1935–1938*, edited by Howard Eiland and Michael W. Jennings, Harvard UP, 2006, 101-133.

Birkerts, Sven. *Changing the Subject: Art and Attention in the Internet Age*. Graywolf Press, 2015.

Blanchot, Maurice. "Kafka and Literature". *The Work of Fire*. Translated by Charlotte Mandell, Stanford UP, 1996, pp. 12-26.

_____. "Kafka and the Work's Demand." *The Space of Literature*. Translated by Ann Smock, U of Nebraska P, 1989, pp. 57-83.

_____. "Reading Kafka." *The Work of Fire*. Translated by Charlotte Mandell, Stanford UP, 1996, pp. 1-11.

Eiland, Howard. "Reception in Distraction." *Walter Benjamin and Art*, edited by Andrew Benjamin, Continuum, 2005, pp. 3-13.

Frederick, Samuel, and Nilima Rabl. "Dividing Zero: Beholding Nothing." *SubStance*, vol 35, no. 2, 2006, pp. 71-82.

Greenberg, Jack. "From Kafka to Kafkaesque". *Franz Kafka: The Office Writings*, edited by Stanley Corngold, Jack Greenberg, and Benno Wagner, Princeton UP, 2009, pp. 355-371.

Howitt-Dring, Holly. "Making micro meanings: reading and writing microfiction." *Short Fiction in Theory and Practice*, vol. 1, 2011, pp. 47-58.

Jarrell, Randall. "Stories". *The New Short Story Theories*, edited by Charles E. May, Ohio UP, 1994, pp. 3-14.

Kafka, Franz. *Aphorisms*. Translated by Willa and Edwin Muir, Michael Hofmann, Schocken, 2015.

_____. *Diaries*. Translated by Joseph Kresh, Martin Greenberg, and Hannah Arendt, Schocken, 2011.

_____. "Clothes." *The Complete Short Stories*. Translated by Willa and Edwin Muir, Schocken, 2011, pp. 382-383.

_____. *Letters to Friends, Family and Editors*. Translated by Richard and Clara Winston, Oneworld Classics, 2011.

_____. "Passers-by." *The Complete Short Stories*. Translated by Willa and Edwin Muir, Schocken, 2011, pp. 388.

_____. "Poseidon." *The Complete Short Stories*. Translated by Tania and James Stern, Schocken, 2011, pp. 434-435.

_____. "Rejection." *The Complete Short Stories*. Translated by Willa and Edwin Muir, Kafka, Schocken, 2011, pp. 383-384.

Lyons, Martyn. *A History of Reading and Writing in the Western World*. Palgrave Macmillan, 2010.

Matthews, Brander. "The Philosophy of the Short-Story." *The New Short Story Theories*, edited by Charles E. May, Ohio UP, 1994, pp. 73-80.

Nelles, William. "Microfiction: What Makes a Very Short Story Very Short." *Narrative*, vol. 20, no. 1, 2012, pp. 87-104.

Pasco, Allan H. "On Defining Short Stories." *The New Short Story Theories*, edited by Charles E. May, Ohio UP, 1994, pp. 114-130.

Plug, Jan. "Shame, on the Language of Robert Walser." *MLN*, vol. 120, no. 3, 2005, pp. 654-684.

Pratt, Mary Louise. "The Short Story: The Long and the Short of It." *The New Short Story Theories*, edited by Charles E. May, Ohio UP, 1994, pp. 91-113.

Reid, Ian. *The Short Story: The Critical Idiom*. Methuen & Co Ltd, 1977.

Ryan, Judith. "Kafka before Kafka: The Early Stories." *A Companion to the Works of Franz Kafka*, edited by James Rolleston, Camden House, 2006, pp. 61-83.

Sontag, Susan. "Walser's Voice." *Selected Stories*. Translated by Christopher Middleton et al., Farrar, Straus and Giroux, 2012, pp. vii-ix.

Thiher, Allen. *Franz Kafka: A Study of the Short Fiction*. Twayne Publishers, 1990.

Walser, Robert. "The Boat." Translated by Tom Whalen. *Selected Stories*. Translated by Christopher Middleton et al., Farrar, Straus and Giroux, 2012, pp. 28-29.

_____. "A Little Ramble." Translated by Tom Whalen. *Selected Stories*. Translated by Christopher Middleton et al., Farrar, Straus and Giroux, 2012, pp. 30-31.

_____. "Hercules." *Speaking to the Rose: Writings, 1912–1932*. Translated by Christopher Middleton, U of Nebraska P, 2005, p. 22.

Living Together, Living Apart: Jews under Oppressive Russian Regimes in Isaac Babel's Flash Fiction

Eric Sterling

> And it will be the birth of the style of our epoch. I do not see any room for verbiage in our epoch, in the ability to ramble on at great length while the thought beneath is so brief.
>
> (Isaac Babel)[1]

Isaac Babel's flash fiction is valuable in part for its powerful characterizations of precarious Jewish life under Tsarist and Revolutionary Russian rule in the first three decades of the twentieth century. Babel's critique and portrayal of oppressive Russian governmental policies that inhibited and endangered Jews made the author a heroic and popular writer yet also rendered him a target of dictator Joseph Stalin, who arranged for his arrest on May 15, 1939 and his murder by firing squad on January 27, 1940. Babel's stories are rich in local color, providing readers with a window into the lives of oppressed Jews trying to survive in the Pale of Settlement,[2] St. Petersburg (later known as Petrograd and Leningrad), Odessa, and other parts of Russia; in these cities and towns, Jews were invariably unwelcome and periodically subjected to forced exile or brutal and deadly pogroms, such as the Odessa pogrom that occurred on October 18–22, 1905. Babel writes about the hardships Russian Jews encountered on a daily basis; even the term "Russian Jews" is a misnomer because many Russian government policies and Russian citizens made it clear that although the Jews were born and raised in the country, they were not citizens, and thus they were treated horribly. My essay will analyze four of Babel's best and representative flash fiction stories (and one longer story for the sake of juxtaposition) to demonstrate how the author employs this genre effectively to manifest the ongoing struggle of Russian Jews to survive under brutal anti-Semitic conditions, including physical and emotional displacement.

Babel is known for his minimalist approach to writing, for leaving much implied, ambiguous, and up to the reader's imagination. His greatest influences as a writer were Guy de Maupassant, Rudyard Kipling, Gustave Flaubert, and Alexander Pushkin. Babel assumed his readers' familiarity with the characters' situations in Russia, so he omitted details that he expected them to know, which was fine for his contemporary readers in Russia. Charles Baxter notes that for writers of "the abruptly short-short story, familiar material takes the place of detail" (229). Part of the reason for Babel's excellence in flash fiction is that out of respect for his readers, he eschewed wordiness and repetition. Zsuzsa Hetényi observes that Babel keeps his sentences short "to provide a total visual impression of a scene or place" (183).

Furthermore, Babel believed that good prose writers shorten their stories by minimizing their word count through an economy of style. In "Reminiscences of Babel," Soviet author Konstantin Paustovsky notes that Babel once told him:

> "A short story must have the precision of a military communiqué or a bank check.". . . Babel would go up to his desk and stroke his manuscript cautiously as though it were a wild creature which had still not been properly domesticated. . . . He would always find a few unnecessary words and throw them out with malicious glee. He used to say, "Your language becomes clear and strong, not when you can no longer add a sentence, but when you can no longer take away from it." (34, 38)

One ramification of Babel's thirst for very short stories is that the action in his flash fiction is often unresolved and left purposely ambiguous, a trait that generally distinguishes European fiction from American fiction. American literary critic and writer Lionel Trilling, for one, found Babel's short prose fiction superb and exceptional but disturbing: "for me it was all too heavily charged with the intensity, irony, and ambiguousness from which I wished to escape" (312). Trilling was intrigued by the brevity and conciseness of Babel's fiction but the concomitant open-ended, ambiguous treatment of characters and events proved unsettling to the literary critic, who preferred the closure offered by American fiction writers. Trilling concedes that because Babel made his fiction short by refraining from moralizing and sharing his opinions with his readers, it is unclear how the author felt about brutality or "Jews; or about religion; or about the goodness of man. He had—or perhaps—for the sake of some artistic effect, he pretended to have—a secret" (312). Whether he wrote about violence, brutality, rape, or anti-Semitism, the author did not judge his characters and seems detached and objective.

Babel's initial flash fiction story, and the first story he ever wrote, is "Old Shloyme" (1913), a poignant tale about an elderly man who, like many of Babel's characters, is ordinary and forgettable. In fact, Old Shloyme's son and daughter-in-law often forget that he lives with them. His only concern is eating and his existence in his own small corner of the house—until his son and daughter-in-law start crying and becoming upset. Despite his deafness and indifference to the world around him, Shloyme discovers that he and his family have been threatened with eviction from their house (where Shloyme has lived for six decades) unless they renounce their Jewish faith. The laconic narrator says tersely that "Shloyme knew why they were being kicked out" (Babel, "Old Shloyme" 4), but he does not reveal the reason; it is implied to, and understood by, Babel's contemporary reading audience, who endured anti-Semitic acts frequently. Shloyme's family is being evicted because they have been maintaining their Jewish faith while attempting to survive in this anti-Semitic and unforgiving Russian culture. It is noteworthy that Babel wrote this story in exile, having been forced to leave his home in Odessa for Kiev, after having been prohibited from attending the University of Odessa because he was Jewish (Freidin 1053). He also wrote "Old Shloyme" in the same year as the famous trial of Mendel Beilis, the Russian Jew who was persecuted and falsely accused of blood libel (murdering a Christian for his blood) (Van de Stadt 36). The irreligious Shloyme is shocked to learn that his son is morally weak and has renounced his faith in order to keep the house. Embittered that "his son wanted to leave his people for a new God . . . to leave one's God completely and forever, the God of an oppressed and suffering people" (5), Shloyme hangs himself in protest. Shloyme's defiance initially seems ironic because he has previously lived his life as a godless man. However, this interpretation falsely assumes that he is a Jew because he has faith in God and divine law; rather, Shloyme is a Jew because he identifies with Jewish people, heritage, and culture. Janneke van de Stadt correctly notes that the titular character's Jewish identity:

> is inexorably tied to the physical space Shloime [an alternative spelling of Shloyme] has inhabited for so long. . . . [H]is house for the past sixty years is now controlled by his son and daughter-in-law, who now are rationing the physical and mental space he occupies just as they do his food . . . [F]or Shloime, personal space is incontrovertibly tied to, indeed, defined by, his identity as a Jew. Thus, even if he were to choose a material home [religious conversion] over cultural heritage, or vice versa, the result would be identical; he would be homeless, either spiritually or physically. (38, 41, 43)

Flash fiction is intriguing and challenging because it sometimes leaves the reader with more questions than answers. For instance, in this story, does the son "want to leave his people," or does he do so with great reluctance to save his family home? How can one show one's faith in God by committing suicide, thus violating one of the Lord's most sacred commandments in the Decalogue? And why would one want to be a member of a faith whose God allows its people to be oppressed and to suffer? The abrupt, unresolved ending that leaves readers speculating and wanting more is a superb example of the power of flash fiction.

Babel's "Guy de Maupassant" (1922), which also contains an unresolved ending, serves as the author's self-conscious examination of flash fiction; Babel offers commentary on the subgenre while writing about an effort to translate the works of the renowned French storyteller, himself a master of flash fiction. In other words, one flash fiction author writes a flash fiction story about another flash fiction writer who profoundly influenced him. As in many of Babel's stories, the protagonist is an unfortunate and impoverished Jew being victimized in oppressive Russia. As a Jew, he lives in a restricted area, fearing arrest and living there illegally "with forged papers and without a kopeck to my name" (Babel, *"Guy"* 44). He lacks a home and personal space, the same unfortunate fate with which Shloyme is threatened. The narrator envies his friend Kazantsev, a Hispanophile who had never been to Spain. The narrator admits that amongst his disenfranchised friends, "the happiest of us all was Kazantsev. He had a motherland—Spain" (45). Here Babel's minimalistic approach saves words but signifies so much. Because of Russian oppression, Kazantsev's only motherland must be a distant country he has never visited. It is implied, therefore, that the narrator, being a Jew in anti-Semitic Russia, can never have a homeland. Babel's stories often deal with Jews who lack a home. The fact that the narrator is nameless is telling, for it suggests that despite his talent as a writer, as a Jew, he has no rights, citizenship, or value. This story of a talented writer and translator who feels threatened and afraid for his safety in his own country because he is Jewish seems autobiographical; Babel was warned for years to flee Russia because of its rabid anti-Semitism and the political restrictions on his writing, but he declined, only to be arrested on trumped up charges and executed, on Joseph Stalin's orders. Although Babel understood that his safety in Russia was precarious, he remained in the country because he felt that his success as a writer emanated from his stories about Russian culture.

The nameless and stateless narrator finds work helping a beautiful, large-breasted Jewish woman named Raisa translate the complete short stories of Maupassant. The narrator ventures from his miserable attic living space to her mansion to meet her, discerning that her elegant but vulgar house is typical of tacky homes owned by "bankers without family or breeding—Jewish converts to Christianity who grew rich through trade" (Babel, "Guy" 45). The house, complete with pink columns and stuffed bears standing on their hind legs gracing every staircase, is owned by Raisa and her lawyer husband, who, because of Russian oppression, have, like Shloyme's son, been compelled to convert from Judaism to Christianity. Fascinatingly, Babel's story and the fiction of Maupassant merge.

Raisa and "the narrator inhabit Maupassant's fiction, either reflecting or consciously reenacting it . . . [In both, the] protagonists are seen to embark on a journey, which, besides conveying them from one physical location to another, also transforms them somehow, taking them to a different place existentially." This occurs because of Babel's correlation "between translation [translate = *perevesti* in Russian] and travel [transport = *perevezti* in Russian]" (*Van de Stadt* 636). Soon the translator ventures often from his dingy attic to a beautiful house in a nice part of town in order to translate, and he and Raisa become lovers.

A translator, Raisa has the job simply because her husband owns a publishing house and because she loves the French author's short fiction. She confesses to the narrator, "'Maupassant is the one passion of my life'" (Babel, "Guy" 46). In a longer story or a novel, a narrator would point out at length that the woman does not love her husband, that she married him only for his money, and he for her physical beauty. Yet because this is flash fiction, Babel leaves the reader with this pregnant line regarding Maupassant being the *one* passion in Raisa's life. If she has love in her heart *only* for the French author, logic dictates that she cannot have any passion for her husband. With this one brief sentence, along with the narrator's references to Raisa "bearing her large breasts before her" (45), Babel foreshadows their sexual encounter. Despite Babel's insistence that authors should avoid repetition to keep their fiction short, he strays from his mantra by mentioning Raisa's breasts several times in order to connect translation and excellent prose with seduction. The translator's obsession with breasts in Babel's story correlates with the well-documented lust for which Maupassant was known. The narrator suggests that beautiful Jewish women like Raisa "transmute the money of their resourceful husbands into the lush pink fat on their bellies, napes, and round shoulders" (46). In exchange for her body (but not her love or fidelity), her husband allows her to live in opulence and publish her translation of Maupassant, despite her lack of talent and need to pay the narrator to repair her translation.

Raisa's translation of "Miss Harriet" lacks "Maupassant's free-flowing prose with its powerful breath of passion. [Raisa]

Benderskaya wrote with laborious and inert correctness and lack of style—the ways Jews in the past used to write Russian" (Babel, "Guy" 46). Her use of language and style seems verbose and mechanical. The narrator fixes Raisa's translation, informing her that a good idea in a fictional text should be mentioned once—and only once—for the sake of emphasis and brevity: "One's fingertips must grasp the key, gently warming it. And then the key must be turned once, not twice" (46). He adds that in fiction, good style requires "an army [of words] in which every type of weapon is deployed. No iron spike can pierce a human heart as icily as a period in the right place" (46). The narrator suggests that cleverly placed punctuation creates emphasis and can allow writers to use words more economically and keep fictional texts short. The iron spike also might be considered a phallic symbol. Raisa is so awed by the narrator's clear and concise prose that she becomes sexually aroused as "the lace between her struggling breasts swerved and trembled" (46). Furthermore, when she listens to the narrator speak of excellent style and concise writing, her "legs, with the strong, delicate calves, were planted apart . . ." (46), as if to welcome his iron spike. As in Maupassant's "Miss Harriet," the reader might discern "the theme of seduction through art; in each case, the female protagonist lacks linguistic skills and is given lectures on art" (Zholkovsky and Yampolsky 59). The aforementioned passages about translation and literary style consume merely a quarter of a page yet indicate how the narrator's skill with language excites Raisa sexually, with talent in the brevity of style being erotic and leading to their illicit affair.

"Elya Isaakovich and Margarita Prokofievna" (1916), like the preceding tales, concerns a Russian Jew who is in danger because of his religion. Babel tells the short tale of an elderly man named Elya who, like the Maupassant translator, is in danger because he is a Jew living in a city (in this case, Oryol) illegally, without a housing permit. Elya, however, is not ready to be deported to the dreadful Pale of Settlement, so he hires a prostitute and briefly takes refuge at her house. Neither character is a bargain physically; he is an old Jew, and she is an obese whore with pimples. They bargain over the price he will pay, even though he hires her simply to have a place to stay since he would be deported without a housing permit. They initially agree upon two and a half rubles for her services, but her price escalates to ten rubles when she learns that he is Jewish. However, she comes to respect and admire the old Jew when he shares with her his positive Talmudic view of human nature, which conflicts with her negative outlook on people. Rather than Babel's narrator discussing at length Margarita's transformed view of human nature and Jews, the author, in his typical minimalistic manner, simply points out that she bakes pies for Elya to take with him as he takes the train to Odessa. Babel employs this unlikely relationship to demonstrate that Jews and Gentile Russians can live harmoniously together if they can get to know one another and that it is governmental oppression, not human nature, that separates different groups of people and allows prejudice to flourish. The remarkable aspect of Babel's observations and perspectives is that he shares his subtle point of view in less than a thousand words.

Russian oppression of Jews is clearly apparent in Babel's "The Story of My Dovecote" (1925). This story, which contains 4,300 words, is far longer than any other Babel story discussed in this essay but is included for the sake of comparison. By looking at a longer story, readers may discern how flash fiction can be limited both thematically and dramatically. Babel's flash fiction occurs when the action is urgent and covers a short period of time; because these two qualities do not apply to "The Story of My Dovecote," it is considerably longer than the author's flash fiction. The nine-year-old Jewish protagonist and narrator longs desperately for a dovecote (a house for doves or pigeons). His father promises him one provided that he earns admission to a prestigious lycée. The young narrator's problem lies in that he needs a perfect score on the exam because the virulent anti-Semitic educational system in Russia allows no more than five percent (two students) of the entering class to be Jewish.[3] This Jewish quota clearly demonstrates prejudice. Although the boy is highly intelligent and has studied hard, the "teacher would come up with the most cunning questions for the two [Jewish] boys [they would ultimately accept]; nobody was given the kind of complicated questions we [Jews] were. . . . The teacher tried every trick" (Babel,

"The Story" 348) to prevent Jews from being admitted to the lycée. The boy earns a perfect score nonetheless and wins a coveted spot, only to lose it because of a bribe. Determined to win a spot for the following year, the boy studies incessantly and memorizes whole books on Russian history and literature. The story must be longer to show the long, tedious nature of the boy's studying. "The Story of My Dovecote," unlike other Babel stories, does not constitute flash fiction because the author uses many more words in an effort to show all the narrator must do to try to gain entrance into the school. Babel must make the story longer to show that the boy, longing for his dovecote, has remained extremely dedicated to his academic task during this year. A flash fiction cannot adequately convey the drudgery the narrator endures for twelve months as he literally memorizes important textbooks. When asked questions during the second entrance exam, he recites many of Pushkin's poems by heart and selections from a history book that deals with Peter the Great. The anti-Semitic teachers reluctantly admit him to the school, with one teacher grumbling that in order to be good students, Jews sell their souls to the devil: "What a nation! The devil is in these Yids!" (348).

The boy's tutor, Old Liberman, celebrates his admission, considering it a cultural victory over an oppressor; the tutor claims that "by passing the examination, I had won a victory over all my foes. I had won a victory over the fat-cheeked Russian boys. . . . [J]ust as I [like David] had triumphed over Goliath, so too would our people, through its sheer power of mind, triumph over the foes that surround us, eager for our blood" (Babel, "The Story" 350). Liberman's comments prove ironic given the looming 1905 Odessa pogrom. This Babel story differs from "Old Shloyme," and "Elya Isaakovich and Margarita Prokofievna" in that the passage of time is significant to the plot because the author wants to demonstrate that his intense studying for an entire year proves wasted. At the end of the story, the boy's doves are cruelly crushed to death when smashed against his own body. The boy will never forget the massacre of his beloved new pets, the murder of his grandfather, and the destruction of his father's store during the pogrom. The narrator's "dovecote itself becomes a symbol: a home for the bird symbolizing peace and reconciliation, antagonistic to the violence of the pogrom," it is destroyed. The dovecote's destruction symbolizes the precarious nature of peaceful Jewish life, as they, because of rabid anti-Semitism, cannot find a safe home (Hetényi 179). Babel's details vividly show how this pogrom has affected him; these details consume many words, even for a writer of laconic prose such as Babel.

In contrast, "Old Shloyme" satisfies the requirements for flash fiction because the titular character wants to commit suicide as soon as possible so that he does not have to witness the shame of his son's forced conversion to Christianity. In other words, Shloyme's desire to end his life quickly correlates with the author's desire to end the story abruptly. Babel creates the sense of Shloyme hurrying by wrapping up his story expeditiously. In "Elya Isaakovich and Margarita Prokofievna," Elya must flee the city immediately, for he has been warned that he will be imprisoned for not possessing a housing permit; therefore, Babel focuses his story on one evening and the next day as the Jew prepares to flee the city where Jews are forbidden. Both flash fiction stories, unlike "The Story of My Dovecote," show merely one day in the life of a Jew. Both works are flash fiction because the plot is focused and the Jews must act quickly. Unlike the dovecote story, these two flash fiction works show special urgency and are not traumatic autobiographical works that Babel feels compelled to tell in painstaking detail.

"First Love" (1925), a continuation of "The Story of My Dovecote," is flash fiction and considerably shorter than its predecessor. This story portrays the aftermath of the devastating pogrom, which resulted in the murder of more than four hundred Jews and the destruction of more than one thousand, six hundred Jewish houses and businesses. The pogrom destroyed all the Jews had worked for over the years and left them at the mercy of the Russians. The boy is devastated by the murder of his grandfather and traumatized by his cherished doves literally being crushed to death against his face. Helpless and with nowhere to go, the boy ends up at the house of a beautiful adult neighbor on whom he has a crush. The narrator goes to Galina's house to escape the pogrom; her house is safe because she is a Gentile. As with Shloyme, Elya, and the Maupassant narrator, this ten-year-old narrator cannot find a safe and peaceful home because his family is Jewish. Here, as in the other stories discussed in this essay, Babel manifests his concern for safety and home in a brutally anti-Semitic Tsarist and then Communist Russia. With his trademark detachment, in this autobiographical story, Babel describes himself as a ten-year-old boy who witnesses his father get on his knees in the mud and beg a disinterested Cossack soldier to stop rioters from destroying his store. The anti-Semitic Cossack agrees to help stop the looting of a Jewish store but instead rides away, ignoring the genuflecting Jewish shopkeeper. It is unclear whether the boy admires the Cossack for looking powerful and admirable on his horse or is embarrassed by his father for begging in the mud. In keeping with his sparse prose, Babel describes the action but offers no sense of where the readers' sympathies should lie. Unlike the longer dovecote story that occurs during a year, this story contains a much more narrow focus and occurs over a few hours, thus enabling the author to keep the story short.

Babel's flash fiction regarding the persecution of Russian Jews correlates with the oppression the author experienced in his professional life, which is apparent in his esoteric speech to the Congress of Soviet Writers in Moscow on August 23, 1934. Babel advocated a new writing style—writing sparsely, using Stalin as an example because Stalin was a sparse writer (in a desperate effort to curry favor). Babel recognized, perhaps, that he was speaking toward the end of his writing career because of censorship and his arrest, which he knew was inevitable, for writing short stories that insulted several prominent Soviet military generals and even Stalin himself. In particular, General Semyon Budenny,[4] a Stalin favorite, was outraged by Babel's *Red Cavalry* stories about the Cossacks' brutal attacks on Poles and Jews. Budenny wrote several articles defending the honor of his Cossack army and attacking the reputation of Babel, whose flash fiction he called "a cowardly, pornographic, effeminizing libel upon the honor and history of the Red Cavalry Army" (Winokur 63). Budenny was enraged not only by the short fiction that portrayed his soldiers as violent murderers and rapists but also by "The Story of a Horse," which depicted the general as petulant for his emotional breakdown and threat to leave the army and the Communist Party after someone took his white stallion and replaced it with a different horse. Babel was disturbed by:

> Stalin's forced collectivization of agriculture, which resulted in deportations, requisitions, starvation, and the destruction of peasant traditions. Babel's observations provided rich material for a book of connected stories, titled *Velikaia Krinitsa* after a thinly disguised village in the Kiev district. The two extant chapters, "Kolyvushka" and "Gapa Guzhva," named for colorful local characters, are eloquent examples of Babel's new restrained voice that spoke of horror in a village where no dog dared to bark. (Sicher)

The publication of these stories endangered Babel's life, yet he refused to flee Russia because he believed that his success as a writer depended on his observations of Russian culture.

Writing sparsely is an essential component of flash fiction, but Babel had to write so sparsely that he could not write at all. Babel joked to the Congress of Soviet Writers audience that the Soviet government gave authors everything—except the right to write badly. Some audience members, knowing Babel's penchant for laconic writing, must have thought he referred to verbosity, yet others believed that he referred to anti-Soviet fiction, such as his politically dangerous *Red Cavalry* stories. Babel joked about his new genre of writing—an extreme form of laconic flash fiction: he was "the master of the genre of silence" (Trilling 314). Lionel Trilling speculates that "it is as if Babel were addressing his fellow writers in a dead language" (313), but perhaps a more accurate assessment is that Babel was implying during his speech that his writing career was being silenced and he soon would be dead. Babel had been censored and became afraid to write, despite his longing to compose fiction. The murder of this writer was meant to silence a Jew, a writer whose very short fiction was ultimately not sufficiently laconic.

Notes

1. Isaac Babel, "Speech given by Babel at the Congress of Soviet Writers in Moscow, August 23, 1934." *The Lonely Years 1925–1939: Unpublished Stories and Private Correspondence.* Farrar, Straus, 1964, p. 398.

2. The Pale of Settlement was an area in Western Imperial Russia to which Jews were restricted to live. They were subject to arrest if they tried to live outside this area.

3. This restriction might remind current readers of educational restrictions, *Numerus clausus*, in Nazi Germany and even Jewish quotas in American medical schools. Historian David M. Oshinsky observes that Jonas Salk could not gain admission to "[m]ost of the surrounding medical schools—Cornell, Columbia, Pennsylvania, and Yale—[, which] had rigid quotas in place. In 1935, Yale accepted seventy-six applicants from a pool of 501. About 200 of those applicants were Jewish and only five got in." Dean Milton Winternitz of the Yale School of Medicine demanded of his medical school staff: "Never admit more than five Jews, take only two Italian Catholics, and take no blacks at all" (Burrow 107 ff).

4. The general's name is also spelled "Budyonny" by some scholars.

Works Cited

Babel, Isaac. "Elya Isaakovich and Margarita Prokofievna." Isaac Babel's Selected Writings, edited by Gregory Freidin, translated by Peter Constantine, W.W. Norton, 2010, pp. 6-9.

_____. "Guy De Maupassant." Isaac Babel's Selected Writings, edited by Gregory Freidin, translated by Peter Constantine, W.W. Norton, 2010, pp. 44-50.

_____. "First Love." Isaac Babel's Selected Writings, edited by Gregory Freidin, translated by Peter Constantine, W.W. Norton, 2010, pp. 355-60.

_____. "Old Shloyme." Isaac Babel's Selected Writings, edited by Gregory Freidin, translated by Peter Constantine, W.W. Norton, 2010, pp. 3-5.

_____. "Speech given by Babel at the Congress of Soviet Writers in Moscow, August 23, 1934." *Isaac Babel: The Lonely Years, 1925–*

1939: Unpublished Stories and Private Correspondence, edited by Nathalie Babel, Farrar, Straus, 1964, pp. 396-400.

_____. "The Story of My Dovecote" Isaac Babel's Selected Writings, edited by Gregory Freidin, translated by Peter Constantine, W.W. Norton, 2010, pp. 347-55.

Baxter, Charles. Afterword. *Sudden Fiction: American Short Short Stories*, edited by Robert Shapard and James Thomas, Gibbs-Smith Publisher, 1986.

Burrow Gerard N. A History of Yale's School of Medicine: Passing Troches to Others. Yale UP, 2002.

Fredin, Gregory. "Isaac Emmanuelovich Babel: A Chronology." The Complete Works of Isaac Babel, edited by Nathalie Babel, translated by Peter Constantine, W.W. Norton, 2002, pp. 1052-58.

_____. "Two Babels—Two Aphrodites: Autobiography in Maria and Babel's Petersburg Myth." The Enigma of Isaac Babel: Biography, History, Context, edited by Gregory Freidin, Stanford UP, 2009, pp. 16-62.

Hetényi, Zsuzsa, "The Child's Eye: Isaac Babel's Innovations in Narration in Russian-Jewish, American, and European Literary Contexts." The Enigma of Isaac Babel: Biography, History, Context, edited by Gregory Freidin, Stanford UP, 2009, pp. 175-92.

Oshinksy, David M. Polio: An American Story. Oxford UP 2006.

Paustovsky, Konstantin. "Reminiscences of Babel." *Dissonant Voices in Soviet Literature: Post-Revolutionary Russian Writing*, edited by Patricia Blake and Max Hayward, Pantheon, 1962, pp. 33-51.

Sicher, Efraim. "Babel, Isaac." *The Yivo Encyclopedia of Jews in Eastern Europe*, 2010, www.yivoencyclopedia.org/article.aspx/Babel_Isaac/. Accessed 25 July 2016.

Trilling, Lionel. "Isaac Babel." The Moral Obligation to be Intelligent: Selected Essays. Farrar, Straus and Giroux, 2000, pp. 311-30.

Van de Stadt, Janneke. "The Poetics of Transit: Miss Harriet and "Guy de Maupassant." *The Slavic and East European Journal*, vol. 50, no. 4, Winter 2006, pp. 635-54.

_____. "A Question of Place: Situating 'Old Shloime' in Isaac Babel's Oeuvre." *The Russian Review*, vol. 66, no. 1, 2007, pp. 36-54.

Winokur, Val. *The Trace of Judaism: Dostoevsky, Babel,Mandelstam, Levinas.* Northwestern UP, 2008.

Zholkovsky, Alexander, and Mikhail B. Yampolsky. *Babel'/Babel.* Carte Blanche, 1994.

Latin American Flash Fiction: Julio Cortázar and Luisa Valenzuela

Laura Hatry

> I usually compare the novel to a mammal, be it wild as a tiger or tame as a cow; the short story to a bird or a fish; the microstory to an insect (iridescent in the best cases).
>
> (Luisa Valenzuela)

In Latin America, flash fiction emerged with the epoch-defining wave of modernist prose during the febrile, and fertile, early years of the avant-garde. In the beginning, it surfaced only hesitantly and sporadically, for example, in Ruben Darío's *Azul* from 1888, some of whose poetic prose could be seen as a precursor to the flash fiction pieces of our own time. The 1924 publication of Leopoldo Lugones's *Filosofícula*, which was inspired at least in part by modernist literary experiments, already signaled in its title the notion of a change in its conception of the extensive field of its concerns. By using the suffix -ícula, which implicitly recovers the word *partícula*, or particle, Lugones closely connects tininess and fragmentariness to short-short stories, as if they are minus*cule* components of an imaginary larger fabric. Julio Cortázar would later use the same tactic in calling his own flash fiction pieces *texticulos*. We see crucial figures of the twenties and thirties, such as Felisberto Hernández, Macedonio Fernández, and Oliverio Girondo, toying with this new form of literature as well, and in the avant-garde journal *Martín Fierro*, one finds a great number of miniature texts, among them Jorge Luis Borges's first flash fiction, "Leyenda policial" (Police Legend) from 1927, which is often referred to as a mere "vignette."

Nevertheless, it isn't until the second half of the twentieth century that the new genre—although not yet considered a genre and still devoid of a specifying designation—really asserts itself as such, specifically in the 1953 anthology, *Extraordinary Short Stories* prepared by Borges and Adolfo Bioy Casares. This volume includes examples of both Spanish and foreign-language texts that, as they state in their prologue, are brief and written in prose. According to Laura Pollastri, Borges's own work "with his tendency to verbal concision and precision, makes the *microrrelato* (microstory) visible, endows it with esthetic legibility, and provides it with literary density"[1] (13). From a more macroscopic perspective, he might indeed be the author whose work raised the short story from a minor genre, the novel's little brother, as it were, to one that could be taken seriously as a literary endeavor in its own right. Famously, one of the shortest example of flash fiction, Augusto Monterroso's *hypershort* of nine words (including the title), "The Dinosaur," was published in 1959 and extensively scrutinized and commented upon, to such an extent that even an entire annotated edition was composed about those mere nine words.[2] Both academia and publishing houses began paying closer attention to the phenomenon in the 1980s and 1990s, when systematic theories, categorical distinctions, and canonization of the genre arose in the Hispanic world (Siles 42-49) and when there was an obvious increase in the publication of anthologies explicitly devoted to flash fiction, which led to more public attention in the form of writing contests and scholarly conferences that focused on the subject.

This article will discuss two of the most prominent Argentinian writers, both of whom have produced a prolific amount of flash fiction within their opus: Julio Cortázar (1914–1984) and Luisa Valenzuela (1938–). Cortázar, the "modern master of the short story" (Weiss), made flash fiction popular in Europe with the publication of his *Cronopios and Famas* (1962) (Gracia Fernández-Cuesta 9). But this is not the only time he made use of the genre: he also included *microrrelatos* in Último *round* (Last round) (1969), and even his famous novel *Hopscotch* (1963) contains many passages and sections that are critically regarded as flash fiction. However, it was in 1950, with "Continuity of Parks," in *End of the Game*, that his first short-short story was published. Cortázar has had a pronounced influence on later authors, among them Luisa Valenzuela, one of the most significant of living Argentinian writers, who has shown great interest in flash fiction, not only as creator, but also as a valuable theorist of the field. Her production begins early, with the inclusion of flash fiction in her first collection of short stories, "El abecedario" ("The alphabet") in *Los heréticos* (*The Heretics*) from 1967 and extending throughout her opus, culminating in the recent *ABC de Microfábulas* (*ABC of Microfables*) (2009). Both *Strange Things Happen Here* (1976) and *Libro que no muerde* (*Book that does not bite*) (1980) contain a large number of flash fiction pieces. Her first collection devoted specifically to the genre was published in 2004 with *BREVS: microrrelatos completos hasta hoy* (*SHRTS: complete microstories up to the present*), and she expanded this pursuit with *Juego de villanos* (*Game of villains*) in 2008; both books are the result of her taking on the role of editor and extracting from previous collections texts that might be considered *microrrelatos*. There has been a long dispute regarding the nomenclature of these tiny pieces of writing among scholars and writers of Latin American flash fiction, ranging from descriptive possibilities, such as *minicuento* (ministory) or *cuento brevísimo* (briefest story) through options like 'miniature' or Luisa Valenzuela's own 'miniminis' to, finally, such "literary" extravagances as Iwasakis' definition of Roas's stories, as "minuscule rice croquets with Poe and Borgesian fibre that maintain the hair Wilde and turn out to be ideal to make Kafka in space"[3] (Iwasaki). However, while the quest for a common designation is in Irene Andrés-Suárez words "a pending task" (16-21), critics do seem to agree that the Hispanic term *microrrelato* unites a series of shared and necessary characteristics. Firstly, of course, there is brevity, and although it is a relative concept, it should be pointed out that:

> very short fictions in Latin America are, on the whole, shorter than in the United States, and questions about them are often concerned less with how short stories can be than with whether very short fictions need to be stories at all. At the same time, a *micro* or *minificción*, like a sudden or a flash, can be voiced in any known mode—realism, metafiction, fantasy, allegory, parable, anecdote. (Shapard)

It is this apparent need for synthesis that brings Valenzuela, in a magnificent chapter of *Escritura y secreto* (*Writing and Secrecy*), to argue that flash fiction does not, as most critics claim, derive from an oral tradition because that is a form of narrative that precisely does not require compression, but rather tends to an abundance of details (*Escritura* 93-94). The comparison she makes is with *quarks*, the minute elementary particles or, if you will, qualities of matter that are so small that they don't even have a size. This borrowing of terms from physics, although they were once borrowed themselves from literature,[4] reminds one of Cortázar's definition of stories in his essay "Aspects of the Short Story," in which he argues that "a good theme is somehow atomic, like a nucleus with its orbiting electrons"[5] ("Aspectos"). The two authors also resort to very similar notions when referring to what a *microrrelato* is, which, conceivably, explains something of the similarity of their work. Cortázar argues that "short stories of this type afflict every reader who deserves it like permanent scars: they are living creatures, complete organisms, closed cycles, and they breathe"[6] ("Del cuento"). Of course, many writers have compared their productions with organisms from both the animal and the plant kingdoms, but it is striking that Valenzuela also uses the figure of closed cycles, and therefore self-sufficient organisms, when she defines the *microrrelato* as "a unicellular organism, alive, that sometimes manages to reproduce by parthenogenesis, transforming and enriching itself through a process of change until it becomes a multiple and complex animal"[7] (*Escritura* 98).

Although the famous "Continuity of Parks,"[8] at a little over 500 words, is a rather lengthy example of flash fiction within the Latin American panorama, for the time when it was composed it is still very concise, and it is clearly a forerunner of Cortázar's later short pieces, the shortest of its type being "Love 77," which starts *in medias res* and consists of only thirty-seven words. Here, Cortázar applies poetic prose to Ernest Hemingway's Iceberg Theory,[9] which is based on the fact that, just as only one-eighth of the iceberg is visible, a text should also not reveal everything, but rather omit things in a way that the reader will be able to go below the surface. This, in turn, is closely related to Cortázar's notion of the "reader-accomplice,"[10] who is defined as an active reader who helps to reconstruct the story through the analysis of strategic allusion. Dolores Koch suggests ten different means of achieving significant brevity in *microrrelatos*,[11] and both of the authors under discussion have frequent recourse to a number of them. In the present case, Cortázar primarily makes use of: 1) ellipsis, by starting with an anaphora (that is, beginning repeatedly with the same word, "they") without stating who the antecedent is; 2) concise language, by enumerating various actions that present us with a metamorphosis of the characters, who finally "go about going back to being what they aren't" (*A Certain Lucas* 87), a twist that provokes suspense in the reader; and, most notably, 3) the incorporation of the title as part of the narration, fueling speculation as to what "77," for example, might refer to and insinuating a certain element of mystery. Although the title is certainly important and provides the reader with information, it is not completely indispensable, since the story could still be understood without it, and it doesn't, at least overtly, comply with Koch's device of "including in the title elements characteristics of the narration that don't appear in the text of the story"[12] (4). This is certainly the case in "The Lines of the Hand," in which we follow the trajectory of a line. Throughout the story, the word 'hand' is not repeated again, rendering the title essential to a full understanding—from a letter, over furniture, through a city, onto a ship, into a cabin, and finally ending up in the palm of someone who is about to commit suicide. Valenzuela takes this literary device to extremes in a *hypershort* that itself is only two words long, but has almost all its narration in the title, "The Taste of a Croissant at Nine in the Morning in an Old Corner Coffee Shop Where, at 97, Rodolfo Mondolfo Still Meets Up With His Friends on Wednesday Afternoons" (Valenzuela, *Juego* 26)[13] (a perfect example that explains why the words of the title must be considered as well) and thereby transgresses the literary norm that assumes that the title will never be longer than the story that follows. This example comes from *Strange Things Happen Here*, a book that was compiled during a visit to Argentina when the state terrorism under López Rega stirred Valenzuela to jot down those "strange things" she saw around her, or even odd snatches of conversation that she overheard in cafés and which inspired these textual flashes (Noguerol 222). Here we find a similar approach to Cortázar's, in which the title reveals the knowledge necessary for the reader to understand its meaning. In "Politics," for example, a couple coming with "information" from the heartland disappears and, with them, the information, which, as the *microrrelato* continues, hopefully will be deciphered by somebody, someday. Without the title, the reader wouldn't be able to infer that the message Valenzuela wants to transmit makes reference to the *disappeared* and to the problematic politics of the time, as well as to the covert resistance to state terrorism. This method shows Valenzuela's concept of the genre for which, according to her, apart from the obvious brevity, the "first and maybe only (in my view) rule of the *microrrelato* [. . .] consists in being fully and absolutely alert to language, perceiving everything the words say in their various meaning and, particularly, what they DO NOT say, what they conceal or disguise"[14] (Valenzuela, *Escritura* 102-103). That is exactly how one could define *Libro que no muerde*, a book that she confesses is the result of the first time she practiced the genre, long before she knew that it was a genre or could be considered as such (107). As a consequence of her voluntary exile during the military dictatorship, she couldn't take all of her notebooks with her and instead compiled those parts that she thought most interesting, whereupon she realized that "the notes that were intended for a future longer text were in essence already a minimal, coherent text"[15] (108). The nature of this work's origin explains the significance of these silences and the unsaid elements that overtake a large portion of the writing. It also shows that Valenzuela has applied the Iceberg Theory, even to such an extreme that not all of the meaning beneath the surface will always be obvious, or even determinable.

Suppressing certain information is connected to ambiguity, another recurrent characteristic of Latin American flash fiction. The "trick" lies in making the reader believe one thing throughout the story but ending it with a surprise element that one could have understood all along if the ambiguous meaning had been interpreted correctly. This is achieved either by using a word that has various meanings, or by using the reader's predisposition to assume that the outcome will satisfy the most likely or the most ordinary explanation. Cortázar confuses the reader masterfully in "Patio de la tarde" ("Afternoon on the patio"). It consists of two paragraphs; the first clearly gives the impression that a dog is wagging its tail every time a blond girl walks by. Then, in the second paragraph the *cola*—"tail"—turns out to be "glue" that a boy, presumably, and not a dog, is applying onto plywood.[16] The effect is intensified by the fact that all references could be interpreted for both a boy and a dog: his name, Toby; his behavior, moving his head to avoid a fly; or his physical traits, big brown eyes. Valenzuela uses puns or ambiguities in a similar way, as, for example, in "All About Suicide," which consists of a preliminary short paragraph that narrates what seems to be the suicide of the protagonist, Ismael, who "grabbed the revolver that was in a desk drawer, rubbed it gently across his face, put it to his temple and pulled the trigger. Without saying a word. Bang. Dead" (Valenzuela, *Strange Things* 48). But, unexpectedly, the story goes on, and Valenzuela returns—acknowledging by the use of the first person plural the relationship between reader and writer—to an earlier moment, repeating the story in more detail, though the outcome is still the same. We remain under the impression that Ismael has killed himself, which leads to the narratorial assertion that "there's something missing" (48), whereupon she takes us yet further back, twice to a time to when he was an infant, before noticing that this is too far back. But then, the final reconstruction of events reveals that what Ismael actually did was to kill a government secretary. Prior to this final re-narration we have already seen hints that Ismael's childhood friend would become a minister and then a traitor and that Ismael decided that the only solution is death. However, we know with certainty what happens only in the last sentence, which describes Ismael leaving "his office (the other man's office, the minister's)" (49). What the reader may have interpreted as suicide in the literal sense, now turns out to be a figurative kind of suicide, given that Ismael knows what he can expect as a consequence of his having committed murder.

This sort of ambiguity is linked to humor and irony, two elements often identified in the characterization of flash fiction (Pollastri 15), but the humor can move from the playful to a more serious register, as Marta E. Altisent observes regarding Hispanic humor in general:

> Irony is a moral and intellectual relativism that allows us to capture the right proportion of things and ourselves. And black humour, a genuine Hispanic trait that mixes irreverence, skepticism, wit, and cruelty, often culminates in an offer of escape from pain; a moment of indecisiveness and confusion between the comic and tragic senses of life. (33)

Both Cortázar and Valenzuela use darker humor to deal with problematic situations, the latter, for example, in general in *Strange Things Happen Here* and particularly in the already-mentioned "Politics." And there is an especially interesting example, given that it not only exemplifies the simultaneous use of wit and cruelty, but also the intertextuality—another of the critically defining aspects of flash fiction—between the two writers. Valenzuela's "Vision Out of the Corner of One Eye," for example, is a worthy revision of Cortázar's priceless "Super-short Film," which appeared in *Último round*"[17] (Noguerol 221). Cortázar leads the reader to surmise that a girl hitchhiking on the highway is going to be a rape victim, but his surprising ending reveals that she herself is a criminal who kills the driver in cold blood to steal his wallet and, en passant, his car. Valenzuela takes on the topic in a story in which we are first presented with a typical scenario of sexual harassment in a crowded bus, a situation that is turned around by the protagonist who "put [her] hand on his behind" (Valenzuela, *Strange Things* 33), just as he had in the beginning of the story, with the intent of an unconsented sexual advance, but she now does it in order to steal his wallet. Not only are the subject, the tone, and the stolen object the same as in the Cortázar story, but Valenzuela even uses the exact same expression—"watched him out of the corner of one's eye" (33)— that Cortázar employed at a moment when the reader is still in the dark about what is happening. Both stories depict painful realities, but they do so playfully, presenting characters as figures who take a sort of collective revenge for typical and long-standing offenses, and not as the victims we naturally expect them to be. These reversals lead readers toward what Pollastri sees as a typical reaction in experiencing a *microrrelato*, one "not of roaring laughter, but a grin"[18] (15). Also in this case, the sensitive and experienced reader recognizes and responds to an intertextual echo between Cortázar and Valenzuela.

The reference to another existing text is, especially in Valenzuela's case, a common trait, for example in "Serie Tito," in which she toys with Cortázar's "The Dinosaur" and the single comma that that hyper-short text contains, or in "Serie 201"[19] in which she sets her text in dialogue with a *micro* by David Roas. Roas dedicated his "Demasiada literatura" ("Too much literature") to her at a conference in Neuchâtel, relating his experience of being accommodated always in the same room, numbered 201, which as it turned out, Valenzuela happened to occupy during that very conference. Constituting one of the subsections of "Serie 201" is an explanation entitled "Explicación racional de un hecho insólito" ("Rational explanation of an extraordinary event"), though it is anything but rational: all tourists who arrive at a fully booked hotel are directed to the 201, a kind of all-purpose chamber to which the tourist is transported when opening the door with a magnetic key, passing from the "customary three dimensional world to another one with X dimensions"[20] (114). Valenzuela also integrates humorous and absurd elements, such as the notion that, in multi-dimensional space, all tourists sleep in the same bed without noticing the fact, or various "filtrations" from one dimension to another, such as the proverbial orphaned sock.

The absurdity of such stories is a common literary device for both writers, in some cases so intrinsically that they have composed flash fictions in which commonplace or everyday events are described as if they were completely alien to the reader. This is the case in the series entitled "Manual of Instructions," in which Cortázar playfully informs us of the procedure involved in climbing a staircase:

> Said part set down on the first step (to abbreviate we shall call it "the foot"), one draws up the equivalent part of the left side (also called "foot" but not to be confused with "the foot" cited above). [...] The coincidence of names between "the foot" and "the foot" makes the

explanation more difficult. Be especially careful not to raise, at the same time, "the foot" and "the foot." (*Cronopios* 22)

Valenzuela picks up the challenge but transposes the action from the innocent climbing of a staircase or combing one's hair to "The Fucking Game," in which she, as the title suggests, explains the act of "copulation," in a way that is "extremely logical and mathematical, like a chess game, and which, instead of provoking erotic sensations, succeeds in achieving just the opposite. [. . .] We can do nothing but laugh at the absurdities Valenzuela has juxtaposed" (Fores 44) just as we did in response to Cortázar's "Manual of Instructions." When asked in an interview about Cortázar's influence on her writing, especially regarding the way they both play with words, Valenzuela responded that, though she does believe there must be an influence, given her admiration for Cortázar, she started reading him intensely only rather later, when she had already published quite a lot. She therefore attributes their similarities to a different source: the fact that they both were immersed in 'Pataphysics,

> the science of imaginary solutions, that genius creation by Alfred Jarry, who urges you to see the supplementary world to this one. It is not believing in rules but in the exceptions of rules [...] and comes from a subversive logic. I, then, entered the movement which seemed very close to my way of seeing the world, and Cortázar, on his part, was also very involved in 'Pataphysics.[21] (qtd. in Díaz 39-40)

This orientation, which Valenzuela proposes using in order to approach the *microrrelato* (*Escritura* 119), is reflected in many of the flash fiction pieces the two authors have written. It is connected to the absurd and also explains the innovative uses of language we often find, such as, for example, their frequent neologisms. In "Contaminación semántica" ("Semantic Contamination"), as the title already suggests, Valenzuela invents a new word deriving from the noun, "funicular," namely, the verb "to funiculate," and spins a story, which can be understood only through the theory of the absurd, elaborated with this new verb that the reader can interpret at her convenience. Cortázar took the creation of new words to an extreme in chapter 68 of *Hopscotch*, in which, out of the 168 words of the text, a third are invented, components of the imaginary language he called *glíglico*. But the most fascinating thing about the passage is that, although it is impossible to understand the words by themselves, one can still make out some kind of meaning, and after re-reading the passage carefully, it becomes clear that the reader is witnessing an erotic scene, but one that is completely comprehensible only to the lovers themselves through their secret language. Another work in which Cortázar relied heavily on the use of invented words is *Cronopios and Famas*, which tells the story of three types of creatures, the *cronopios*, the *famas*, and the *esperanzas*. While *fama* (fame) and *esperanza* (hope) are Spanish words, there is no relationship between the original meaning of the words and the creature they designate in the stories, revealing that neologisms needn't actually be made-up words, but can be any word that is assigned a new significance. David Lagmanovich, who has divided the micro-story into three sub-types, has categorized this group as "substituted discourses"—the other two being "rewritings or parodies" and "emblematic writings"—whose foundations he locates in the work of poetic avant-garde writers such as Vicente Huidobro and César Vallejo (60). Lagmanovich explains that the reason one is able to understand "at least the general direction of the narration" (61) without recognizing all the individual words is based on the fact that we are "familiar [or become familiarized] with its morphematic components" (62). He adds another piece to the list: Valenzuela's "Zoología fantástica" ("Fantastic Zoology"), which is composed of "a rigorous selection of terms and idioms which everyday language assigns not to humans but to animals"[22] (62), resulting in an extreme cohesion that therefore confronts us as particularly and specifically literary. All this shows that both Cortázar and Valenzuela have mastered the art of what Valenzuela has described as "catch[ing] the unknown monster, angel or demon, or demon-angel, which dozes in some hideaway of our un/consciousness, alive"[23] (*Escritura* 91) through their ability not only to play with language and use it however they please, but also to forge it as if from its primordial sources to create powerful and evocative *flashes*.

Notes

1. "Con su tendencia a la concisión y precisión verbal, hace visible el microrrelato, lo dota de legibilidad estética, le provee espesor literario" (Pollastri 13).

2. Zavala, Laura. *El dinosaurio anotado: edición crítica de "El dinosaurio" de Augusto Monterroso*. Universidad Autónoma Metropolitana, 2002, p. 135.

3. "Minúsculas croquetas literarias de arroz con Poe y fibra borgeana, que mantienen el pelo Wilde y resultan ideales para hacer Kafka en el espacio" (Iwasaki).

4. Luisa Valenzuela lays this out in the same essay where she reminds us that "quark" is the name that was borrowed by microphysics from James Joyce, who coined the term from the word "quirk."

5. "Un buen tema tiene algo de sistema atómico, de núcleo en torno al cual giran los electrones" (Cortázar, "Aspectos").

6. "Los cuentos de esta especie se incorporan como cicatrices indelebles a todo lector que los merezca: son criaturas vivientes, organismos completos, ciclos cerrados, y respiran" (Cortázar, "Del cuento").

7. "Un organismo unicelular, vivo, que logra a veces reproducirse por partenogénesis, transformándose y enriqueciéndose en el camino del cambio hasta constituir un animal múltiple y complejo" (Valenzuela, *Escritura* 98).

8. In this flash fiction piece, Cortázar presents the reader with a protagonist who is reading a mystery story about a murderer who wanders through a park into an apartment and approaches, with a knife, the very same protagonist reading his story and thereby masterfully sums up "the kind of enigma bordering on the fantastical (and perhaps a metaphor for the act of reading) that people love in Latin American fiction" (Shapard).

9. In *Death in the Afternoon*, Hemingway lays out his theory as follows: "If a writer of prose knows enough about what he is writing about he may omit things that he knows and the reader, if the writer is writing truly enough, will have a feeling of those things as strongly as though the writer had stated them. The dignity of movement of an ice-berg

is due to only one-eighth of it being above water. A writer who omits things because he does not know them only makes hollow places in his writing." (153-154).

10. Cortázar, *Rayuela*, p. 414: "[. . .] con puertas y ventanas detrás de las cuales se está operando un misterio que el lector cómplice deberá buscar (de ahí la complicidad) y quizá no encontrará (de ahí el copadecimiento). Lo que el autor de esa novela haya logrado para sí mismo, se repetirá (agigantándose, quizá, sería maravilloso) en el lector cómplice". ("[. . .] With doors and windows behind which there operates a mystery which the reader-accomplice will have to look for [therefore the complicity] but might not find [therefore the cosuffering]. That which the author of this novel achieved for himself will be repeated [on a bigger scale, maybe, and that would be fabulous] in the reader-accomplice.")

11. Dolores Koch proposes the following literary devices in order to achieve this brevity: using well-known characters, such as biblical, historical, mythological, literary or popular figures; including in the title parts from the narration; incorporating a title in another language; ending the story with an unexpected colloquialism; using ellipsis; using concise language; applying an unexpected format for familiar elements; employing non-literary formats; parodying familiar texts or contexts; and making use of literary intertextuality.

12. "Incluir en el título elementos propios de la narración que no aparecen en el texto del relato" (Koch).

13. "El sabor de una medialuna a las nueve de la mañana en un viejo café de barrio donde a los 97 años Rodolfo Mondolfo todavía se reúne con sus amigos los miércoles a la tarde" (Valenzuela, *Juego* 26).

14. "La primera y quizá única (a mi entender) regla del microrrelato [. . .] consiste en estar plena y absolutamente alerta al lenguaje, percibir todo lo que las palabras dicen en sus muy variadas acepciones y sobre todo lo que NO dicen, lo que ocultan o disfrazan" (Valenzuela, *Escritura* 102-103).

15. "Los apuntes para algún futuro texto largo eran en sí ya un texto, mínimo, coherente" (Valenzuela, *Escritura* 108).

16. We might note the lineage of Raymond Roussel here, whose influence on both the Surrealists and the Pataphysicians, would naturally have affected Cortázar as well.

17. "'Visión de reojo', digna revisión del impagable 'Cortísimo metraje' incluido por Julio Cortázar en Último round" (Noguerol 221).

18. "No apunta a la abierta carcajada, sino a la sonrisa" (Pollastri 15).

19. As Sandra Bianchi points out, the fact that Valenzuela refers in this piece of flash fiction to the producers of microfiction as a "strange sect" reminds one of Cortázar's writing which is filled with "secret societies" (Bianchi 55).

20. "De este consuetudinario mundo de tres dimensiones a otro de dimensiones X" (Valenzuela, *Juego* 114).

21. "La ciencia de las soluciones imaginarias, la creación tan genial de Alfred Jarry, que te insta a ver el mundo suplementario a éste. Es el no creer en las reglas sino en las excepciones a las reglas [. . .] y viene de una lógica subversiva. Entonces yo entré en un movimiento que me resultaba muy afín a mi manera de ver el mundo y Cortázar por su lado también estaba muy involucrado en la 'Patafísica'" (Valenzuela qtd. in Díaz 39-40).

22. "Por lo menos la dirección general" (Lagmanovich 61); "familiarizado con sus componentes morfemáticos" (62); "una selección rigurosa de los vocablos y modismos idiomáticos que el lenguaje corriente asigna, no a actores humanos, sino a animales" (62).

23. "Cazar vivo al desconocido monstruo, ángel o demonio o demoniángel, que dormita en algún repliegue de nuestra in/conciencia" (Valenzuela, *Escritura* 91).

Works Cited

Altisent, Marta E. "Spanish Shorter-than-Short Fiction: Subverting Tradition." *Hispanic Research Journal*, vol. 4, no. 1, 2003, pp. 19-39.

Andres-Suárez, Irene. *La era de la brevedad: el microrrelato hispánico.* Menoscuarto Ediciones, 2008.

Bianchi, Sandra. "Abierta al misterio: la 201 de Luisa Valenzuela." *Cuadernos del CILHA*, vol. 12, no. 15, 2011, pp. 51-60, www.scielo. org.ar/pdf/ccilha/v12n2/v12n2a06.pdf/. Accessed 24 July 2016.

Cortázar, Julio. *A Certain Lucas.* Knopf, 1984.

_____. "Aspectos del cuento." *Ciudad Seva*, n.d., www.ciudadseva. com/textos/teoria/opin/aspectos_del_cuento.htm/. Accessed 24 July 2016.

_____. *Cronopios and Famas*. Translated by Paul Blackburn, New Directions, 1999.

_____. "Del cuento breve y sus alrededores." *Ciudad Seva*, n.d., ciudadseva.com/texto/del-cuento-breve-y-sus-alrededores/. Accessed 20 Nov. 2016.

_____. *Rayuela*. Biblioteca Ayacucho, 2004.

Díaz, Gwendolyn Josie, and María Inés Lagos. *La palabra en vilo: narrativa de Luisa Valenzuela*. Editorial Cuarto Propio, 1996.

Fores, Ana M. "Valenzuela's Cat-O-Nine-Deaths." *The Review of Contemporary Fiction. Luisa Valenzuela Number*, vol. 6, no. 3, 1986, pp. 39-47.

Gracia Fernández-Cuesta, María. "El microrrelato: origen, características y evolución." *Universidad de Málaga*, 2010, www.mecd.gob. es/dctm/redele/Material-RedEle/Biblioteca/2013-bv-14/2013_ BV_14_21Gracia_F.pdf?documentId=0901e72b8163adfe/. Accessed 25 July 2016.

Hemingway, Ernest. *Death in the Afternoon*, Scribner, 2002.

Iwasaki, Fernando. "Back Cover Blurb." *Distorsiones* by David Roas, Páginas de Espuma, 2010.

Koch, Dolores M. "Diez recursos para lograr la brevedad en el microrelato." *El cuento en red: estudios sobre la ficción breve*, vol. 2, 2002, 148.206.107.15/biblioteca_digital/articulos/10-644-9328yqi.pdf/. Accessed 24 July 2016.

Lagmanovich, David. *El microrrelato hispanoamericano*. Universidad Pedagógica Nacional, 2007.

Noguerol, Francisca. "*Juego de villanos*: Luisa Valenzuela, maestra de intensidades." *Las fronteras del microrrelato: teoría y crítica del microrrelato español e hispanoamericano*, by Ana María Revilla Calvo and Javier de Navascués, Iberoamericana, 2012, pp. 221-33.

Pollastri, Laura. *El límite de la palabra: antología del microrrelato argentine contemporáneo*. Menoscuarto, 2007.

Shapard, Robert. "The Remarkable Reinvention of Very Short Fiction." *World Literature Today*, 22 Aug. 2012, www.worldliteraturetoday. org/2012/september/remarkable-reinvention-very-short-fiction-robert-shapard#sources/. Accessed 23 July 2016.

Siles, Guillermo. *El microrrelato hispanoamericano: la formación de un género en el siglo XX*, Corregidor, 2007.

Valenzuela, Luisa. *Escritura y secreto*. Instituto tecnológico y de estudios superiores de Monterrey, 2003.

_____. *Juego de villanos*. Thule, 2008.

_____. *Strange Things Happen Here*. Translated by Helen Lane, Harcourt Brace Jovanovich, 1979.

Weiss, Jason. "Julio Cortázar, The Art of Fiction No. 83." *The Paris Review*, vol. 93, 1984, www.theparisreview.org/interviews/2955/the-art-of-fiction-no-83-julio-cortazar/. Accessed 24 July 2016.

"Art is not in some far-off place": Lydia Davis's "one-paragraph freedom"_____

Julie Tanner

Breaking it Down

"I thought it was a kind of terrible thing that we did in our family. Because it made writing . . . oh, the text became full of emotion" (*Paris Review* 188). Here, Lydia Davis recalls her family's curious habit of writing brief notes to one another in order to examine and resolve disagreements. These self-conscious feud-notes relied heavily on an implicit context as well as lexical precision and concision, and the reader's response was as important as the writer's own input. These qualities are transferable to flash fiction, which Davis has produced consistently for forty years.

Davis and her family's notes show the power of short fiction to express thought and emotion amidst the many aspects of our lives. Davis believes that short forms of writing correspond with the distracted nature of modern life and claims that they are successful because they are fresher, "more recently begun" in the mind of the reader (*Sudden Fiction* 230). She adds:

> What is certain, in any case, is that we are more aware of the great precariousness and the possible brevity of our lives than we were in the past [. . .] and for this reason, perhaps, we express not only more despair but also more urgency in some of our literature now, this urgency also being expressed as brevity itself. (230)

Each of Davis's story collections has included a higher percentage of flash fiction than the last, and, judging in part by her playful group of recent stories in *Ploughshares* (July 2016), she continues to find inspiration in the potential of extremely short forms. Michael LaPointe posits that "Lydia Davis did not invent flash fiction, but she is so far and away its most eminent contemporary practitioner." Therefore, it is surprising that there is a dearth of critical discussion of her work. To redress this lack of criticism, this chapter examines how Lydia Davis's work continues to reinvent itself by charting the formal and thematic progression of her stories. This examination demonstrates the varieties of expression in Davis's stories and illustrates why flash fiction has held Davis's creative interest and how her innovative fiction continues to affect and liberate her readers.

Extracts from a Life

After graduating from college, Davis worked as a translator in France, where she discovered Russell Edson's very short fiction and began to move away from the traditional short story form that she had grown up with. Davis recalls: "Edson was the one who jolted me out of my stuckness in long conventional stories and into one-paragraph freedom" (McCaffery 67). However, Edson is one of Davis's few contemporary American influences; she cites Europeans, such as Kafka, Joyce, Altenberg, and Beckett, more frequently, the latter of which she first read at the age of thirteen (Prose 84).

By the time of her first publication, *The Thirteenth Woman and Other Stories* (1976), Davis had returned to New York married to Paul Auster and expecting son Daniel. *Sketches for a Life of Wassilly* (1981), and *Story and Other Stories* (1985) followed. These three collections were produced in limited runs and thus remain difficult to obtain. However, many of these stories appear in later collections, either in their original form or reworked into alternative versions. Davis published *Break It Down* (1986) in the wake of her separation from Auster, and the book deals intermittently with the breakdown of relationships.

Davis's next collection, *Almost No Memory* (1997), was released almost a decade later. During the interim, she released her only novel to date, *The End of the Story* (1995), which, in part, reimagines some of her earlier stories, such as "Story" from *Break It Down*. Thus, this period of Davis's career is characterized by a blend of long and short forms that inform one another in terms of content, concern, and style. In a 2006 interview, Davis discusses writing her novel alongside raising her two sons (Lawless). She remembers: "I did feel that when I had my first child my work became more focused because I had less time in which to daydream or agonize about what I might write." Davis also mentions that during this time, she used a Kaypro computer for her writing. She recalls that the machine, long out of date when she was using it, could not hold more than ten pages of text per memory disk. The restriction of length imposed by the dated Kaypro allowed her to focus on smaller chunks of writing within the snippets of time she could take away from her children and her translation work (Lawless).

This writing schedule influences how Davis treats her stories in both long and short forms; she often focuses on a small idea or observation and unpacks it. Her flash fiction during this time depicts a mind that is preoccupied with the analysis of a premise. The analytical process, rather than the situation itself, absorbs Davis's narrators. "Ethics" represents this methodical approach, as a woman reconsiders the phrase, "Do unto others as you would have others do unto you" (Davis, *Collected Stories* 289). She realizes that someone she knows would prefer others to be as hostile towards him as he is to them, so that it would justify his hostility towards them. She then sees that, in his own way, he is already doing as the biblical ethic of reciprocity intends. The end of "Ethics" is similar to other stories of this period in its revelatory tone: "he may still be quite within some system of ethics, unless to feel something toward someone is to do something to that person" (290). These types of conclusions to analytic flash fictions are important in their own right, even if they do not fully resolve the narrator's predicament. The analysis does not just open up more questions, but, specifically, opens up bigger questions that surpass the personal circumstances that created them. In this way, Davis reinforces flash fiction's tendency to transcend its initial premise. Davis's narrators ponder questions that are both philosophical and personal, and for each protagonist, they provide a kind of intellectual escape from the context of the story. Breaking down the key phrases of these stories actually builds them up to something much more than they initially were. With an emphasis on the power of short phrases, the reader is reminded that the shortest stories can often be the most powerful ones.

Analysis of oneself, of others, of words and texts, is not always a fruitless task. Sometimes it provides answers, or at least catharsis; at others times, it opens up other lines of inquiry. The image of the narrator sniffing the ink on the page of "The Letter" (a story in which a woman receives a handwritten French poem from her ex-lover, without an accompanying note) could be said to represent the futility of analysis where feelings are involved (Davis, *Collected Stories* 46). However, unpredictability and entanglement with raw emotion represent the nature of analysis in Davis's fiction. Analytical and often obsessive processes are animated by Davis's narrators' strength of feeling. In her analysis of "A Few Things Wrong with Me," a story in which the narrator ruminates on aspects of her character that her ex-lover has admitted disliking, Maggie Doherty notes that "we sense that the narrator is writing this story for her own understanding rather than ours" (162). This feature of many of Davis's analytic early-career flash fictions heightens their realistic appeal. As the characters grapple with analysis, we recall our own experiences with obsessive logic, language, and meaning. For these characters, the way that they rehash their own stories is the *only* story because what has happened is inextricable from how they feel about it. Having characters work over things that have already happened is a surreptitious way to develop the dramatic aspect of these situations, and Davis achieves surprising new results with every application of this method that draws her flash fiction closer to our lives.

The Slipperiness of Language

The collections that followed *Break it Down—Samuel Johnson Is Indignant* (2001) and *Varieties of Disturbance* (2007)—signify a further turn inwards. The proportion of flash fiction to longer stories shifts once more in favor of the former, and both groups of stories are inclined towards one's relationship with oneself and the workings of the world, rather than direct relationships with other people. This results in flash fictions that are increasingly playful with language and form, perhaps in order to signal and express the variety of these experiences. Davis was awarded the MacArthur Foundation's

"Genius" Grant in 2003, which may account for the formal freedom evident during this period of her career.

Her artistic freedom was also influenced by her work in this period as a translator, which often accounts for the formally and linguistically innovative elements of her flash fiction. Davis began to earn a living as a translator as soon as she graduated from Barnard College, and she became renowned for this early work, such as her translations of Maurice Blanchot's essays. She continues to be celebrated for her acclaimed Penguin translations of Proust and Flaubert and her more recent work on short pieces by A. L. Snijders and Peter Bichsel. Davis translated Proust's *The Way by Swann's* in 2003. *Samuel Johnson Is Indignant* and *Varieties of Disturbance* bookend this significant project. During this time, Davis furthered her experiments with very short stories as a "reaction to Proust's very long sentences" (qtd. in Skidelsky). As with her writing in the mid-1990s, she once again found herself with "almost no time" for her own work, "but didn't want to stop" (Skidelsky). These anecdotal reflections suggest that the most renowned aspect of Davis's stories, their brevity, sprung from two concurrent stimuli. Firstly, there was the necessity to utilize time economically amidst a large translation assignment, and, secondly, there was an augmented awareness of time because of Proust's own fiction—the miniature units of time that punctuate Swann's memories-within-memories. However, Davis seemed to welcome such constraints as freeing. Translating Proust (as with using a Kaypro for her novel in the 1990s) could hinder progress. But the nature of creative confinement heightens productivity by reinforcing the need to produce the best work in the allocated time (and disk space). Davis applied this method to her experiments with very short fiction with fruitful results.

Davis's flash fiction in her mid-career work draws on a translator's attention to detail; the stories snatch at time, revel in the charming oddities of everyday lexical choices, and exploit layers of meaning with unexpectedly profound results. These stories focus on types of loss—moments when the slipperiness of both time and language is apparent. This is depicted throughout *Samuel Johnson*

Is Indignant and *Varieties of Disturbance* and is represented by the distinct gap between the experience of emotions and how to express them.

Davis often foregrounds the separation of thought and speech more prominently than the circumstances that they are borne of. "Grammar Questions" supports this interpretation, since the story consists of an extended consideration of appropriate grammatical constructions in relation to the death of a father. In bypassing an extended rumination on the nature of grief, Davis's short piece offers an unfamiliar lens through which to examine loss, resulting in a powerful story that is both compact and expansive. The narrator asks:

> [. . .] when he is in the form of ashes, will I point to the ashes and say, "That is my father"? Or will I say' "That was my father"? Or, "Those ashes were my father"? Or, "Those ashes are what was my father"? (Davis, *Collected Stories* 528)

In an ironic twist, parsing the difficult language associated with bereavement moves beyond the problem of grammatical variations. The perspective seen in "Grammar Questions" can seem extreme, even cold, considering the context of the story. However, the story develops into a profound linguistic exercise that taps into the heart of the narrator's universal worry about how to think of and talk about loved ones after their death. In a discussion of "Grammar Questions," Davis comments that the way that emotion is controlled in the story "can imply that this narrator cannot deal with it" (qtd. in Wachtel). She also explains that: "Really, of course, what I was wrestling with was the age-old questions and quandaries: is this person, as he dies, really still a person? Are these ashes still a person? What happened to my father?" (qtd. in Gunn).

"Letter to a Funeral Parlor" also confronts both language and death, addressing the insensitive portmanteau "cremains," the term used to describe the writer's father's ashes (Davis, *Collected Stories* 380-1). LaPointe notes that in "quibbling with the word, the narrator conveys a palpable fear that in cheapening her speech, she loses the ability to adequately cherish the dead." As a genre, letters of complaint typically contain a measured argument and, sometimes, a stern tone. The author of the letter to the funeral parlor adheres to these generic conventions by complimenting the representative's politeness before addressing their complaint (380). As in "Grammar Questions," the writer of the letter attempts to create a constructive form of expression. In both stories, controlled exposition provides an outlet of consolation. "He" or "it," "is" or "was" are problematic in "Grammar Questions," but the exercise itself is cathartic, and while "cremains" is a painful term, the ability to complain is a relief. Davis acknowledges unusual responses to loss, and this unusual story marks her insistence upon the aptness of certain forms to express grief, as a riposte to the difficulties of individual language choices. Flash fiction in particular proceeds directly to the core of the story's pain. Davis's short forms of writing observe lexical choices at close range to push the boundaries of the story and of language itself.

Davis returns to this method throughout this period, notably in "Head, Heart":

> Heart is so new to this.
> I want them back, says heart.
> Head is all heart has.
> Help, head. Help heart. (Davis, *Collected Stories* 705)

Davis explains: "When I came to try to express this particular grief, a poem was what I wanted. No 'story', no talk, but that distillation" (qtd. in Aguilar and Fronth-Nygren 194). "Head, Heart" is one of the only poems to be included in Davis's story collections because a poem is just what that speaker requires; the compact language of the poem distills the speaker's pain. This "difficulty speaking" is expressed in the poem as it is elsewhere in Davis's flash fiction; via the choice of a form that reduces language to its necessities (194). On deciding the length of a story, Davis says "I think I have a sense right in the beginning of how big an idea it is and how much room it needs" (qtd. in Martin). This distinction is crucial to Davis's work; the synthesis of form and content is justified by how long is needed to represent the idea, rather than an outright preference for short forms. Davis decided to write a novel because she felt "it was necessary, if the story was to have its full effect, for a reader to live with that narrator for a long time" (qtd. in Johnson). This sensitive application of form is also apparent in every story collection Davis has published. "The Seals" (*Can't and Won't* 146-70), a twenty-four-page piece on the death of a half-sister, is one of Davis's longest stories, particularly noticeable among the high concentration of flash fiction in *Can't and Won't*. The speaker evidently needs to delve into the experience of bereavement, and the story stands out for its form and content among the other stories that deal with more everyday experiences. Davis matches her stories about separation and grief with a fitting form in order to express the personal nature of each individual loss. In Davis's delicate treatment of the relationship between form and content, she constructs startlingly empathetic stories and conveys circumstances that are simultaneously personal and universal.

Found Materials and the 'Retired Imagination'

The publication of Davis's *Collected Stories* in 2009 (USA) and 2010 (UK) with Penguin increased readership, and appreciation of her work filtered through literary publications to mainstream media, with the brevity of her work as a frequent focus for reviewers. In 2013, Davis won the Man Booker International Prize. A year later, she released *Can't and Won't* (2014), which signals the maturation of her style while advancing the experimental quality of her work. It is possible to identify a Lydia Davis story if it is up to 1,000 words long, deals with a form of loss, and involves analytic processes or foregrounds problems with language. However, with her recent work, knowing for certain whether we are reading a Lydia Davis story is an increasingly problematic task. Even if the cover of the book reads "by Lydia Davis," you are just as likely to encounter an extract from Flaubert's letters as you are a short story by Davis herself.

The centrality of such "found materials" demonstrates the importance of intertextuality (the relationship between texts), borrowing and context in Davis's recent flash fiction, indicating a development in inspiration. On the emergence of these sources in her stories, Davis observes:

> I realized that you could write a story that was really just a narration of something that had happened to you [. . .] In a way, that's found material. [. . .] if a friend of mine tells me a story or a dream, I guess that's found material. [. . .] But then if I notice the cornmeal making little condensations, is that found material? (qtd. in Aguilar and Fronth-Nygren 177)

The notion of "found" sources is not necessarily new to Davis's style, but it is much more prevalent in her most recent collection, *Can't and Won't*, where it is taken to further extremes. Davis conjures her material from numerous sources: anecdotes, dreams, friends' dreams, Flaubert's dreams, letters, Flaubert's letters. Davis also admits to taking notes while on the phone with family members (Prose 93). Davis's critics have met this stylistic development with skepticism; for example, LaPointe claims that "*Can't and Won't* does feel like the work of a partially retired imagination." To an extent, Davis would agree: "It is true that over the years I have become less interested in the wholly invented fictional story" (qtd. in Winters 111). However, rather than a retreat of the imagination, these stories arguably represent even further refinement of the possibilities of storytelling.

Thirteen stories in *Can't and Won't* are extracts from the work of Flaubert. However, they are also stories by Davis in the sense that she sees the texts, isolates them, translates them, and lends a new context to them, making each work a strikingly effective and arguably original act. When Davis started to experiment with these stories, she spoke of her enjoyment of "shaping [self-contained stories] into stories" (qtd. in Yeh). As with stories from the middle of her career and their relation to Proust, it seems that her later preoccupation with Flaubert also translated to her fiction. Davis observes: "I like the fact that it's Flaubert's story as much as mine [. . .] I like sharing it that way" (qtd. in Mathews). Indeed, as Kasia Boddy notes, "Each one starts as Flaubert and ends as Davis." The stories are always designated with "story from Flaubert" (once as "rant from Flaubert" in "Industry," *Can't and Won't* 215). The clear labelling of Flaubert extracts is notable, since they are often strikingly similar to Davis's own compositions. This can easily be accounted for; perhaps Davis selected them because of this similarity. It is also possible that her translation could lend them this feel. However, the similarity is markedly thorough, and extends all the way back to Davis's earliest stories. The austere tone, bizarre, exclamatory conclusions, and philosophical ruminations derived from daily life are all integral aspects of Davis's style. For example, the line from Flaubert "I wonder if thoughts are fluid, and flow downward, from one person to another, within the same house" (qtd. in "The Visit to the Dentist," *Can't and Won't* 31) could be from either writer. Using Flaubert in such a direct, unedited manner is a bold assertion of the intertextual nature of writing about daily life and representing the ordinary. Furthermore, this technique of intense intertextuality affirms the universality of experience, even across significant periods of time. This method is especially effective when using flash fiction because the stories mingle thoroughly on account of their brevity; in *Can't and Won't*, an original Davis story immediately follows Flaubert's personal musings, and dreams and anecdotes circulate through the collection. This flow of stories creates vivid textual links in the mind of the reader and reminds them about the possibilities of observation and common experience.

"Art is not in some far-off place"

Throughout her career, Davis's extraordinary powers of reflection have transformed normal, even mundane experiences into thoughtful pieces of writing. This is achieved by tweaking certain details, or fictionalizing other parts. Davis's later work strays from this process as there is often no transformation of the material, but rather a pointed isolation, and re-contextualisation that allows the text to speak for itself. Davis explains: "More and more my interest as a writer goes in the direction of taking real material and making something from it. [...] my interest, more and more, is in what really happened" (qtd. in Farsethas). "Example of the Continuing Past Tense in a Hotel Room" is exemplary of this impulse. The full story is: "Your housekeeper *has been* Shelley" (*Collected Stories* 715). Davis italicizes the aspect that she finds remarkable, highlighting the oddness of this grammatical construction, and reinforces this in her chosen title. Here, her authorial input is minimal, but instead her insightfulness as a reader is just as important. She unpacks the story in an interview:

> It may be the name "Shelley," I don't know why. It may be the precise use of the "has been." In other words, "We assume you're leaving now, and this is who your housekeeper has been," not "is about to be" or "is." And then the presumption or the intimacy of saying, "Your housekeeper." And the word "housekeeper." You know, she's not really my housekeeper. (qtd. in Wachtel)

How much a reader enjoys a Lydia Davis story relies on their willingness as a reader; as Jessica Jernigan argues, there is work to be done. Davis is an accomplice in this process, and the potential to find stories-within-stories abounds in her later work that expands the possibilities of the story form by involving non-writers and challenging the reader to dig deeper into each small pocket of text. Thus, her work with flash fiction refines our understanding of the form without narrowing its possibilities.

Found materials also provide a challenge for Davis herself because it is her responsibility to notice and select interesting pieces of life. Perhaps the most difficult is the representation of dreams, which Davis depicts for the first time in *Can't and Won't*. The telling of one's dreams is associated with a story that is more interesting for the teller than for the listener, and Davis admits:

> Part of the challenge was stylistic—to get back to your initial point about the danger of boredom: in the shadow of that danger, of our association of dream narratives with boredom, how to shape each account in a tight and compelling way, and how to narrate the dream in language that had the tension of reality. (qtd. in Winters 110)

There are twenty-nine dream stories in *Can't and Won't*. These stories bridge the gap during Davis's gravitation towards found materials, as some are derived from Davis's dreams and some are borrowed from friends (Winters 110). She pinpoints the difficulty in listening to other people's dreams: "to them the dream is still half real, and emotional, while to you [the listener] it is not, and you look on from the outside as they re-experience something in which you had no part" (Winters 110). The dream stories in *Can't and Won't* overcome this by recreating the dream and vivifying it for the reader to experience. "The Child" is a piece that demonstrates this:

> The child is laid out in state on a table. She wants to take one more photograph of the child, probably the last. In life, the child would never sit still for a photograph. She says to herself, "I'm going to get the camera," as if saying to the child, "Don't move." (Davis, *Can't and Won't* 27)

Thus, the found and the fictional are combined to produce a new endeavor for Davis, but one that fits within her body of work thus far.

Davis's dream stories are integrated well within *Can't and Won't* because dreams are often a central feature of the extracts she picks from Flaubert's letters and diaries. Furthermore, Davis makes extensive use of the letter genre in other stories beyond her borrowing from Flaubert, thus increasing the blend of materials in the collection. In contrast to Flaubert's letters to friends, Davis terms her own "letters of complaint" (qtd. in Mathews). The letters appear to bypass their intended audience, as if plucked from their context and mixed in with the other found pieces in *Can't and Won't*. Davis admits that she has, in fact, sent most of them (Aguilar and Fronth-Nygren 176). *Samuel Johnson Is Indignant* includes one letter of complaint, "Letter to a Funeral Parlor," and Davis explains that she wrote more in *Can't and Won't* "because I realized that I had a lot to complain about" (qtd. in Mathews).

In the same interview, Davis describes her attraction to the more playful letter form:

> I think it allows you to take on this artificial, over-pedantic or over-correct voice. It's sort of like the letters to the editor you'll read in the

paper sometime—a slightly absurd tone and that allows you to voice your opinion about one particular thing or another in an entertaining and extreme way and I just found it a lot of fun. (qtd. in Mathews)

Most of Davis's letters exaggerate and fictionalize something that has occurred to her, taking it to a more extreme extent, which creates a humorous effect. For instance, in "Letter to a Frozen Peas Manufacturer" (Davis, *Can't and Won't* 33), the writer suggests that the company use different artwork on their packaging, since their current choice makes the peas look less appetizing than they are in real life: "Please reconsider your art" (33), the writer implores. Some of Davis's other epistolary stories, however, are still humorous but are more understandable as complaints, such as "Letter to a Marketing Manager" (*Can't and Won't* 80-1). In this letter, the objection is to a biographical error in a bookshop's newsletter, which wrongly claims that the writer is an alumnus of McLean's, a psychiatric hospital (80). This misprint is originally addressed seriously, but Davis cannot resist ending the letter with:

> [. . .] no other explanation occurs to me for your mistaken identification, unless your buyers assumed on the basis of the contents of my book, its title, or my admittedly somewhat wild-eyed photograph that at some time in the past I was an inmate of McLean's. (Davis, *Can't and Won't* 81)

Davis advises young writers not to "cave in to the pressure of publishers or agents": "Do what you want to do, and don't worry if it's a little odd or doesn't fit the market" (qtd. in Lund). With her letters of complaint, as with the rest of *Can't and Won't*, Davis is taking her own advice and having fun with different forms and sources. With 111 out of 122 stories being flash fiction, she is also championing formal free will and encouraging a broader market for flash fiction. Earlier in this discussion of Davis's work, I referred to LaPointe's criticism of *Can't and Won't* and what he perceives as Davis's "partially retired imagination." Perhaps *Can't and Won't* is a form of retirement after all, though not from the imagination, as the deftness of her found pieces proves. In retirement, many people choose to indulge in what they truly wish to do; what they love doing and what they want to learn. The found materials in *Can't and Won't* are a way for Davis to experiment and to represent her increased interest in other people's writing, a lifelong passion of hers as a translator. They represent the concerns of her recent work and also her future work, since she has indicated that she is working intermittently on a nonfiction, source-based project, involved in tracing history and genealogy—alongside other stories (Farsethas).

The Lydia Davis Effect

Our understanding of what constitutes Lydia Davis's short fiction expands alongside the progression of her career. Thus it is necessary to accept that, although we can recognize recurrent themes and genres in her work, our understanding of Davis's art will need to be refined upon the release of her next story. Flash fiction is such a suitable mode for Davis's fiction because of its reputation for reinvention and the open manner in which readers and writers of flash fiction approach new stories and new ways of telling them.

Several of Davis's critics evince that when you read Lydia Davis, you start to think like Lydia Davis. LaPointe discusses the notion of "looking for myself in her work" and the ultimate revelation of "finding her work in myself." In his review for the *New York Times*, Peter Orner warns his readers: "Read enough Lydia Davis and her stories start happening to you." This is a shared experience of reading Davis's stories, which leaves the reader wondering how she would articulate these observations, how she could transform them. But beyond this admiration of her skill, the reader takes on the observational yet active role of the writer, noting both touching and bizarre aspects of their everyday world.

Works Cited

Aguilar, Andrea, and Johanne Fronth-Nygren. "Lydia Davis, Art of Fiction No. 227." *The Paris Review*, Spring 2015: 168-195.

Boddy, Kasia. "Lydia Davis." *The Telegraph*, 5 Nov. 2010, www.telegraph. co.uk/culture/books/8113668/Lydia-Davis.html/. Accessed 12 Jul. 2016.

Davis, Lydia. "AfterWord." *Sudden Fiction: American Short-Short Stories*, edited by Robert Shapard and James Thomas, Gibbs-Smith Publisher, 1986, p. 230.

_____. *The Collected Stories of Lydia Davis*. Penguin, 2013.

_____. *Can't and Won't*. Penguin, 2014.

_____. *Ploughshares*, vol. 42, no. 2, Summer 2016, pp. 38-41.

Doherty, Maggie. "Cool Confessions." *n+1 Magazine*, vol. 21, pp. 158-168.

Farsethas, Ane. "Lydia Davis at the End of the World: on Learning Norwegian and Writing the Beauty of the Dying World." *Literary Hub*, 9 Apr. 2015, lithub.com/lydia-davis-at-the-end-of-the-world/. Accessed 17 Aug. 2015.

Gunn, Dan. "The Lydia Davis Interview." *The Quarterly Conversation* 10 Mar. 2014 Web. 15 Jul. 2016.

Jernigan, Jessica. "Putting the Reader to Work." *The Women's Review of Books*, vol. 27, no. 4, 2010, pp. 22-23.

Johnson, Bret Anthony. "2007 National Book Award Fiction Finalist Interview With Lydia Davis." *National Book Foundation*, Oct. 2007. Web. 15 Jul. 2016.

LaPointe, Michael. "The Book Gets Fatter: Lydia Davis's *Can't and Won't*." *Los Angeles Review of Books*, 2 Apr. 2014, lareviewofbooks. org/article/book-gets-fatter/#!/. Accessed 5 Jul. 2016.

Lawless, Andrew. "Samuel Johnson Is Indignant: TMO meets Lydia Davis." *Three Monkeys Online Magazine* 1 Mar. 2006. Web. 12 Jul. 2016.

Lund, Christian. "Lydia Davis: Advice to the Young." *Louisiana Literature Festival*, Louisiana Museum of Modern Art, Denmark, Aug. 2014. Accessed 14 Jul. 2015.

Martin, Rachel. "Lydia Davis' New Collection Has Stories Shorter Than This Headline." *NPR Books*, 6 Apr. 2014, www.npr. org/2014/04/06/299053017/lydia-davis-new-collection-has-stories-shorter-than-this-headline/. Accessed 13 Jul. 2016.

Mathews, Brendan. "Lydia Davis: 'I kind of like the fact that my work isn't for everybody.'" *Salon*, 29 Apr. 2014, www.salon.com/2014/04/28/lydia_davis_ i_kind_of_like_the_fact_that_my_work_isn%E2%80%99t_for_everybody/. Accessed 11 Jul. 2016.

McCaffery, Larry. "Deliberately, Terribly Neutral: An Interview with Lydia Davis." *Some Other Frequency: Interviews with Innovative American Authors.* U of Pennsylvania P, 1996, pp. 59-79.

Orner, Peter. "Illuminations: *Can't and Won't* by Lydia Davis." *New York Times* 4 Apr. 2014. Accessed 16 Jul. 2016.

Prose, Francine. "Lydia Davis." *BOMB: The Author Interviews*, edited by Betsy Sussler, Soho Press, 2014. 81-96.

Skidelsky, William. "Lydia Davis: My style is a reaction to Proust's long sentences." *The Guardian*, 1 Aug. 2010, www.theguardian.com/books/2010/aug/01/lydia-davis-interview-reaction-proust/. Accessed 7 Jul. 2016.

Wachtel, Eleanor. "An Interview with Lydia Davis." *Brick Magazine*, Summer 2008, brickmag.com/an-interview-with-lydia-davis/. Accessed 20 Aug. 2015.

Winters, David. "Interview with Lydia Davis." *The White Review*, Feb. 2014, pp. 104-12.

Yeh, James. "The Story Becomes About Seeing: an Interview with Lydia Davis." *Gigantic Magazine*, no. 4, Jan. 2013, thegiganticmag.com/magazine/articleDetail.php?p=articleDetail&id=159/. 19 Jul. 2016.

Shameful Secrets and Seducing the Whole World: Amy Hempel's Flash Fiction and Female Sexuality_____

Laura Tansley

Amy Hempel's "Housewife," just a single sentence long, illustrates many of the characteristics we have come to expect from flash fiction. In forty-three words, we learn of a housewife who, whenever she sleeps with her husband, always sleeps with another man as well. The story ends by explaining that to pass the time with what remains of her day after these events, the housewife incants, "*French film, French* film" (Hempel 221).[1] "Housewife" is a taut, compact piece that alludes to layers of complications and explanations that exist within the space around the text and between the reader. It's the example that was given to me in my first-ever flash fiction workshop, and at the time, I remember feeling slightly suspicious of it. Its dark humor, casual sexuality, and the ease with which it wryly depicted a life, made me wonder if it was maybe a little unsympathetic. Outside of the context of Hempel's collected stories, this piece felt like a dare to prove something about storytelling (which, of course, it does) with a smug sense of humor (my own initial interpretation). But getting to know Hempel's writing is to understand how completely concerned she is with people; they are not just pithy little characters incanting tropes that she employs to portray something witty. Hempel's people are often desperate, grasping for something and employing a gallows humor that is funny principally because this slant view towards life-experiences reveal unexpected truths, which illuminate the ordinary. She understands how we live through a mix of clichés, cultural capital, and pop psychology; how our knowledge of ourselves is shaped by what we learn, which often clashes with the inherited wisdom that surrounds us. Hempel's shortest pieces employ the contradictions of the flash fiction form to explore how stripping away the unnecessary leaves something that could be regarded as scant when the number of words used is considered but, upon closer inspection, reveals complexity and a multifaceted consideration of character and story. When it comes to themes and issues within women's lives in particular, this multiplicity allows Hempel to explore what lies beneath and beyond the dramatic because her shortest fiction is often more interested in the repercussions and reverberations of an event rather than the depiction of the event itself. Rick Moody, in his introduction to Amy Hempel's *Collected Stories*, suggests this focus is opposed to the masculine writing of Hempel's contemporaries during the minimalist realist period of mid-1980s fiction, which "raged or postured" about men fighting, hunting, and "coke-snorting" (Moody x). Instead, Moody suggests that Hempel's "sentences, with their longing and their profound disquiet . . . ache" (Moody x). Aching is key for me when it comes to understanding Hempel's writing; it is a quieter kind of pain but in its consistency can be devastating. It is internal and is inextricable from the body. Hempel herself suggests that a corporeally-connected experience is what she seeks to achieve in her writing, that she knows when a piece of writing is complete because she feels it viscerally: "I trust the body. You can admire something intellectually, but how much better if you respond to it bodily!" (Hempel 1997). The body, then, and very often the female body (her protagonists are, for the main part, women), is placed at the center of Hempel's writing and is "rent open in the search for identity" (Moody xv). Secrets and history and illness and accidents elicit this exploration, revealing psychological purpose, personal contemplation, and a reconciled appreciation of the world and its randomness. If, as Moody suggests, this is all in opposition to grandiose, masculine narratives, it would seem appropriate to associate Hempel's precise and exacting writing with a kind of femininity. However, Hempel developed her craft under the tutelage of Gordon Lish, an infamous editor arguably responsible for the rise of minimalism in short fiction, whose instructions to emerging writers such as Hempel couldn't have been clearer: "Remember, in reaching through your writing to a reader, you are engaged in nothing so much as an act of seduction . . . Seduce the whole fucking world for all time" (qtd. in Blumenkranz 211). The strength of Hempel's portrayal of women is perhaps undermined by the knowledge that a man at the helm of her minimalism was calling for writing to work as a sexual metaphor in order for it to be effective. This essay, however, intends to complicate this understanding by considering the relationship between gender and form and exploring notions of creative process through Hempel's own shortest fiction and the multiplicity inherent within it.

Gordon Lish, editor at Knopf and *Esquire* and Creative Writing teacher out of New York, had a profound influence on the American short story and literary scene in the 70s, 80s, and 90s. He is renowned for his work with authors such as Mary Robison, Barry Hannah, and Richard Ford, and his editorial influence on Raymond Carver has been much discussed.[2] His teaching methods were notorious, as Carla Blumenkranz documents in her essay "Seduce the Whole World: Gordon Lish's Workshop." Hempel, who sought out Lish's writer's workshop at Columbia University after moving to New York in 1975, recalls his first class "vividly":

> The assignment was to write our worst secret, the thing we would never live down, the thing that, as Gordon put it, "dismantles your own sense of yourself." And everybody knew instantly what that thing, for them, was. We found out immediately that the stakes were very high, that we were expected to say something no one else had said, and to divulge much harder truths than we had ever told or ever thought to tell. (Winner)

Lish's tactic, it seemed, was to break writers down in to their vulnerable pieces and build them back up again with the technical skills required to have authorial control over their most sensitive but truest material. This vulnerability, devised to make his class uncomfortable (after everyone had revealed their worst secrets he's reported to have said, "did I say that this secret doesn't have to be true?"), is bound up with Lish as he positioned himself as figurehead, writer's savior and part-time tyrant (Blumenkranz 216). Writers created work to please him, impress him, and attract him: "if he really liked what you were doing, he might sleep with you, or he might publish your book" (Blumenkranz 211). This ensured that his students' "literary motivations and erotic motivations [were] impossible to extricate from each other" (Blumenkranz 213). His tutelage, then, seemed wrapped up in a kind of masculine sexuality where his authority was unquestionable and all-powerful, and steeped in muddied notions of erotic control:

> "The best writers are those who put themselves at risk—first destabilize yourself, then restore yourself," Lish said. How did they restore themselves? By dramatizing their confessions in a way that commanded attention: that was tense, taut, and confident, that had the feeling of an emotional striptease about it. . . . Writing is not about telling; it is about showing, and not showing everything. (Blumenkranz 216-17)

"Tense" and "taut," adjectives often used to describe minimalist writing such as flash fiction, also align with the striptease, an act orchestrated by a male authority figure firstly for his own pleasure then for potentially the rest of the reading world. The art of the flash, revealing just enough to take readers the rest of the way themselves, in the context of Hempel's development as a writer and her subsequent work, suddenly takes on issues of a gender-rooted power struggle. With this context in mind, our reading of "Housewife" becomes centered on a woman's problematic self-actualization. The sexual encounters of this housewife start to seem perfunctory, suggesting a rigid routine rather than a series of liberating experiences or an existential quest. The character of housewife is contained by men; the moments that are truly hers, whatever's left of her day after all the sex she feels she has to have with men, she spends trying to find agency in the fictional and fictionalized women that might fully realize themselves through these encounters. It is a lonely but deliberate act that could suggest a shame, not for her actions, but for not enjoying these experiences as much as she should. There is a longing, rooted in her body, to create a different meaning for the space she occupies; the italicized, repeated emphasis of "*French film*" becomes desperate and any humor evoked from the allusion to stereotypes in European cinema is nullified. So if, as Moody suggests, Hempel's stories are opposed to the more masculine work of her contemporaries, does "Housewife" empower women by giving them voice? Or is it part of a masculine tradition of erotic tantalization that her work mimics and/or explores from a woman's point of view?

When considering gender and genre, Mary Eagleton has suggested that "the intimacy of the [short story] form . . . or [its] focus on a manageable, single incident, is, on the one hand, to recognise women's social experience in our culture . . . on the other hand, it is to confine women once again in the personal, the closely detailed, the miniature" (64). Eagleton sees the short story as a venue capable of expressing the marginalization of women in society because it is, in comparison to novels which have a greater market and mainstream stature, a marginalized form. But she also acknowledges that suggesting the short story is a gendered form is simultaneously a creatively expressive and limiting gesture because although it may allow for an exploration of liminality (an experience of alienated or isolated people perceived to be outside of accepted conventions), it perhaps also seeks to reinforce the notion that women (and the short story) are essentially liminal. If we take a "single incident" to mean the capturing of a moment, one segment or experience within a life, then this sentiment is equally applicable to flash fiction and with the definitions of the form we have come to know. It's possible, then, to extend the idea to suggest that literally smaller forms like flash fiction (a liminal form) written by women (whose experiences can be liminal) contain stories that are considered to be metaphorically smaller, more intimate, focused, with a finer tuning or, as in Doris Lessing's description of feminine writing: "intense, careful, self-conscious, mannered" as opposed to "straight, broad, direct" (8). But does this always have to be the case? With Hempel's writing in mind, it's perhaps true that the big events that have disrupted or that will disturb the lives of the protagonists contained within her very short stories are inferred, referenced to, or are looming on the horizon, after the last sentence has been read. As Cynthia Whitney Hallett suggests, Hempel's stories are almost always "never about the 'what' that happened, but rather about the protagonist's behaviour and thoughts in response to the occurrence"

(68). But this would be a very oblique way of suggesting that epic, grand incidents are, therefore, not the purview of Hempel's writing or of very short forms of writing by women. The word count relies on writers addressing themes and topics with a singular focus, but one that can suggest the multiplicity of experience and the infinite number of moments, which make up this experience. Broad topics can be addressed by flash fiction through a process of distillation, fragmentation, dissection or disintegration, which is not necessarily a scaling down but a microscoping of a theme, event, or authorial intent. That is to say that Hempel, I suspect, does not begin a story with a word count in mind; the brevity of her writing is an intrinsic part of her voice and her process:

> Sometimes it just means taking things out, and it happens when you ask yourself, as you go along, "Is this essential?" I mean every sentence, every word. It means leaping past anything that would slow things down for the ideal reader. You know, embellishment that is there just to be "writerly." I never liked the term "minimalism." I prefer Raymond Carver's term. He called Mary Robison and myself "precisionists." And that's what he was doing too, of course. (Small)

"Precision" is an important choice of words for Hempel to make here. To define her work and her intent as precise is very different from defining it as minimalist, a word that suggests something diminutive and of a traditionally feminized size and stature. A precisionist's writing is not small, it's specific and accurate. Hempel says, "the story provides every challenge I could want in writing, and endless possibilities. It comes naturally, and lends itself to the way I experience life—or, to make this more manageable, the way I experience a single day" (Small). Hempel's precision, as well as her choice to focus on short stories because of how the form reflects her own experience of life (days rather than years, small plates rather than platters), creates the form of her work.[3] The content of this form has been described by Whitney Hallett as an exploration of the "poetics of exclusion," again perhaps choosing to emphasize the peripheral aspects of the story form and identifying this writing with ancillary women (66). Although Whitney Hallett goes on to suggest that "gender has little to do with the effect of [Hempel's] fiction," understanding her writing in these terms associates her stories with the social and literary constraints of which Eagleton wrote (137). Instead it seems equally apt to understand Hempel's work as concerned with the poetics of the specifics of inclusion, where the white space that surrounds whole pieces, as well as fragment-paragraphs within a story, opens up understanding rather than closes it down. Hempel suggests that "the connective tissue of a story is often the white space, which is not empty"; we understand this space to be full of the ways readers can makes associations and how the mind of the narrator assembles a story (Winner). By choosing to align her fiction with precision rather than minimalism, Hempel seeks to move her writing away from a particular and perhaps limiting understanding of women's expression and experiences. For Hempel, precisionist flash fiction exemplifies her understanding of life and its creative interpretations as open to endless moments of possibilities that are inclusive rather than exclusive, not necessarily marginalized, constrained, or singularly experienced.

Hempel has suggested that more women tend to write extremely condensed, extremely short, extremely stylized short-short stories, the likes of which she herself is known for, and she lists authors Lydia Davis and Sarah Manguso, among others, as examples (Small). Hempel doesn't speculate on why this might be the case, but it's worth looking briefly at Davis and Manguso to consider any apparent connections with how Hempel perceives her relationship to very short forms. For example, the fundament of Lydia Davis' extremely short writing is "seeing the thing in isolation, apart from the normalizing context" and allowing a single image, idea, or interaction the space to become all encompassing (Goodyear). In an interesting comparison to Hempel (who describes filtering out the unnecessary), Davis seems to be seeking out the smallest parts of an incident first in order to extrapolate them. Davis has also located the precision of her work as sprung from a female family tradition of scrupulousness: "my grandmother, my mother, and me—we were always making do and saving, very economical. I like the idea that the writing would belong to that practical tradition." Although she appreciates the idea of economy, she has struggled with it as well:

> In general, it is true that I am always examining how I live my life. Always. It's sort of relentless. Not just, Have I had a healthy breakfast? But everything. There is a constant judge. Maybe it's my poor mother who lives on in my head. She was always judgmental, and her mother was judgmental. (Aguilar and Fronth-Nygren)

This constant examination reveals not only a frugal awareness but also a consistent desire for personal evaluation. Each of these ideas feeds into Davis's writing, as her female family members provides a simultaneous freedom from the superfluous, but with the burden of excessive self-analysis. In a similar vein, Davis has also spoken of the "very constrictive, very constraining" form of the traditional short story by authors such as Katherine Mansfield, suggesting that the very short stories she began to write in her mid-twenties were liberating because they weren't as well-established as a literary form (Goodyear). But her writing seems to chime with the ethos of modernist, epiphanic short stories because by "dwelling on minutiae . . . [which masks] problem[s] of unspeakable magnitude," stories are disproportionately focused to skew and reveal flawed perceptions and to encourage new understandings (Goodyear). Authors such as Mansfield "draw attention consistently to the realm of interstices, of the not-said; a contingent world of possibility which reveal[s] itself in momentary glimpses of uninhabitable domains and dilemmas which, by their nature, lack clear solutions" (Drewery 121-122). Davis does avoid the scenes, conversation, and sustained arc of the traditional short story in order to focus on the singular, magnifying the minutiae, but this responsive approach to the traditional short story becomes a springboard for her work in which scenarios are taken to their extremes, existing in "uninhabitable domains." It's possible then to see Davis as simultaneously following and breaking away from what she establishes as her own female conventions, both familial and literary.

Sarah Manguso, too, suggests that her very short prose writing is tied inextricably to how she understands herself as an individual:

The only thing I've consistently been interested in in the last twenty-five years is writing very short texts. That continues to interest me as a project, to contain some part of reality, which is chaotic by definition, in a contained space. I like small apartments. I like getting rid of stuff. I went through my files yesterday and spent hours shredding things. It was great. (Seley)

Manguso, like Hempel and Davis, suggests that the brevity of her work is an aspect of her psychology but also something that she has chosen to pursue because it best represents her reality. She has also acknowledged how "pregnancy and motherhood were triggers for a new understanding of the position of the self in time" and the effect this had on her process when she was writing exacting diaries of everyday occurrences (the content of which formed *Ongoingness*, a poetic essay-memoir which explores memory). She has also written about her rejection of the term "woman writer" on the grounds that she was unwilling to "choose femaleness as [a] principal category of identity" (Manguso and Zucker). She continues:

The female archetypes available in our culture are few. Mother, wife, spinster, whore. All of these identities depend upon the sexual organs. . . . A man can become a husband and father and still be a writer first in the public imagination, but it seems a woman must choose. (Manguso and Zucker)

These discussions of her process begin to suggest that there are many facets at work for Manguso when she writes; most significantly, she "feel[s] neither confinement nor inspiration [from writing a story with such an extreme economy of words] . . . short texts seem stolid in my character, inextricable from my personality. It's just what I do: I write short and edit shorter" (Krefman).

What's clear when considering these authors' processes is that they are placed specifically within the realm of their own experiences. Each writer sees a tie between herself and the form her writing takes. Each chooses to write in the way that suits their creative explorations and expressions; the form itself is not inherently feminine or female, but it is an important part of their expression as women who write, and their gender identity is constantly linked to but not always the leading focus of their work. These authors' discussions of their writing demonstrate the impossibility of wholly associating a form with a gender, particularly when intersectionality, diversity, and knowledge of what it is to exist in the world can contradict any singular understanding of femininity or female. Each individual has her own, very specific set of experiences, which sit within a wealth of other cultural, racial, societal, and linguistic contexts. Instead, Hempel, Davis, and Manguso assert an appreciation for the very short form because of its ability to mirror experiences as built of many different, viable parts. For these writers, very short stories have a distinct appeal over sprawling tomes that leave no space for silence, the unsaid or the unsure. If Gordon Lish asked for the "*whole* world" to be seduced for "*all* time," for readers to be in an unyielding state of arousal, Hempel and others have responded to this dictum by puncturing solidity, seeking out chaos and contradictions, variability and multiplicity.

It is, then, perhaps more constructive to consider the ways Hempel *uses* or *employs* the very short story form to explore particular experiences of women. If we consider "Housewife" one more time with this in mind, once again different elements of its construction and content are highlighted. Yes there is certainly a stripping away of additional elements of this character to reveal something hidden, something intimate about her. And through this stripping away, the reader is invited to consider this intimacy and imagine the rest of this person's life through what is alluded to. However, we are also encouraged to consider our own initial interpretations because the piece, in its brevity, draws attention to how readers construct story. As the housewife incants "*French* film, *French* film" in an attempt to understand the story of her own life, "Housewife" draws attention to the contradictions between the reality of lived experience and its portrayal, what we're taught and what we learn, what we know to be true and what we tell ourselves. In this case, a woman, known only as a housewife (which seeks to place her in an interior, feminized space), puts italicized emphasis on the French in "*French* film," placing another frame around herself, one that is equally wrapped up in perceptions of female sexuality, and one that contradicts the traditional monogamy of a housewife. This creates complexity, preventing "Housewife" from being easily reduced to one reading or another. What is clear is that her sex life is consuming, somewhat fantastic and her reasoning, secret. Whatever else we decide about her is up to us.

Critical analysis of very short fiction is often end-oriented and a flash fiction reading can become focused on the moment of realization or revelation that occurs as a story comes to a close creating a corkscrew that sends a reader back in to the story. Again, the "single incident" complements the brevity of the flash fiction form, giving the moment focus and light, as well as emphasizing the instant of change through a twist, or a stab in the back, or a last line that insists that the reader's perception of what has come before is re-evaluated. This can allow the life of a piece of flash fiction to exist beyond the borders of a web/page. But I would argue that Hempel's shortest fiction is equally concerned with sustained, associative experiences, which are often unpredictable but eminently interconnected, mirroring the act of creating a story itself and moving beyond the singular. "Beach Town" is a particular example of this, placing a narrator neighbor as a witness to next-door summer holiday renters and an extra-marital affair, the sounds and scenes of which seep through the gaps in the hedge that separate their two beach houses. The narrator doesn't know these neighbors but learns about them through the things that pass between the two spaces they occupy: Corona bottles thrown over the hedge into the garden, loud music, voices travelling across the water of their swimming pool, and concern for the next-door orchids the narrator thinks are going untended. Through these sounds and actions, the narrator builds a picture of this couple, but because after three months they haven't introduced themselves, the narrator feels no loyalty or any particular sense of duty when one day s/he hears a woman's voice that isn't the wife's. There is a prevailing sense in "Beach Town" of something close but simultaneously removed, emphasized by an outsider's perspective and a series of absences. The narrator, after hearing "the voice of a woman *not* the wife," wonders about phoning the wife at work to "hear what she would sound like *if* she answered" (Hempel 305, my emphasis). While the husband is away, the wife invites friends over to court advice and receives wisdom such as "no regrets . . . if you are even the type of person who is given to regret, if you even have that type of wistful temperament" (Hempel 306). Here regret becomes the absence of an opportunity taken advantage of. Finally, the husband and wife make a joke bet on the weekend they first move in next door. The bet is won by the wife, although the narrator expects her to "collect nothing" in return, which is neither moral judgment nor pity, but an awareness of the wife's experience in that moment of meaninglessness in the face of her husband's affair (Hempel 306-307). The story becomes about not only what occupies a space when it is left open—the possibilities and the potential—but also about how the act of viewing this space can affect it. The narrator plays no role in the relationship, but by being witness, she is privy to an understanding that the wife, the husband, and the woman-not-the-wife are incapable of. She becomes both participant and voyeur, the body that links them, but with no real place between them. When the narrator witnesses a sex act between the husband and not-his-wife, s/he says "I watched the woman do something memorable to him with her mouth" (Hempel 305). The "memorable" moment becomes a scene that will live on in story as it's replayed or retold, mythologizing the status of the act while the couple are in the midst of it. As something memorable, it ceases to exist in the moment and becomes a performance. In Hempel's writing, sexuality is formed of a series of instances, a web that is assembled into a story that makes sense, for the moment, until something disrupts it (often the reality of an experience versus the impression, although the impression is still very compelling).

The construction of story is literally presented in "Memoir," the shortest of Hempel's pieces in *Collected Stories* at just seventeen words long. A thought cut short, a resigned resolve, "Memoir" transitions from a common complaint, "Just once in my life," to an admission that momentary respite is not really what's sought; the narrator has never needed anything just 'once' (Hempel 373).[4] The broken phrase, something to be uttered when we feel hard done by, is interrupted by the reality for the narrator in which nothing is ever good enough and that s/he isn't looking for a single thing, but a series of ongoing reliefs. It highlights that we often meet the same challenging circumstances over and again and so the ache here becomes an acknowledgment of longing springing from an insatiable body. By calling the piece "Memoir," Hempel alludes to the construction of our life stories—what we omit and what we'd have to admit if we are being honest. She makes us wonder what single sentence might comprise our own memoir. The task is, of course, impossible, which is why Hempel disrupts the attempt to single out one thing. Instead, once again, she is able to point out the contradictions between lived experience and what is presented in the world, encouraging readers to examine their own embodied experiences which can be more truthful, accurate, and *precise*.

Notes

1. Hempel's story "Housewife" can be found in full in Camille Renshaw's seminal 1998 article "The Essentials of Micro-Fiction" for *Pif Magazine*.

2. *The New Yorker* article "Rough Crossings" by Simon Armitage illustrates Lish's influence by reproducing Carver's story "What We Talk About When We Talk About Love" with Lish's edits over-scored. It's clear that Lish's suggested severe cuts changed the emphasis of the story, prompting many to wonder who exactly is responsible for the minimalist short story movement of the 80s, the editors or the authors?

3. Hempel has written two novellas, *Tumble Home* and *The Dog of the Marriage* (although there are many short, self-contained pieces within these two novellas that could arguably make them equally definable as flash fiction sequences), both published within story collections and *Collected Stories*, and has cowritten a full-length crime novel with Jill Ciment as AJ Rich, called *The Hand That Feeds You* (2015). But she acknowledges these forms as very different and of "doing different things" (Winner).

4. The full text of Hempel's "Memoir" can be found in a BookForum. Com review of *Dog of the Marriage* by Darcy Cosper from 2005.

Works Cited

Aguilar, Andrea, and Johanne Fronth-Nygren. "Lydia Davis, Art of Fiction No. 227." *The Paris Review*, no. 212, Spring 2015, www.theparisreview.org/interviews/6366/lydia-davis-art-of-fiction-no-227-lydia-davis/. Accessed 30 July 2016.

Armitage, Simon. "Rough Crossings: The Cutting of Raymond Carver." *The New Yorker*, 24 Dec. 2007, www.newyorker.com/magazine/2007/12/24/rough-crossings/. Accessed on 30 July 2016.

Beck, Julie. "When Diary-Keeping Gets in the Way of Living." *The Atlantic*, 27 Feb. 2015. www.theatlantic.com/health/archive/2015/02/when-diary-keeping-gets-in-the-way-of-living/386321/. Accessed 30 July 2016.

Blumenkranz, Carla. "Seduce the Whole World." *MFA vs NYC: The Two Cultures of American Fiction*, edited by Chad Harbach, n + 1 / Faber and Faber, 2014.

Cosper, Darcy. "Leash on Life: Darcy Cosper on Amy Hempel". *Book Forum*, Apr/May 2005, www.bookforum.com/archive/apr_05/cosper.html/. Accessed 30 July 2016.

Drewery, Claire. *Modernist Short Fiction by Women: The Liminal in Katherine Mansfield*. Routledge, 2016.

Goodyear, Dana. "Long Story Short: Lydia Davis' Radical Fiction." *The New Yorker*, 17 Mar. 2014. www.newyorker.com/magazine/2014/03/17/long-story-short/. Accessed 30 July 2016.

Hempel, Amy. *The Collected Stories*. Introduction by Rick Moody. New York: Scribner, 2007.

Krefman, Adam. "Interview: Sarah Manguso, Author of *The Two Kinds of Decay*." *Smith Magazine*, 3 June 2008, www.smithmag.net/memoirville/2008/06/03/interview-sarah-manguso-author-of-the-two-kinds-of-decay/. Accessed 30 July 2016.

Lessing, Doris. *African Stories*. Simon and Schuster, 2014.

Manguso, Sarah and Rachel Zucker. "Woman Writer + Writer Mother: A Conversation between Sarah and Rachel Zucker." *Candor Magazine*. 12 October 2009, candormagazine.tumblr.com/post/211502843/woman-writer-writer-mother-a-conversation/. Accessed 30 July 2016.

Renshaw, Camille. "The Essentials of Micro-Fiction." *Pif Magazine*, 1 June 1998, www.pifmagazine.com/1998/06/the-essentials-of-microfiction/. Accessed 30 July 2016.

Sapp, Jo. "An Interview with Amy Hempel." *Missouri Review*, vol. 16, 1993, muse.jhu.edu/article/409804/pdf/. Accessed 30 July 2016.

Seley, Melissa. "Imperfect Tools." *Guernica Magazine*. 1 Mar. 2013. www.guernicamag.com/interviews/imperfect-tools/. Accessed 30 July 2016.

Sherman, Suzan. "Amy Hempel." *BOMB*, no. 59, Spring 1997, bombmagazine.org/article/2058/amy-hempel/. Accessed on 30 July 2016.

Small, Tim. "Amy Hempel." *Vice*, 1 Dec. 2010, www.vice.com/en_uk/read/amy-hempel-644-v17n12/. Accessed 30 July 2016.

Whitney Hallett, Cynthia. *Minimalism and the Short Story: Raymond Carver, Amy Hempel, and Mary Robison*. Edwin Mellen Press, 1999.

Winner, Paul. "Amy Hempel, The Art of Fiction No. 176." *The Paris Review*, no. 166, Summer 2003, www.theparisreview.org/interviews/227/the-art-of-fiction-no-176-amy-hempel/. Accessed 30 July 2016.

"a few very pleasant shocks": Diane Williams and the Art of Flash Fiction

Matthew Duffus

In a June 2014 interview with *The White Review*, American flash fiction writer Diane Williams described one of her goals as "to provide some mystery, a place to meditate, where I might be nearing a new insight, if in fact I haven't reached it" (Pittard). This is an apt description of flash fiction's purpose, in general, as its length often precludes resolution. For writers like Williams—whose work is often considered experimental, though she declares her dislike of the term in the same 2014 interview—introducing mystery or only the possibility of insight often takes the place of the story arc of traditional fiction. In keeping with this aim, Williams highlights characters and situations in ways that elicit emotional responses from readers at the same time that they refuse to provide easy solutions to the problems these women and men encounter. Her extreme brevity and idea-driven concepts appeal to readers of fellow experimental writers, such as Lydia Davis and Robert Coover, while her use of conventions including character, conflict, and clearly-drawn scenes keeps her from alienating a broader audience. This successful balancing act is most evident beginning with her 2007 collection, *It Was Like My Trying to Have a Tender-Hearted Nature*, where she begins to expose the cracks in characters' relationships, one of her most common preoccupations.

Born in Chicago in 1946, Williams studied with Philip Roth at the University of Pennsylvania and continued her apprenticeship, years later, with Gordon Lish, known for his editorial work with Raymond Carver and Barry Hannah, among others. Throughout her early adulthood, she worked as a dance therapist at Bellevue Hospital, as a secretary at Doubleday publishing house, and as a textbook editor and writer for Scott Foresman, in her hometown, where she also joined the *StoryQuarterly* editorial team. In 2000, she founded the journal *Noon*, a prominent venue for avant-garde work that she continues to edit. She has published seven books of original fiction, beginning with 1990's *This Is About the Body, the Mind, the Soul, the World, Time, and Fate*, and continuing through *Fine, Fine, Fine, Fine, Fine* in 2016. Taken as a whole, her body of work is certainly one of the most impressive of recent American flash fiction writers.

"Lady," the first story in *This Is About the Body*, Williams's debut collection, presents a clear picture of what to expect from the book in general. The story opens *in medias res*, without any of the scene-setting one might expect from a longer work: "She said *please*. Her face looked something more than bitter, with hair which it turned out was a hat, which came down over her ears, which was made of fake fur, which she never removed from her head. She had glasses on. Everything she wore helped me decide to let her in" (Williams, *This* 3). Readers are presented with observations about this woman as they come to the narrator, without benefit of hindsight to arrange them into a clearer, more streamlined form. Neither of the women in this story is given a name. The lady of the title has simply turned up at the wrong address, seeking use of the narrator's phone to clear up her confusion. Nevertheless, "[w]hat this woman had done to me was incalculable, and she had done it all in a period of time which had lasted no more than five minutes" (5). The narrator has been affected in some way by the lady's pleading, shouting voice on the phone. At least that is the narrator's justification for "jamm[ing] her up into the corner with the jumble by the front door and [holding] her in there, exhausting myself to keep her in there" (5). Williams rarely connects all of the dots in her stories, leaving it to readers to fill in gaps, but in this tense moment, one that "hurt her more than it hurt me," she comes close when she admits, "[v]iolence is never the problem. Love at first sight is" (5).

Love is never a simple emotion in a Williams story. In "All American," also from *This Is About the Body*, the narrator explains, "I have to force myself to love the ones I am supposed to love, and then I have to force myself on the ones I am not supposed to love" (Williams, *This* 13). Here, she's referring to her desire, as a married woman, to have an affair with a married man. When she thinks about this man, "she thinks *force*, and then whoever has the man already is her enemy" (12). Once again, a woman resorts to violence, or at least the possibility of violence, to get the object of her affection. At the end of this two-page story, the narrator remembers an encounter with her sister, as children, when she "must have been getting rough, because [her sister] was getting hysterical. I remember I was surprised. I remember knowing then that I was applying force and was getting away with it" (13).

Getting away with it, whatever *it* may be, is a common desire in this collection. In "Hope," yet another unnamed female narrator, when faced with visiting her dying father in the hospital, states, "[i]t was unbelievable, unbelievable that a daughter such as me [. . .] should deliberately ask my father a question after the doctors had rendered him positively without the power of speech" (Williams, *This* 69). The question she posed is never stated outright, though readers can understand its import based on the story's final lines: "I felt so incredibly nervy. He was down in his bed. I was at the end of it. My father put his head forward toward me, crazy to tell me the most essential thing I will ever need to know" (70). The father is as unable to articulate an answer as the narrator is to account for her behavior. Readers are left with the sense that this "nervy" event has left a mark on the narrator that has outlived her relationship with her late father.

The title of Williams's second collection of stories—1992's *Some Sexual Success Stories Plus Other Stories in Which God Might Choose to Appear*—is meant to be taken ironically. In "The Good Man," while the title character achieves "his dream come true" by "produc[ing] ultra-pleasure for Darlene," he dies in the next paragraph (Williams, *Some* 8). The narrator of a later story, "Turning," suspects that, even as she embraces her lover, "he cannot tolerate being confined by a woman" (12). And in "Ore," readers learn that "[t]he wife had been making her husband miserable for years" (55). Even though this couple "agreed how excellent their sexual satisfactions together were," they also acknowledged "that every other aspect of their life together [. . .] was so unsatisfactory in such extreme" (55). In all three of these cases, and many more, characters fail to achieve a lasting, or even fleeting, connection. The brevity of the flash-fiction form enhances these disconnections, as Williams is able to leave characters dissatisfied and in limbo without feeling the pressure to bring her characters closer to the kind of resolution readers of longer fiction have come to expect. In this way, the stories are bleaker, and often funnier, than they would be if expanded to fill more space. As Laura Sims explains in *The Review of Contemporary Fiction*, the characters in this second collection have "broken free from the bonds of intimacy." The question, though, is what remains once they've done so.

One answer to this question relates to Williams's increasing dissatisfaction with conventional storytelling. "They Were Naked Again" provides a rare third-person perspective on events. Even so, the authorial "I" continually asserts its control over the story in a way that tilts towards metafiction, with lines such as, "I'll get her into his bed," or, "I would never say that to him in this situation" (Williams, *Some* 37, 37-8). By the end of the story, Williams makes it clear that this narrator does not like to be overshadowed by her characters. As the man and woman discuss the carpet in his bedroom, the narrator reports that the woman "says something obscene, which happens to be clairvoyant" (38). But instead of providing readers with the woman's "clairvoyant" thoughts, which we could then judge for ourselves, she turns the tables on them, ending the story with a rant of her own:

> Then I say, 'I gave my own carpet away like that, *bitch*!'
> But they cannot hear me.
> I'll threaten suicide!
> You—you think about a carpet.
> *Me*. (Williams, *Some* 38)

This roughly 250-word story has been hijacked by its narrator, who refuses to give the man and woman the room they need to become fully-fledged characters. While writers like John Barth and Robert Coover have found ways to do this in longer-form fiction, Williams's flash fiction provides readers with much the same thrill without nearly the investment, in terms of pages. Williams seems to be challenging herself to escape from realism as quickly as possible, thereby breaking down the barrier between reader and story and highlighting the fictive, crafted qualities behind the story her narrator will not allow us to read uninterrupted.

A more extreme version of such an interjection occurs in "The Band-Aid and the Piece of Gum." The story's set-up is mundane: the narrator believes that this is the day she will hear from a man named Walter. In expectation of this event, she has used both the band-aid he gave her the last time they met and chewed the piece of gum he'd also given her. All of these are portents of her belief that "*today* would be the most important day of my life*" (Williams, *Some* 62). But Walter never calls. In fact, after the story's first paragraph, which contains more than half of its roughly 300 words, the occasion for the telling is jettisoned in favor of the following ending:

> That's it. Usually they start where a person was born, then their parents, their parents' parents, where they were born, occupations, so that includes dates, names, locations, character traits of all the parties concerned, chronology, trauma, wishes, dreams, eccentricities, real speech, achievements, including struggle, the obstacles, someone's dementia, another chronic illness, a centrifugal drama, certainly all the deaths, photos, paintings if any—likenesses of many of the parties concerned, plus summary statements made periodically throughout to sum up the situation at any given time. (Williams, *Some* 63)

This critique of conventional, realistic stories succeeds by distilling such works down to their essences. Anyone who has ever stifled a yawn while reading competent, workmanlike fiction that fails to transcend its generic qualities cannot help but smile at this attack on the form. While *Some Sexual Success Stories* does not succeed in offering an alternative to such conventions often enough, it shows her increasing confidence as a purveyor of nontraditional narratives and points toward the preoccupations that she will continue to explore in later collections. Ultimately, *Some Sexual Success Stories* demonstrates Williams's growing maturity as a writer. At the same time that she is able to tell a straightforward story when the desire strikes her, she is even more at home expanding the flash-fiction format to include not just vignette-style stories but metafictional stories that lean towards postmodernism in their concern with the nature of fictional discourse.

The Stupefaction appeared in 1996, four years after *Some Sexual Success Stories*, and continues to highlight many of the previous book's successes, as is evident from the story titles: "A Moment of Panic," "The Guider of the Prick," "A More Detailed Account of This Is Out of the Question," "The Masturbator," and so on. These stories continue Williams's interest in male-female relationships, most broadly, and sex, specifically. Interestingly, while continuing to share these similar themes, the stories in *The Stupefaction* are even more extreme in their brevity (paradoxically, this is also the first of Williams's books to include a novella). As Williams continues to pare down her stories to their essence, she shows that a satisfying story does not require an expansive word count. "My Reaction to Life," for instance, introduces three characters—the narrator, Harry Winch, and Chet Henry—and relays a terse conversation between the narrator and Henry, in under 250 words. As is almost always the case in a Williams story, the specific details stand in for what readers can only intuit. We learn that the characters are riding "half-broken horses," but little else about them, or the purpose of the trip (65). The unnamed narrator is simply "one of those who keeps expecting the dark heart of human desire to be revealed to [her]" (Williams, *Stupefaction* 65). Similarly, the narrator describes Chet Henry as "a man who may have temporarily gotten off of his horse so that he could be loved, or so that he could be hated, or so that he could hate me" (66). Though Williams's concision is often a strength, in this case, she goes too far. Without a greater understanding of the dynamic between Henry and the narrator, it becomes difficult to see what this brief story details about the narrator's "Reaction to Life." Finally, we're left wondering the same thing that Henry did—"[n]ow what?"—as the story concludes with, "[t]he traveler in me is full of hope. She is a splendidly bland and a smug woman" (67). Like many other stories in *The Stupefaction*, the narrative technique is direct and to the point. The narrator, whether first- or third-person, prefers to tell us what's on her mind outright rather than leave such thoughts for readers to intuit.

This technique is on display in an earlier story from the collection, entitled "The Transformation." In the second paragraph of this one-and-one-half page story, readers learn that:

[a]fter [the main character's] bath, she feels she is significant. She eats some biscuits. The leftover biscuit morsels she goes ahead and she scrapes off of her plate into the garbage can. The stain on her shoe is hot blue or has been caused by some hot glue. To tell you a lie, even about this last, would be such a waste of everybody's time. (Williams, *Stupefaction* 43)

The character's perceived significance, newfound or not, hints at the transformation of the title, which is only made explicit at the end of the story. But the rest of the paragraph, quoted in full above, frustrates readers' desire to learn more about what has gone on. Instead, we end with another address to the reader, assuring us of the narrator's veracity. Typically, a narrator earns such trust, but Williams uses the mundanity and specificity of the narrator's observations as evidence that what we are about to learn is factual as well as fictional. This is a ruse, however, as we learn in the final paragraphs, which begin, "[t]ruthfully speaking, the above marvel has been described irresponsibly, without any perception on my part as to the why, the wherefores, or even any of the heretofores, or even why I thought to make the whole thing up" (Williams, *Stupefaction* 44). The narrator's protestations of fidelity to reality have been a trick. Furthermore, the narrator states, "[a]nd I am not sorry for it at all. You deserve everything you get, I am sure, even the crap you have to read" (44). The narrator's assault on her readers pays off, at least in terms of satisfying the story's title, as it is only in the middle of this rant that she tells us, "of course, this fake woman hasn't died; she has just transformed herself into me" (44).

Here, we discover that the transformation has nothing to do with the bath or with the conversation with her "loving friend" that led to the near-death incident. The transformation is even more dramatic, as a character who has remained relatively flat on the page becomes the narrator—whose voice, in its consistency across stories, can be conflated with the author's, creating a three-in-one metamorphosis that convincingly declares: "I am of royal blood and huge intellect and I enjoy myself immensely, *come hell or high water!*" (Williams, *Stupefaction* 44). Readers leave the story wondering if this enjoyment comes from merely telling stories or from the added thrill of manipulating readers' reactions in the fewest words possible. Regardless, *The Stupefaction* shows Williams's growing penchant for extreme conciseness, which reinforces the need for readers to remain on their toes. At this point, reading Williams is akin to reading poetry. Every word counts, and the briefest lapse in attention can ruin a story's effect. As her stories have gotten shorter, Williams has jettisoned much of traditional scene-setting and narrative progression in favor of fiction that truly does work in a flash. The insights arrive quickly and not always for the characters. Often, it is the reader, who, after putting together the disparate elements of the story, perceives a change in the world of the characters, though such changes are never large or overly dramatic.

Published in 2001, *Romance Erector* includes a novella as well as two other uncharacteristically-long stories. In spite of these, the rest of the collection continues to push the boundaries of flash fiction. In "I Freshly Fleshly," the unnamed narrator describes a presumably sexual encounter with a butcher, behind the shop's counter. Faced with whatever is going on between the narrator, who "tug[s] on myself and [cries] out as if making quite an effort" (Williams, *Romance* 81), and the butcher, one customer "took what she ordered and she vowed she would never return" (82). While the juxtaposition between the butcher's wares and the erotic encounter might be enough to satisfy many flash fiction writers, Williams adds a final paragraph post-encounter, in which the narrator asserts, "[w]hen I started seven years ago I was a very shy person. I don't think anyone would guess it now. The ability to meet people and to talk to anyone will be an asset all of my life. I have learned a lot about people and I have made some great friends" (82). Readers do not know what "started seven years ago," nor do we get much evidence of the narrator's ability "to talk to anyone," but ending the story with such blandly self-affirming language allows Williams to send-up the situation—the tryst between the characters is interrupted by customers seeking German bologna and half a ham, as though nothing untoward is occurring—more subtly than would be possible if she ended the story in the moment. The narrator's self-help speak is as empty of meaning as the sexual exchange.

"Actual People Whose Behavior I Was Able to Observe" does an excellent job of explaining the writer's role in creating compelling fiction. The story begins, "I want to act as if I love them and then I want to hurt at least those two during the next period of my life" (Williams, *Romance* 39). While the title suggests that this is in reference to the narrator's feelings towards "Actual People," this is as good a definition of a writer's purpose as one could hope for. What better way to create compelling fiction than to take characters one pretends to love and place them in danger? As is often the case in Williams's work, the story takes an abrupt turn after this opening paragraph, this time a turn towards the confessional: "I will kill you if you tell anybody that I have no anal intercourse, no art treasures" (39). What relationship exists between "anal intercourse" and "art treasures"? Williams leaves it up to readers to determine the connection, as she shifts gears once again, focusing on mundane items like a "water jug with the goldband lilies inside of it" (40), cake, and the narrator's wardrobe. At times such as this, the lack of obvious, logical connections between the parts of a story can be frustrating, as it leaves readers feeling like they've been given a series of pieces that do not fit into a coherent whole. Ultimately, we encounter a series of rare finds that are significant to the character but not particularly enlightening for reader. What we are left with, in this story and several others in this collection, is a narrator who is far more self-involved than she is interested in the "Actual People" of the title. This solipsistic tendency can be off-putting, even more so when left with the added puzzle of the story's final line: "[t]here is a slim chance that anything is unable to be unmoved" (40). Ultimately, each reader must decide whether or not to be moved by these mundane details—including not just the narrator's wardrobe but the contents of her refrigerator and her frequency of urination. Again, like poetry, flash fiction often forces readers to make meaning out of the disparate parts of a story for themselves. Williams seems to be telling readers that the preoccupations and biases of a narrator should be considered as significant as the qualities that narrator imbues in the characters she creates.

It Was Like My Trying to Have a Tender-Hearted Nature, from 2007, marks the point at which Williams's preoccupation with interpersonal relationships and her experimental, often metafictional, techniques coalesce to create truly memorable, enduring flash fiction. In these stories, Williams's brevity and her interest in human psychology come together to create unusual situations and stories, such as "A Dramatic Classic Leap," which opens with the line, "[m]ost of my romances are like this, so that I must conclude my behavior produces the poor result" (*It Was* 59). What makes these relationships "poor" is never revealed, but based on others' reactions to the narrator's story—"[t]hey want to talk to me about sex, what I should know about fortune-telling, how to think logically, how to improve my conversation" (59)—the narrator's ideas cannot be easily categorized. In typical Williams fashion, what begins as a story about one thing—relationships and sex—metamorphoses into something else, a story about an unnamed person learning small talk: "I took to fluffing my speech with the details of the day, with some unrelated subjects about my health, my salary, with absolutely worthwhile questions on poetry and art" (59). As such, the title of the story refers to the leaps in conversation that lead to the narrator's minor epiphany: "I learnt that being partially helpful and light feels as if I am a dear, and, that whatever else I do I expel this" (59). Williams's use of the word "expel" suggests that what has been learned is not necessarily desirable, that the narrator would rather gain an understanding of why her romances fail so often, instead of discovering the advantages of making small talk, though even this information could come in handy.

Williams's penchant for upending the traditional elements of short fiction is on display in the story "Rice," which opens with another unnamed woman and man arguing over the lack of trust in their relationship. As in "A Dramatic Classic Leap," readers are never told what has caused this problem. Instead of continuing the argument, Williams shifts to the woman's actions in the kitchen, to the arrangement of chops in a pan and the preparation of "long slender grains of roughleg" (Williams, *It Was* 73). Distancing readers even more from the argument, Williams ends the story with a description of the woman's attire, chosen before the man's arrival, and a reference to "the deafening ring of troubles in the air" (74), a result of someone's once saying, "'I have so appreciated serving you. I look forward to many years of giving you the highest standard of excellent service'" (74). Just like that, the story ends. Readers aren't told who the "someone" is in the above quotation, nor are we told how the disagreement between the man and woman is resolved. Williams is less interested in resolving conflicts than she is with posing them in a way that elicits an emotional response, both from the characters and the reader. Readers of longer fiction have come to expect resolution at the end of a story, but one of the unique properties of flash fiction, and of Williams's work, in particular, is its ability to leave characters with possibilities or reactions that have yet to clarify themselves via a pronounced denouement. The same leaps that the narrator of "A Dramatic Classic Leap" learned to make in conversation are deployed by the narrative, which shifts effortlessly from trust issues to dinner preparations to the dangers of high expectations. By refusing to make the connections between these elements, Williams leaves readers as frustrated as the characters are. As the woman's voice grew "baby-small" during the argument, "it was no longer the most beautiful sample in existence" (73). Similarly, as the story grows more diffuse, it loses its focus on romantic troubles but gains a broader emotional resonance, something that could be said about many of the stories in *It Was Like My Trying to Have a Tender-Hearted Nature.*

The best story in Williams's excellent sixth collection, *Vicky Swanky Is a Beauty* (2012), is "The Emporium," about the past coming back to haunt the present in the form of Kevin Crosstick, a former acquaintance of the narrator's. The story is atypical of Williams's work at this stage; it contains more of the features of a traditional story than she has incorporated since early in her career. Even so, it still makes some of the "dramatic classic leaps" readers have come to expect from her work. The story opens with the narrator racing through the store of the title, her body "stretched . . . into a dart" for maximum efficiency, only to be interrupted by a man who used to be married to a woman the narrator "more or less respected" (Williams, *Vicky* 53). Now he seeks only "peace, prosperity, and freedom" (53). In typical fashion, these grand ideas are presented without elaboration, as though such concepts are easily attainable. Instead of dwelling on Crosstick's goals, the narrator focuses on the former wife: "I didn't like her at first. She is not very nice. She's odd, but that's the whole point" (53). This oddity reminds her of a piece of jewelry she owns that she didn't like at first, either. Though it's not made of real jewels, it's still "very rare and the colors are not nice and I get lots of enjoyment from that" (54). Readers can be forgiven for thinking, at this point, that they've encountered yet another Williams narrator who revels in the difficult, conflicted aspects of life. However, as she leaves the store, a child manning a lemonade stand asks a nearby adult, "Why is she crying?" (54). Unlike so many of Williams's narrators, whose confidence borders on arrogance even in the face of life's confusions, she "trie[s] to hear the answer, but could not have heard the answer, without squatting—without my getting around down in front of the pair, bending at the knee, so that the proverbial snake no longer crawls on its belly" (54). This woman, so sure of her mission at the beginning of the story, is left bewildered, looking to a stranger to explain her sudden, unexpected reaction.

Williams offers readers a clue as to the reason for this reaction in the final paragraph, where the narrator focuses on the "gumdrop cookies" the girl "had hoisted for sale" (Williams, *Vicky* 54). Their presence "brings back memories of Spritz and Springerle and Cinnamon Stars—party favors—attractive, deliciously rich, beautiful colors, very well liked, extra special that I made a struggle

---

to run from" (54). Surely, these "party favors" date back to the days when the narrator was friendly with the Crossticks, a life she has fled in favor of "Glad Steaming Bags and Rocket Cheese" (54). Where the rarity of her fake jewelry inspires enjoyment, the thought of these cookies, "extra special" in their own way, leads to tears and distress. Like Kevin Crosstick and his search for "peace, prosperity, and freedom," the narrator seems to be in search of a life outside of the emotional tumult of the past. To Williams's credit, she refuses to provide easy answers, which is reminiscent of the prayer offered in a later story, "A Man, An Animal": "Please forgive our confusion and our failures. We make our petitions—say our prayers. It's like our falling against a wall, in a sense" (106). The male narrator of this story concludes by explaining, "I've given my wife a few very pleasant shocks, too" (106). While the narrator of "The Emporium" may not view the encounter with Kevin Crosstick as a "pleasant" shock, she certainly dwells in the world of confusions and failures mentioned in the latter story. That Williams is willing to leave her characters in this state instead of seeing them through to "peace, prosperity, and freedom" tells readers volumes about her outlook on the world.

Diane Williams's most recent collection, *Fine, Fine, Fine, Fine, Fine,* offers a masterclass in flash fiction writing. In this book, she expounds on the same preoccupations and themes in fresh, new ways. The opening story, "Beauty, Love, and Vanity Itself," begins in familiar Williams territory, with a narrator in search of love: "As usual I'd hung myself with snappy necklaces, but otherwise had given my appearance no further thought, even though I anticipated the love of a dark person who will be my source of prosperity and emotional pleasure" (Williams, *Fine* 13). And while "[t]he real thing did come along" (14), the narrator must first endure several false starts that are dealt with briefly. For all of this focus on the beauty and love of the title, Williams introduces vanity "[p]oolside at the Marriott Courtyard" (14), where the narrator and a lifeguard watch a group of Chinese women drown. Instead of acting, "[their] eyes were on the surface of the water—the wobbling patterns of diagonals. It was a hash—nothing to look at—much like my situation—*if you're not going to do anything about it*" (15, emphasis added). Like the "stomach muscles gone slack" that the narrator hides in an expansive swimsuit (14), neither the woman nor the lifeguard, whose job it should be to save these women, can rouse themselves from their self-absorption long enough to save the women.

The inability to connect with others is clearly on display in "When I Was Old and Ugly." In this story, a wife and her husband live "unhappily married" (Williams, *Fine* 123). While the dialogue is limited to the wife's unanswered questions and statements—"Are you all right? What do you want? You're looking at me" (124)—she twice attempts to forge a connection with animals. The story opens with a "creature" who "looked and looked at me and looked, ardently," thus reminding her "how to fall in love by meeting its eyes" (123). Her husband fails to meet her eyes in the way that this creature has. But a "creature" cannot offer the kind of relationship the narrator seeks. At the end of the story, she is reminded of a bird she saw in the park that day, one "who wasn't interested in talking to [her]" (124). Undeterred, she realizes that "[l]ust and temptation are sometimes personified. I heard the bird cry—*Chew! Chew!* I took pains to say *Chew! Chew!*—loudly too" (124). But personification is in the eye of the beholder, who yearns for a connection that none of the men in the story can provide. While many of the women in Diane Williams's stories would insist that they are as Fine, Fine, Fine, Fine, Fine as the title of this collection, it is clear at the end of "When I Was Old and Ugly" that they would talk to as many birds as necessary if it would bring about the type of connection this narrator attempts but is unable to make.

As a genre, flash fiction has flourished in recent decades, thanks to the influence of precursors as diverse as Kate Chopin, Ernest Hemingway, and Franz Kafka, as well as the proliferation of journals, both in-print and online, that feature such works. Williams, herself, has contributed to this phenomenon as both a writer and as the founder and editor of *Noon*. Her more than quarter-century career as a writer and publisher of flash fiction helps to show the breadth and possibilities inherent in this short, demanding form. No matter their length, Williams's stories will bedevil, fascinate, and entertain any reader open to "a few very pleasant shocks."

Works Cited

Pittard, Harriet. "Diane Williams: Two Stories and an Interview." *The White Review*, June 2014, thewhitereview.org/interviews/diane-williams-two-stories-and-an-interview/. Accessed 4 Mar. 2017.

Sims, Laura. "Diane Williams." *The Review of Contemporary Fiction*, vol. 23, no. 3, Fall 2003, p. 7.

Williams, Diane. *Fine, Fine, Fine, Fine, Fine*. McSweeney's Books, 2016.

_____. *It Was Like My Trying to Have a Tender-Hearted Nature*. FC2, 2007.

_____. *Romance Erector*. Dalkey Archive Press, 2001.

_____. *Some Sexual Success Stories Plus Other Stories in Which God Might Choose to Appear*. Grove Weidenfeld, 1992.

_____. *The Stupefaction*. Knopf, 1996.

_____. *This Is About the Body, the Mind, the Soul, the World, Time, and Fate*. Grove Weidenfeld, 1990.

_____. *Vicky Swanky Is a Beauty*. McSweeney's Books, 2012.

Kathy Fish's Flash Fiction: Fishing for Meaning in a Diminished World_____

Randall Brown

Of the loud singing of the oven bird, Robert Frost writes, "The question that he frames in all but words / Is what to make of a diminished thing" (13-14). After their first encounters with flash fiction, readers might initially ask a similar question, often framed as *So what?* Flash fiction's diminished word count, its focus on the tiniest of moments, and its urgent rush to end—all these might add to that sense of diminishment. As do writers of longer fictions, flash writers employ narrative strategies to avoid such reactions, but these traditional narrative techniques might be less obvious in smaller fictions. Kathy Fish, for example, is a contemporary flash writer whose small stories overflow with deeper significance, and in looking at ways to read her fiction, readers can discover specific ways—such as stakes, reader identification, conflicts, internal struggles, and resolutions—writers make their flash fictions sing out with significance. These particular strategies, and the ways they function, can be seen in selections from Fish's flash collection *Together We Can Bury It*.

Why Kathy Fish? Readers have the same question, perhaps, when discovering a flash fiction focused on a small, intense moment: *Why this moment? Why these people? Why now?* Fish has been influential for many contemporary flash fiction writers—through her workshopping at Zoetrope Virtual Studio, her work as editor of the flash fiction journal *Smokelong Quarterly*, her four collections of flash, her online flash fiction workshops, and her current position on the faculty of the Mile-High MFA at Regis University in Denver, where she teaches flash fiction. Her work itself—appearing in numerous print and online journals, such as *Yemassee Journal, Elm Leaves Journal, Slice, Guernica, Indiana Review, Mississippi Review, Denver Quarterly, New South, Quick Fiction*, and various other journals and anthologies—continues to influence many writers.

She's been involved in contemporary flash fiction as a writer, teacher, editor, reader, workshop leader, and mentor and is thus one of the most respected and influential members of the current flash fiction literary community.

To understand the considerable craft Fish brings to flash fiction, it is useful to begin with what writers of longer stories traditionally use to make their writing matter. Let's begin with the basic narrative structure. As Kurt Vonnegut so succinctly put it, "The story is 'Man in Hole' but the story needn't be about a man or a hole. It's: somebody gets into trouble, gets out of it again" (par 3). To increase the significance of that story, writers create situations in which the "character in the hole" can win or lose something. If readers think that what's to be won and what's to be lost are significant things, then the story will seem more significant. Oftentimes, the stakes are important to the protagonist, so the more the reader identifies with the protagonist, the more the reader will care about getting or not getting. With something important to be gained or lost, characters then act, and the force that arises to prevent them from achieving their desired outcomes similarly creates the sense that something important is afoot.

Thus, the protagonist's desires are met with a force that acts in opposition to those desires, and now the desired goal becomes more challenging. Add to that struggle the sense that this antagonistic force represents a need or flaw of the protagonist, and the story becomes particularly challenging. As John Yorke writes of narrative, "Structure at the level of scene, act and story conspires to bring the protagonist[s] face to face with their darkest fear, or weakest link— and at the crisis point, forces them to confront it" (82). Finally, at the end, a resolution that brings new awareness about an aspect of the world to both the character and reader gives the story significance. "They have returned," writes Yorke, "from whence they came with a truth they must deliver to their tribe—and not always a truth the tribe wants to hear." The antagonistic forces are "an embodiment of the protagonist's flaw, making external and internal battles one and the same" (101-2). The resolution gains significance by connecting the protagonist's battle to deeper internal issues and by connecting those flaws and issues to those in society, so that the reader gains insight and truth.

In short, there are a number of narrative elements that writers can use to have their stories be read as being significant: (1) the "hole" or trouble characters find themselves in; (2) what's to be won or lost by trying to resolve the trouble; (3) the conflict created by opposing forces; (4) the connection between the character's psyche and the trouble; and (5) the resolution. All of these elements become weapons in a flash for fending off the dreaded *So what?* of readers. Yet flash's extreme brevity requires writers to tweak these elements—to rely more on filling in the holes with singularly focused details, on embedding the "stakes" within its web of word choices and images, on creating as much conflict in the language as in the story, on connecting strongly and intimately with the protagonist's psyche, and on finding resolutions that feel significant even though they happen in under one thousand words.

Let's begin with focusing on the hole characters find themselves trapped inside. In Fish's flash "Cancer Arm," the fear of cancer metastasizes into the protagonist's life, creating "cancer leg," "cancer arm," "cancer head," "cancer throat," "cancer, cancer, cancer" (138). The story begins with a wish—your wish actually, since the story is told in second person: "You think you might grab hold of [your mother], bury your face in the folds of her neck, but you look up and she's gone" (137). At the end, the story returns to your initial desire: "Exasperated, [your mother] flutters away, but you catch her wrist, draw her hand to your lips and kiss it, just in time" (140). The second person protagonist wants to grab hold of a mother who keeps disappearing, fluttering away, until at the end, for the briefest of moments, she is able to be caught, just in time.

So, let's gaze more closely into this "hole"—or trouble—the character finds herself stuck inside; namely, lets look at the way Fish creates a very specific, detail-filled world for the narrator to be immersed within. "Cancer Arm," is overstuffed with detail; everything is oversized. There's the *Big Book of Cancer Symptoms* (Fish 137), even "dwarfing" Rocky Mountain sunsets. It's Thanksgiving—a holiday associated with excess, and this one doesn't disappoint: "clotted with voices," filled with "all these people" and "way too much food," "the [table] crowded" with relatives and "slabs of steaming turkey breast, the outsized mounds of mashed potatoes" (140). She can't keep fearful thoughts from entering her mind, wants to grab hold of her mother to stop them, perhaps desiring to retreat from this too-big world, perhaps wishing for protection from it.

For readers of flash, Fish's stories work as a how-to-book on how to glean meaning and find these narrative elements—such as the specific trouble—in compressed stories. The flash rewards a close reading. As readers search through both the writer's choice of details and their various options of filling in the blanks, readers can discover the exact nature of the world the character has entered why it might constitute trouble. In "Cancer Arm," a reader might initially miss the nature of this invasive, pushing, overgrown world. She has entered a world where things—like cancerous cells—multiply and try to fill her with their malignancies. The small space of flash increases the urgency of this trouble, deepens the sense of the character being confined within this specific "hole." The writer's singularly focused details and word choices direct the reader's attention to the specific nature of that trouble, creating an almost supernatural sense that everything encountered in this "hole" has been specifically created to create trouble for the character.

Next, let's add to this mix of narrative strategies not only "the trouble" but the stakes. Think, for example, how film narratives often raise the stakes. In *Billy Madison*, for example, Billy (Adam Sandler) must pass every grade in twenty-four weeks or lose his multi-million-dollar inheritance. Oftentimes, in movies as varied as *Donny Darko* or *The Dark Night Rises*, the existence of an entire city, nation, world, or universe is at stake. Within larger narratives, those stakes rise to meet the grand expectations and space such stories inhabit, but within the very tiny space of flash fiction; stakes that large are likely to feel melodramatic, too big to be solved. In *Serious Daring: Creative Writing in Four Genres*, Lisa Roney interestingly defines *melodrama* (and the closely related *sentimentality*) as "too muchness" (257). So stakes within flash are fraught with challenges—to have enough at stake by the characters' winning or losing for the story to feel important but not so much so that the stakes feel artificial. One might think of stakes, as Yorke does, as "a risk/ reward ratio: a character gains something vital, but in doing so ramps up the jeopardy around them" (59).

Fish's "Disassembly" tells the story of a distant daughter among seven brothers who returns home for her father's funeral at the bar in the Knights of Columbus, only to be confronted by a stranger, Barbara Lee, who is there, she tells our protagonist, because "[she's] got to see this poor girl" (131). That encounter leads to their absconding from the funeral to Walgreens for necklaces, returning without them, singing "along with Aretha in loud and fantastically off-pitch voices" (134). In the final paragraph, the protagonist is reminded of how her "brothers insist that [she] stand right in the center for all family photos"; in particular, she is reminded of an old photo of her as a baby, "sitting on [her] oldest brother's lap, arms outstretched, like Ta-Da!" (134).

Here, the stakes—made all the more urgent by a father's death—involve a family photo, which has begun its process of subtraction from the family. The stakes are also increased by the fact that the family photo is a rare thing, "because . . . the sister . . . moved so far away" (Fish 132). Her putting that photo at risk happens directly after the brother's call for the photo:

"Say where'd you get those necklaces," I ask. "I want some."
She appraises my clothes; I dress like a communist.
"Walgreens. They're on sale."
"Will you take me?" (Fish 132)

So what? you say. *A family photograph won't be taken. Big deal.* Literally, the reward for leaving the bar is (1) a necklace and (2) not having to take that picture; the risk is (1) not getting a necklace and (2) her continuing that role of someone whose absence makes family photos missing from photo albums. Her role as the person responsible for such things appears to have already been cemented. She doesn't need the necklace and doesn't seem to need the photo. *So who cares, then, about the photograph?*

A closer look—something Fish's flash always rewards—reveals the "hidden" stakes. While at Walgreens, the narrator ponders the consequences of her actions, imagining the scene back at the Knights of Columbus:

> My brothers have probably stopped wondering what happened to me. Maybe the thing is over by now. They have gathered up all the pictures and mementos of our dad's life and hauled them away.
> I take off the necklace and hand them to her. "I should get back." (Fish 134)

She removes the necklace—a chain, a noose, a yoke—and chooses the photograph, as implied by the future tense in the final paragraph: "My brothers insist that I stand right in the center for all family photos. It is our custom. And one of them will say, *a rose among thorns*! And another will forget to put down his can of Bud" (Fish 134). They encircle her, the way a necklace surrounds a neck, the way thorns ring a rose, the way a hand enfolds the Bud. She's chosen to be the neck of this family, its centerpiece, for that moment its "Ta-Da!"

To recap, characters find themselves trapped in holes, with a risk/reward for getting out. But characters can't just easily step out, can they? That might again lead to a sense of diminishment: *Why are we getting this story? The character just stepped out of trouble no problem? What was the point of that?* Conflict—some force that makes stepping out of the hole more challenging—arises to create a greater sense of importance to make the resolution hard-earned and valuable. Things increase in worth in proportion to the obstacles overcome to achieve them; or at least in story world, such a dynamic appears true. Readers conditioned by longer narratives and classroom instruction might look for a *versus* to identify conflict: a character *versus* self or other or animal or nature or some supernatural force and so on. But conflict in flash can also occur at the language level, within words, between what is said and what is suggested; and among words, too, within a network of meanings, implications, and connections. Yes, this dynamic can happen in conventional stories, but flash does it more, with that conflict sometimes meeting or surpassing the tension in the narrative. And, once again, the flash writer must work within the confines of compressed space to make these "small" conflicts feel meaningful to readers.

For example, tension is created through language in Fish's "Tenderoni," in which a young couple on bikes come across a dead kitten and must make decisions about what action to take next. The young man's decision to try and move the dead body leads to a search for something to move it with, an attempt to use cardboard that doesn't work, traffic that smashes the cat's body and head, and an attempt to scoop up the smooshed remains that leads the young female narrator to this revelation: "I hate watching him struggle, but he struggles a lot so I'm getting used to it" (Fish 54). The final solution to the problem of the dead kitty—"together, we walk to the side of the road and I watch as he chucks the remains, hard, into a patch of high weeds" (55)—is also the final line of the story. Thus, the story follows a fairly traditional narrative arc: it gives the characters some trouble and then has them struggle to resolve the trouble.

Here, the conflict arises out of Fish's use of language, symbolism, and precise details to reveal the young man's lack of tenderness toward the narrator. Consider, for example, his comment when she mentions the uselessness of ponchos against the rain: "Stop goading me" (Fish 53). He tells her that, if she needs to get away, she can "go clog her lungs under the viaduct" (54). The use of goading—with its implication of someone poking someone with a stick—seems particularly connected to the problem of the kitten. And isn't *kitten* also a term that lovers use in tenderness toward one another? *Clog*, too, might be associated with hairballs, with stickiness, with that kitten clogging the road, stuck to the street. As stated above, within the confined space of flash, without the necessary space for a series of failed, thwarted actions to solve a problem, the conflict might seem too small—or, on the other hand, might seem too big, too melodramatic or sentimental. To solve that challenge of flash, Fish puts words in conflict, creates tension between the *tenderoni* of the title and the crushed *tenderoni* on the road, between the image of going under and the clogged burial of the kitten. That conflict is resolved by this moment at the end: "He pats my head and he's never patted my head before" (55). The patting of the head is how someone might show tenderness to a kitten, and that use of *never before* emphasizes that something has changed between them.

Stakes also get raised by Fish's creating greater subtext by connecting the character's psyche to the trouble. In "Wren," for example, the neighbor girl Renee Chu—"but she was always Wren to me" (Fish 48)—absorbs the narrator's attention and thoughts, though they have almost no contact, except for seeing "Mr. and Mrs. Chu moving up the street, each holding onto one of Wren's tiny hands, their bodies curved inward on either side of her like parentheses" (49). One night, the narrator says, "it seemed [Wren] was looking at [her]" (50). At the end, the narrator learns that Wren is "going to live in a home for sick children," and in that lyrical final paragraph, the narrator dreams of Wren: "I dreamed that I had hammered together a home for Wren. She would live there forever, surrounded by a thousand bright blue butterflies. And she would emerge from time to time to smile at me from behind a window of cracked glass" (50).

Here, there seems little at stake for the narrator—her contact with Wren, as shown above, is minimal, and what happens to Wren has no direct effect on the narrator's life. The "hole" that this narrator has fallen into is, at best, quite shallow, if it exists at all. It's Wren who has fallen into a hole—being sent away from her home and parents. Yet, the story feels important to both the narrator and the story's reader; it feels as if something very significant has happened. And that, I'd argue, has to do with Wren's connection to the narrator's deeper self.

The first transformation that occurs in the story is the narrator's changing Renee Chu to Wren. In folklore, the wren "figured as a symbol of eros" (Wentersdorf 196), and as result of ancient fertility rituals, the wren was hunted, sometimes afterwards "treated with reverence, carried around in solemn procession, and even buried, sometimes in hallowed soil" and other times boys "hunt[ed] to death with sticks and stones any unfortunate wren they could find" (192).

The narrator lives "kitty-cornered" (Fish 48) to Wren—and again there's that sense of something being hunted, as a cat would prey upon a bird. On display for the neighbors "like some of the men in the neighborhood displayed their new cars" (48), the narrator's family lives large—tearing into their food (49), playing games in their "large and fenced" backyard (48), "listening to the [large] bug zapper fry [tiny] mosquitoes and flies and moths" (49), watching the Chu family move up the street. The conversion of Renee—a name meaning rebirth—into this hunted, revered, unfortunate thing might have something to do with the narrator's own sense of her place in the world in which the largeness—"there were six of us, including our parents" (48)—has become connected with health. "Wren," the narrator asserts, "was not sick, only very small" (50). Fenced in, struggling in the family games, the narrator transfers her own anxieties onto the neighbor girl.

Thus, significance emerges. At the end, Wren's living inside the narrator's psyche confirms Wren's important connection to the narrator's own secret self. The dream itself—that Wren would only emerge to smile at the narrator—keeps Wren at a distance, a sign of something fragile yet fearful. It suggests the narrator's inability to cross some barrier—that "window of cracked glass"—to grasp Wren fully.

Finally, let's take a look at the resolution, once again turning to Fish's flash collection. Fish's "Moth Woman" begins as a woman comes to pick up clothes, gets to talking to the protagonist and her husband Greg, and hears about the moths in their basement. She comes in to see them—tells them that they are mating Luna Moths that will die within a week and criticizes Greg for swearing at a moth that flies into his face. She rises from the basement, takes the bags, and leaves in "her crappy little car" (Fish 93). The story ends with this remarkable passage: "The next morning I went down to the basement, and just as the woman had said, the moths had all died. At first I thought everything, the floor, the furniture, the shelves, was covered in thick, green leaves. Then I realized" (94). *So what?* (I can't believe you're still asking that question.)

It might very well be that Fish intends for the reader to fill in the object of *realized*. Literally, the narrator has realized that what's covering everything isn't leaves but dead moths. Anything else? She realized the old woman was right, perhaps. But about what? About all that she said about moths—and beyond? Or maybe the character's having "realized" is the point, with no fill-in required. Consider the root of *realized*—to make real—and replace that as the ending: "Then I made real." That's what the visiting woman has done to the moths for the protagonist—made them real by giving them a name, a purpose, a life span.

Here, in the final conversation that takes place in the basement between the woman, Greg, and the protagonist, the visitor continues to make the protagonist to confront the deeper truths of her subconscious, her own internal dark basement:

> One of the moths flew directly into Greg's face and he batted at it, saying Shit. Shit. The woman put her finger to her lips, shushing him, like, Oh no, don't swear in front of the pretty bugs, and we got pissed all over again remembering it later, like how dare she. She said, Words get embedded in a place, they settle into the walls and furniture like ghosts, to which Greg said horseshit and the woman said are you afraid of strange ideas and Greg said, Horseshit, and the woman said, Are you afraid of strange ideas, and Greg said, No, I'm afraid of strange people, and we smirked at each other then because we seriously wanted this Moth Woman out of our basement . . . . (Fish 93)

Yorke tells us that a story's final insight is our own—that of our community, our society, our world—always known, continually forgotten. *I made real.* Words get embedded, the old woman has said. If she were right about the Luna Moths, what else has this woman made real? "How do we get them out of here" (Fish 93), the protagonist asks of the Luna Moths. *I made real.* But that is the wrong question, the old woman makes them understand, because their "journey is a short one" (93). They are, to the old woman, something not to be gotten rid of; they are "pretty," in need, perhaps, of love in their too-short time here on earth. *I made real.* Do you see it, now, protagonist and readers? Love, like the flutter of a luna moth, is set against the inclination of this couple to use hateful words (crappy, shit, horseshit, strange, pissed) that get embedded in everything, coloring the world into something false, something other than it is—"bright green [and] fluttering" (92).

In "Wake Up," the final story under discussion, I'd like to take a look at how all these elements might work together. The story is a deceptively simple one: In the middle of the night, a naked sleepwalking neighbor, Mr. Dorn, begins singing, and the main character has to decide what to do about it: call Mrs. Dorn, wake up Mr. Dorn, and so on. Once more that force that wants to diminish tiny things arrives, barraging the story with all those *So whats?* For this one last time, let's look at how Fish fends them off.

Fish's story begins in the first sentence, with trouble arriving on the narrator's doorstep: "My neighbor, Mr. Dorn, is standing naked on my front steps, singing" (Fish 144). Notice how in all these flashes, reader interest is heightened by making the trouble a bit off-kilter: characters find themselves encountering imagined cancer-parts; smooshed kittens; a funeral-crashing stranger, encircled by Walgreens' necklaces; a moth basement and moth woman; and here, a naked singing neighbor. So right away, readers find themselves in a "hole" that feels a bit unfamiliar and unpredictable, a technique that helps with making the trouble feel "story-worthy." This technique feels especially important to flash, as it has little time to place the reader in a world of disquiet, confronting a world and character in-trouble.

Added to this trouble are stakes, such as the fear that if she wakes him, she'll induce a heart attack. Also, this is her "third night of insomnia," and she's "feeling as close to crazy as [she's] ever have" (Fish 144). It's possible, the narrator tells us, that Mr. Dorn is a hallucination. Or worse, she says, "It's possible I'm not even here" (144). So it's a risk to act, for fear of killing or harming Mr. Dorn or making herself appear crazy. But what's to be gained by helping Mr. Dorn out of this predicament and getting him to bed without incident or harm? Well, she gets to provide aid to a couple she likes.

But surely, from what we've seen previously in looking closely at flash, there must be more to it than that.

It's not easy to get Mr. Dorn to stop singing, a situation made worse by the fact that he "stands holding his penis, looking amazed, as if penises had just been invented and he'd been asked to try this one on for size" (Fish 145). Concern for Mr. Dorn arises to make the conflict more challenging. How easy it would be to act if she didn't care so much! She is crazy herself—unsure of her own reality, her own presence—and that too adds to the struggle to act, to do something for him. So the conflict makes her stay trapped with the trouble, Mr. Dorn continuing his singing, his grasp of himself.

As previously discussed, this specific trouble represents a specific aspect of the narrator's inner and outer life. For example, the narrator's cat is missing the narrator's husband, who has left her. Her own feelings of separation remind her of the time Mrs. Dorn left Mr. Dorn, temporarily on a trip: "She knew Mr. Dorn would be lonely so she built him a snow version of herself standing in front of their house" (Fish 145). The narrator tells us she took a picture of the snow-version of Mrs. Dorn, and when she gave it to Mr. Dorn, "he cried" and "said she'd only been gone three days" (145). The narrator reveals to us that she often calls her husband in the middle of the night, whispering, "Are we going to be okay?" She adds, "I don't want to wake him completely. I read somewhere that people in a semi-conscious state are incapable of lying" (145). The story's title, "Wake Up," might seem to be addressed to Mr. Dorn, but the flash's readers must consider the possibility that it also relates to the main character, as does everything surrounding her. The story elements exist to get her to confront this deeper self, this dark self that hasn't yet awoken to this new life—lonely, anxious, unsure of her okay-ness, her very presence. She is losing a grasp on her identity as all the things that previously defined her are being erased from her life. Yes, she can't sleep, up all night herself, but it's the darker recesses of her psyche that still lie, semi-conscious, beginning to stir. It's you, the story says to her, on the doorstep—you still holding on to what you were, you naked now and vulnerable, you wanting someone to miss you as the Dorns miss each other.

The resolution to this trouble centers on the need to get Mr. Dorn off the doorstep and to his rightful place:

> Mr. Dorn needs to wake up and go home to his bed. I push up the window and lean close to the screen and start singing, "La la la la la la."
>
> He blinks. "La la la la la la." He clears his throat and lets go of his penis. Mr. Dorn and I are singing "My Cherie Amour" together. Maybe he's still asleep or maybe he's not, but I'll say this, the two of us are really something. (Fish 146).

The action works, the implication being that Mr. Dorn is now awake, consciously singing the lyrics to Stevie Wonder's song about a cherished love, for the only one that a heart beats for, and it was, wasn't it?, a heart that she worried about breaking by trying to awaken. The indefinite pronoun "something" and repeated "maybe" add that sense of the unknown to the resolution. Maybe she, too, has begun to let go. Maybe she now sees that love isn't about the desire to have anyone, but to have that unique someone, creating a "two of us" that are really something.

In these stories from *Together We Can Bury It*, one can see Fish's themes emerging—beauty in the world that cannot quite be grasped or held, except for the briefest of moments; the trouble people find themselves in, encircled by a world seemingly turned against them, that trouble a product of their own minds and their families; the stakes of loving, committing, and acting in a world defined by uncertainty. That Fish's flash fictions consistently and elegantly capture these significant, defining moments makes each of her stories worth the careful consideration of a close reading. In doing so, the reader becomes a student in reading not just Fish's very short fiction, but the work of others.

Frost's answer to the question "What to make of a diminished thing?" might have been to write a poem, another tiny thing that rises like a birdsong in a fallen world, its original notes leftover from Eve's songs in Eden. Others write flash, to make real those tiny moments that others might miss, and in doing so, reveal the meaning that flutters around us continually, if only we can grasp it.

Works Cited

Fish, Kathy. *Together We Can Bury It*. Lit Pub Books, 2012.

Roney, Lisa. *Serious Daring: Creative Writing in Four Genres*. Oxford UP, 2015.

Vonnegut, Kurt. "At the Blackboard." *Lapham's Quarterly*, 2005, www.laphamsquarterly.org/arts-letters/blackboard/. Accessed 15 June 2016.

Wentersdorf, Karl P. "The Folkloristic Significance of the Wren." *The Journal of American Folklore*, vol. 90, no. 356, 1977, pp. 192-98. *JSTOR*, doi:10.2307/539700. Accessed 6 June 2016.

Yorke, John. *Into the Woods: A Five-Act Journey Into Story*. Overlook Press, 2015.

The Mathematics of the Heart: Mary Robison Considered as a Flash Fiction Novelist

David Swann

On the dust jacket of Mary Robison's 1991 novel, *Subtraction*, the writer is praised by Frederick Barthelme for the "peculiar squinted view" that she adopts to describe a troubled poetry teacher named Paige Deveaux, who is combing the suburbs of Houston, Texas, in search of her hard-drinking, skirt-chasing husband, who has gone "missing in action again" (150). Shortly after enduring a fleeting reunion with the serial philanderer, who usually returns from his vanishing acts "with new scars, new stories, no excuses" (8), the protagonist encounters a poem written by one of her disenchanted poetry students, a particle physicist who describes his work with a cyclotron as involving the shattering of "*matter into antimatter / Straining meaning through a sieve / Till all the world's a negative*" (97). It's a description that could serve equally well to describe the work of Robison, a writer who, in the decades since her debut collection, *Days* (1979), has been straining characters like Paige Deveaux through the sieve of her peculiar gaze. "Squinted," Barthelme calls it, this intense, ironic gaze—an image that suggests someone dazzled by a fierce light, but steadfastly refusing to look away.

That light is never fiercer, nor more painful, than in Robison's *Why Did I Ever* (2001), a 200-page novel containing fourteen chapters that have been shattered into 536 brief, numbered (and sometimes sub-titled) sections. Here, my aim is to explore these fragmentations and to analyze ways in which *Why Did I Ever* can be considered a "novel-in-flashes." I will describe challenges that may face those who attach the shiny beads of flash fiction to the long thread of a novel. And, along the way, there will be brief detours to consider work by Robison that bears comparison with *Why Did I Ever*, including the three-page story "Yours," as well as her 2009 novel, *One D.O.A., One on the Way* (whose 166 pages are broken, similarly, into 225 numbered sections).

Born in 1949, and said by Cynthia Whitney Hallett to have run away as a teenager to find Jack Kerouac (Hallett, "Mary Robison" 321), Robison was raised a Roman Catholic in Washington, DC, and the Midwest. She studied in the MA program at John Hopkins University, Baltimore, with the experimental novelist John Barth and later worked with the high-profile editors, Gordon Lish and Roger Angell. Her output to date consists of three short story collections, an anthology of her best-known short work, four novels, and a script for the independent movie *Twister* (1989), based on her debut novel *Oh!* (1981).

Brevity is one of the hallmarks of Robison's fiction. Thirty of her stories are accommodated in the 277 pages of the collection, *Tell Me* (2002), which rounds up her career's best short fiction, including the masterpiece "Yours," a story of just over 700 words. Although the novels *Oh!* and *Subtraction* are conventional in their approach to form, *Why Did I Ever* and *One D.O.A., One on the Way* are built from scores of short fragments. Hence, Robison often operates on territory that shares characteristics with flash fiction.

Throughout Robison's work, the prose has been distilled to its essence. Descriptions are brief, and exposition minimal. The immediate scene at hand is asked to do most of the heavy lifting, and the scene itself is generally peopled by characters trading dialogue that is notable for its wit and precision. Often, characters struggle to find meaning and security, but this anxiety is balanced against funds of humor and warmth.

Robison appears to have found this distinctive, pared-back voice relatively early in her career. According to Frederick Barthelme, who was in the same writing workshop at John Hopkins in 1975, fellow participants already "grudgingly admired [her work] . . . noting that the ordinariness of her subject and sentence was offset by the intense particularity of her language." For Barthelme, Robison emerged at a cultural moment when North American writers were suspicious of postmodernism's self-conscious experimentation and of realism's claims to guarantee the truth. In "rolling down the windows, trying to get a good whiff of what's out there," Barthelme argues that writers developed a literary minimalism that left "room for the readers." The result, he says, was work describing "an ordinary planet that looked strikingly like ours." However, he suggests that this planet's creators were just as concerned with artifice as they were with any "one-for-one depiction of a real world." The sense he conveys is that the minimalists were replacing the skeletal trees of *Waiting for Godot* with kitchen-sinks and wardrobes, while disguising their philosophical concerns as everyday transactions in laundries and greengrocers, so that enquiries into the nature of reality were cloaked as recognizably "real" events, and took place in settings familiar from daytime TV. But if it was soap-opera, it was soap-opera directed by Franz Kafka or Samuel Beckett. And if, as Barthelme suggested, it tried "some of this representational stuff," it realized that writing was made from words and could never simply mirror reality.

This was the literary climate in which Robison's work came to prominence, and pretty soon she was being grouped with other writers who shared a miser's attitude towards exposition and material detail. Robison's tendency to work with very short forms (and, later, to deploy fragments), provided another reason why she was linked with the minimalists, whom her tutor John Barth, in 1986, called "the most impressive phenomenon on the current . . . literary scene" (1). For Barth, "minimalism" could describe many qualities, not only the length of a piece, but also its style, vocabulary, and/or rhetoric. And it might equally well be used to describe characterization, plot, action, and imagery (1). Generally, he said that the aesthetic was responsible for:

> the new flowering of the (North) American short story (in particular the kind of terse, oblique, realistic or hyperrealistic, slightly plotted, extrospective, cool-surfaced fiction associated in the last 5 to 10 years with such excellent writers as Frederick Barthelme, Ann Beattie, Raymond Carver, Bobbie Ann Mason, James Robison, Mary Robison and Tobias Wolff, and both praised and damned under such labels as 'K-Mart realism', 'hick chic', 'Diet-Pepsi minimalism' and

'post-Vietnam, post-literary, postmodernist blue-collar neo-early-Hemingwayism'). (Barth 1)

For her part, Robison told *BOMB* magazine that she "detested" the "minimalist" label: "Minimalists sounded like we had tiny vocabularies and few ways to use the few words we knew. I thought the term was demeaning; reductive, clouded, misleading, lazily borrowed from painting and that it should have been put back where it belonged" (Murray). There are sly references to this antipathy in Robison's story, "Mirror," in which a nude life-model reports that a painter has asked her to gain weight "so there'd be less anatomy to draw and more volume" (213). Joking in her characteristically serious fashion, Robison told *BOMB* that she preferred to be called a "'subtractionist'—that at least implied a little effort" (Murray).

It's easy to see why Robison should have disliked being linked with "minimalism," which has been defined as "a flat, spare, and subdued style of writing, characterized by an accumulation of (sometimes apparently random) detail that gives an impression of benumbed emotion" (Burroway et al. 400). In insisting instead on a definition that includes the notions of labor and intelligence, Robison seems to have been keen to emphasize the invisible component of her work, that long process of drafting, which is familiar to all serious writers and which Robison alludes to in a 2003 interview on KCRW Radio, where she describes a rigorous approach to editing that involves root-to-branch re-writes. In that sense, the term "subtraction" restores craftsmanship to her approach and reminds us of the mathematical precision that she requires of her prose. It may also suggest parallels with woodcutting—a discipline that depends upon the removal of material, so that there is ultimately less volume, but more anatomy.

Equally, "subtraction" brings to mind the spiritual quests associated with the *via negativa*, a mystical path that involves "the giving up of sight and sound, the dwelling in darkness and shadow" (Morgan 174). Ascetics who follow this path to enlightenment must retreat from the distractions of the physical world and enter "the deep shadow thrown by blinding light" (175), where the presence of

God is "inferred from the experience of absence" (174). "The soul grows by subtraction," as Rupert Sheldrake and Matthew Fox put it, referencing the German mystic, Meister Eckhart. (74)

It perhaps shouldn't surprise us to enter religious territory when discussing Robison, for there's a yearning for transcendence in her work, as Michael Silverblatt suggests in his 2003 interview on KCRW Radio. He points out that Robison's debut novel *Oh!* was released in the same period as the *Oh, God!* movies in which God (played by George Burns) chooses a supermarket employee to spread his Word. Silverblatt argues that Robison's work often points us towards a God that has been removed from the equation. For instance, her story "May Queen" takes place during a Roman Catholic procession, but any religious overtones are subdued by the squinting, rather frazzled adult characters. Their daughter has been elected at school to lead the parade, but the event descends into slapstick chaos when her dress catches fire on some candles. Afterwards, the parents console the girl by promising her a lavish holiday with friends "who went on television and won a convertible" (Robison, "May Queen" 187). If God can't supply it, maybe a lakeside amusement park will do the trick instead.

Subtraction, then. But multiplication, too. In Robison's fiction, families include many twins and siblings, and it's the proximity of so many bodies that creates a lot of the warmth and comedy. The family members communicate at sardonic angles, but their bickering has a ritual quality, and the humor acts as emotional glue. It's the same with the many best friends who appear in Robison's work, even when they're as clueless as the self-absorbed Hollis in *Why Did I Ever*, whom the narrator describes as "Maybe not the best friend I have in the world. He is, however, the only" (2). Here, we sense that the narrator lacks a talent for enlarging the cast of her life, and this passivity is one aspect of a static tendency in Robison's narratives that I'll discuss later. For the moment, I think it's important to note that, for all the irony in Robison's work and for all its ambivalence towards intimacy, characters like Hollis play an important role. He's irritating, yes. But he's one of the few constants in the narrator's disintegrating existence.

Where there *is* a movement out of stasis, it's generally in the opposite direction, leading not towards addition, but division, as the lovers in Robison's narratives often discover. And while these divisions can create bitterness, as in her novel *Subtraction*, they also have the capacity to be heartbreakingly tender, as in the short-short story, "Yours," where the male character ultimately considers the gulf in experience that prevents him from fully communicating with his partner. Here, it's not infidelity that causes pain, but the realization that even the most successful relationship can never achieve full transcendence.

The divisions and subtractions that appear throughout Robison's work are at their rawest in her 2001 novel, *Why Did I Ever*. Narrated by a troubled mother-of-two named Money Breton, who describes herself as "a script doctor, as far as I know" (5), *Why Did I Ever* is really about the rape and torture of the protagonist's son. However, that terrible ordeal only sporadically surges up out of the novel's seething background. Hence, the novel's fragmentations are reminiscent of what Molly Andrews describes as "traumatic testimony . . . marked by what is not there: coherence, structure, meaning, comprehensibility" (Robison, *Why* 37).

Money supplies this "traumatic testimony" while she is attempting to concentrate on the re-write of a ridiculous B-movie and losing the plot in her personal life. Wired on drugs and addicted to long, insomniac road-trips ("I drive all over the American South, all night long" [Robison, *Why* 18]), Money laments that, "This . . . is not my real life. My real life is still coming up" (59). While Money is waiting for this life, Robison confronts us with a series of brief, imagistic, often hallucinatory fragments, in which children wearing "brown lipstick" appear to be reading the TV news (76) and the narrator is unable to name the objects in her handbag. These uneasy, imagistic moments are always derived from everyday life, but the vivid, dislocated fashion in which they are presented makes them as surreal as anything in a David Lynch movie. At times, the images flow on from each other, but sometimes they loom from the voids between the sections, like faces appearing unexpectedly before a camera. There is a relentless quality in the approach, as if a flash-bulb is popping in our eyes, over and over.

It could be argued that Robison's more recent "flash novel," *One D.O.A., One on the Way* (2009), presents an even more disorientating vision of contemporary society, since its characters are marooned inside the hole that Hurricane Katrina has gouged from New Orleans. Certainly, Robison pours her sociological despair into the 225 fragments that make up the novel, but I would argue that its statistical and journalistic data offer a measure of distance— whereas *Why Did I Ever* simply plunges us, head-first, into the void by concentrating its psychological trauma in one individual rather than scattering it across a city. That said, the later book is interesting for its continuing use of the flash techniques that proved so startling in *Why Did I Ever*.

Robison has suggested, in interviews, that personal circumstances influenced the earlier novel's fragmentations and jump-cuts. In the interview with *BOMB* magazine, she alluded to "various horrible things" that enforced new working practices:

> I was having more than difficulty . . . So to get through, I began scribbling notes. I would go out, take a notebook. Or drive, or park wherever and take notes. I would note anything left. Anything that still seemed funny or scary or involving for four seconds. Some berserk conversation I overheard. The crap on the radio. This big, brilliant cat. Ridiculous weather. Then it was months before I read over the scribbles and realized they had a steady voice, and that there were characters and themes. (Murray)

For all her distress, Robison suggests that she was otherwise operating like many writers of very short fiction, who activate their flash-buttons to illuminate, isolate, and preserve the moments that they have imagined, witnessed, and/or remembered. Usually, the next job is to emblemize this "captured" moment so that it suggests a range of wider meanings. In successful work, the moment then acts like a leaf under a scientist's microscope, revealing, through every vein and wrinkle, an infinite number of tiny trees.

When applied to traditional short fiction, this endeavor is often linked to Hemingway's "principle of the iceberg" (198), in which the writer's task is to imply the hidden "seven-eighths" (198) of the iceberg from the portion that's visible in the story. In facing this challenge, the writer must ask questions about back story. How much exposition can a short story support? Where (if at all) should the back story emerge? How should the exposition be released? These are important questions because the writer otherwise risks simply dumping narrative information and slowing forward momentum.

The shorter the fiction, the more these challenges increase, as there simply isn't time and space to include all the time and space that a story may need. Hence, the flash fiction writer is operating at the very tip of Hemingway's iceberg, and must contend with an iceberg that is itself rapidly dissolving, owing to the sheer brevity of the form.

The best-known "iceberg" in Robison's work can be found in the three-page masterpiece, "Yours," where two late-night pumpkin-carvers, living in a comfortable house on a dark ravine, are revealed to be a loving couple divided by gulfs of age, talent, and experience. Thanks to a few of the "brief expository statements" that Daniel Green identifies as being common in Robison's work, we understand that the lovers have persisted with their relationship in the face of family opposition and that the younger member of the couple is dying. However, most of the story's emotional and informational weight is shouldered by the single scene in which the couple carve the pumpkins. That's the tip of the iceberg on which Robison requires her characters to stand—the fleeting autumnal moments that must emblemise the lovers' relationship and provide some powerful, allusive sense of the wider forces that have carried them to this turning-point. As Green observes, it's a familiar strategy in Robison's work, in which "there are intimations of larger significance . . . [and] fleeting implications of back story or future forward movement, but mostly they seem to be fixated on the depiction of present moments."

In flash fiction, this "fixation" on the present moment is very common, and the writer's job is to suggest significant events that lie beneath the waterline. But it's interesting to ask what happens when those fragments must work together in a novel rather than existing independently, within the frame of a stand-alone story.

When considering Robison's flash novel, *Why Did I Ever*, it may be instructive to reflect upon Stephen Minot's observation in *Sudden Fiction: American Short-Short Stories* that, "as fiction gets longer. . . the emphasis tends to be placed on a different set of concerns: complexities of plotting, subtleties of characterization, and the portrayal of social scene" (Shapard and Thomas 237). To some extent, Robison seems to have resisted the "different set of concerns," as she explains to *BOMB* magazine when describing what she did with the fragments:

> . . . none of the material was organized at all except around my urgent need to distract myself. So I gave the sections different headings and typed them onto index cards, punched and popped the cards into a binder. And looking through, I thought, This is the only writing you're doing. You ought to try to make it interesting for others to read. That meant, to me, a reappraisal, and taking a more fictive approach to the narrative, and then, pretty literally, assembling it. Still, I never did give it a hat or shoes, and if you read the pages in reverse order, they work about the same. (Murray)

Robison's refusal to provide "hat and shoes" explains the novel's capacity to bewilder the unprepared reader, particularly when the imagistic fragments are presented as static, self-contained tableaux (often in short paragraphs, or in one- or two-line phrases).

The fragments allow Robison to stage a series of abrupt transitions, between settings, time frames, and modes of narration. Hence, we can whiz in a few paragraphs from terse details of the son's torture . . . to memories of his childhood . . . to a TV puppet-show . . . to a highway tailgating scene . . . to a series of supermarket visits . . . to driving again . . . to a revelation of shoplifting . . . and then to breakfast (Robison, *Why* 137-140). These seemingly random transitions make it clear that Robison isn't much interested in playing the Hollywood game that her protagonist, Money Breton, increasingly despises. In conventional cinema and literature, the writer would make it easier for us to trace a character arc and for us to connect the events through a plot-chain founded upon principles of cause and effect. Instead, in *Why Did I Ever*, Money simply drifts through a blizzard of moments. "I don't go anywhere," she says— "I'm merely out here practising going somewhere" (40). To that extent, what we're watching is movement rather than action, for, as Janet Burroway et al. suggest, "these terms are not synonymous" (118), and movement fails to become action if it isn't "moving the plot forward" (118).

Robison's novel may well have departed home without shoes and hat, but it's far from naked (even if the clothes aren't always worn in the places we'd expect). Although character, language and imagery finish higher in Robison's hierarchy than plot, she has clearly "plotted" certain elements of the novel, if only in the sense that many of the scenes have been carefully selected and arranged, particularly in the case of the back story, which emerges in sporadic dribbles rather than a convenient splurge.

An important part of the novel's plot is hidden in the white spaces between fragments, so that we must also concentrate on what *isn't* said or dramatized, such as in the sequence where Money arrives late for a script-meeting, afraid she may have "passed out in terror" (Robison, *Why* 69) after sleeping with a producer. If this is true, then it's the first time the reader has heard about it. And Money seems equally clueless. So what we share is the protagonist's blackout—and another troubling realization that important events are happening in the darkness between the popping of narrative flash-bulbs. Ultimately, there's a frightening sense that the gaps are as important as the fragments and that the void beneath the novel is just as real as the stores and highways that Money roams.

Gradually an alert and patient reader will piece together the back story and understand that Money's son is under police protection while doctors assess his health following the rape. However, the unreliability of Money's narration, and the drip-feeding of information, will likely tax the patience of readers who prefer a linear plot, or fewer crooked angles into characters' lives.

For those who find the elliptical approach maddening, it could be that Robison's economy with a huge quantity of brilliantly observed imagery, will act as compensation. And even the harshest critic would probably concede that the novel's formal fragmentations are organically linked to Money's fractured consciousness. There is also the reward of Robison's trademark wit, as dry as it is relentless. Throughout, the terror of the son's ordeal is counterpointed by an extraordinary gallows humor, often conveyed to us through de-familiarizations that serve not only to evoke the narrator's mental state, but also to satirize the corporate, media-saturated landscape through which Money drifts. In her broadest comic-moments, Robison pokes fun at Money's role in the movie industry, particularly when the script that she's trying to improve rapidly succumbs to the same crude commercial forces that have disfigured the roadsides:

> The script used to have a man in love with a wood nymph. Then a version had him in the redwood forest in love with a tree. Now the story's set in Alaska, and is about some dame chasing after Bigfoot. My job, and what I do for a living. (Robison, *Why* 70)

Here, Money's attempts to integrate Bigfoot into the film studio's stupid script can be read, on one level, as what Lindquist calls "Hollywood-bashing . . . and a pointed rejection of almost every storytelling technique that makes movies work." If so, it's a common tendency in Robison's work, in which protagonists on the brink of natural and man-made disasters (hurricanes, twisters, earthquakes, lightning-storms, mine-collapses, etc.) are often psychologically frozen, unable to perform the significant deeds that would change their situations if they were heroes in Hollywood cinema.

A fatalistic worldview is evident throughout Robison's fiction, as in her story, "Kite and Paint," where the sixty-something characters protect their piano from the "fourteen-foot waves" (90) of an imminent hurricane but then lapse into inaction, and plan a kite-flying expedition. In assessing Robison's aversion to decisive action, one is reminded of another writer frustrated by Hollywood's demands—the screenwriter Charlie Kaufman. In his script for the film *Adaptation*, Kaufman has a character seemingly similar to himself declare an ambition to write "a story where nothing much happens, where people don't change, they don't have any epiphanies. They struggle and are frustrated and nothing is resolved" (Kaufman).

Of course, there *are* epiphanies in Robison's work (e.g., the profound ending of her story "Yours," accomplished by a deft shift in perspective, in which we enter the male lover's consciousness to discover that he is dismissive of his own artistic gifts and wants only the comfort of getting drunk with his dying wife). Also, it would be wrong to assume that the characters are always resigned to their stasis. In the story, "Care," we sense the pain felt by a woman who has been warned by her partner that she "ought to start changing" (223), but confesses she doesn't know how because: "He wouldn't tell me." (223)

Despite these moments, some critics have argued that Robison's work would benefit from more commitment to dramatic change and narrative momentum. For Douglas Bauer, the inaction in Robison's fiction amounts to a maddening sanctioning of "self-pitying" behavior by people who "are unable or cynically unwilling to act, or are frozen in states of abdicating adolescence (whether they be 25 or 60)."

More forgiving souls might want to suggest that the fatalism is some residue of Robison's Roman Catholicism, or to argue, along with Thomas Elsaesser, that "the motivated logic" (280) of conventional fiction had been called into question in the 1970s, when Robison was honing her craft. Elsaesser was writing about maverick 1970s cinema rather than literature, but his description of the era's "scepticism about motivations and justifications" (283) and "the fading confidence in being able to tell a story, with a beginning, a middle, and an ending" (280) give us a critical prism for Robison's work and helps us to understand the cultural environment in which her fiction was born.

The stasis in Robison's work may also be connected with qualities intrinsic to flash fiction itself. Faced by the pressures on time and space that were discussed earlier, very short fiction has a tendency to privilege imagery over plot—and to concentrate on frozen moments rather than sequences stretching through hours and days and months. In that sense, flash is a natural vehicle for writers who simply to refuse to believe in story-worlds that bend to the hero's will, and whose plot-chains are logical, and make sense.

When considering Robison's fatalistic streak, it may also be helpful to study the last four items on the nine-point list that Cynthia Whitney Hallett offers as an attempt to characterize 1980s minimalism:

> (6) implications of an existential, often absurd, universe in which "real" communication is impossible and action is useless—to protest is to waste one's breath; to fight is to waste one's energies, "better to say nothing and do even less"; (7) a recognition that words are useless, for most things are unsayable; (8) a perception that time passes without resistance and that the characters exist as audience rather than as participants in their own world and lives, especially since it would seem that nothing they do or say can make a difference; (9) a universe in which no one thing appears innately important, so all worth is artificially conferred, decided by individual values. (*Minimalism* 25)

Seen in this light, Robison's work was born out of cultural exhaustion, and her characters are rather like the passive, pathetic victims who simply sit around waiting for help after being shipwrecked in the original version of *The Poseidon Adventure*. Released in 1972, the year of Watergate and of Richard Nixon's re-election as President, the movie celebrates the battling qualities of those survivors who refuse to wait for the authorities and instead rescue themselves by climbing up through the overturned ship. It was a common narrative quandary in disaster films of the 1970s, when society faced difficult choices over the economy and Vietnam. In essence, the question was: should you trust the authorities, or your own convictions?

Whenever I read criticism that positions Robison's characters as the inert victims of a shipwreck, I feel a strong urge to connect them to a contrary, argumentative quality in Robison that is far from passive, and has much in common with the spikey, rebellious sensibilities of the 1970s that challenged dominant ways of seeing the world—and went on to produce not only experimental cinema and literature, but feminist art and punk rock.

It's true that you sometimes want to shake her characters—but maybe that's part of the point. Subtracted from the heroic realm and divided by their internal doubts, the people in Robison's stories lack the courage and certainty to hunt down Bigfoot. Often endangered by the decisions and deeds of others, they instead seek consolation with people who share the same wacky humor and the same plaguing doubts.

In focusing upon these frail, funny, and frustrating characters, Robison's flash narratives retreat from causal action chains and press the freeze-button. This can lead to dramatic inertia, I agree. But, for those who share Robison's suspicion of plot's bullying, totalitarian tendencies, and who question their own capacity to star as the hero in the movie of their lives, these doubts and vulnerabilities are bound up with an artistic calculus that values the damaged and the vulnerable—and that prefers vivid snapshots of these individuals rather than engineered narratives that resolve their difficulties in ways that real life rarely can.

As in all the best short fiction, the small lives in Robison's startling work are captured with perfect clarity and precision, and their shadows extend into a larger, more frightening darkness beyond the limits of the frame.

Works Cited

Andrews, Molly. "Beyond Narrative: The Shape of Traumatic Testimony." *We Shall Bear Witness: Life Narratives and Human Rights*, edited by Meg Jensen and Margaretta Jolly, University of Wisconsin Press, 2014, pp. 32-47.

Barth, John. "A Few Words about Minimalism." *New York Times*, 28 Dec. 1986, Late City Final Edition Section 7, p. 1.

Barthelme, Frederick. "On Being Wrong: Convicted Minimalist Spills Beans." *New York Times*, 3 Apr. 1988, n.p.

Bauer, Douglas. "New Scars, New Stories, No Excuses." *New York Times*, 24 Feb. 1991, n.p.

Burroway, Janet, et al., editors. *Writing Fiction: A Guide to Narrative Craft,* 8th ed., Longman Pearson, 2011.

Elsaesser, Thomas. "The Pathos of Failure: American Films in the 1970s, Notes on the Unmotivated Hero." 1975. *The Last Great American Picture Show: New Hollywood Cinema in the 1970s,* edited by Thomas Elsaesser et al., Amsterdam UP, 2004, pp. 279-292.

Green, Daniel. "Mary Robison." *Daniel Green's The Reading Experience: Literary Criticism and Commentary,* 1 July 2016, www.thereadingexperience.net/tre/blog_index.html/. Accessed 4 Mar. 2017.

Hallett, Cynthia Whitney. "Mary Robison (1949–)." *Contemporary American Women Fiction Writers, An A-to-Z Guide,* edited by Laurie Champion and Rhonda Austin, Greenwood Press, 2002, pp. 323-29.

_____. *Minimalism and the Short Story. Raymond Carver, Amy Hempel, and Mary Robinson.* Edwin Mellen Press, 1999.

Hemingway, Ernest. Interview. *Writers at Work, 2nd Series. The Paris Review.* Martin Secker & Warburg, 1968.

Kaufman, Charlie, screenwriter. *Adaptation,* Columbia Pictures, 2002.

Lindquist, Mark. "A Life through Flashbacks and Dialogue." *Seattle Times,* 13 Jan. 2002, n.p.

Morgan, Christopher. *R.S. Thomas: Identity, Environment, and Deity.* Manchester UP, 2003.

Robison, Mary. "Care." *Tell Me: 30 Stories.* Counterpoint, 2002, pp. 217-27.

_____. Interview with Maureen Murray. "Artists in Conversation: Mary Robison." *Bomb Magazine,* 77, Fall, 2001, n.p.

_____. "Interview with Michael Silverblatt." *Bookworm.* KCRW Radio, Santa Monica, California, 23 Jan. 2003. Radio.

_____. "Kite and Paint." *Tell Me: 30 Stories.* Counterpoint, 2002, pp. 88-94.

_____. "May Queen." *Tell Me: 30 Stories.* Counterpoint, 2002, pp. 183-87.

_____. "Mirror." *Tell Me: 30 Stories.* Counterpoint, 2002, pp. 208-16.

_____. *One D.O.A., One on the Way.* Counterpoint, 2009.

_____. *Subtraction.* Alfred A. Knopf, 1991.

_____. *Why Did I Ever*. Counterpoint, 2001.

_____. "Yours." *Tell Me: 30 Stories*. Counterpoint, 2002, pp. 275-77.

Shapard, Robert, and James Thomas, editors. *Sudden Fiction: American Short-Short Stories*. Gibbs Smith, 1986.

Sheldrake, Rupert, and Matthew Fox. *Natural Grace*. Bloomsbury, 1996.

Thomas, R. S. *Collected Poems 1955–1990*. Phoenix Giants, 1993.

Nanofiction and the Limits of the Form: Insights from the 420-Character Fictions of Lou Beach___

Jarrell D. Wright

> We read the lines; the words enter us. The poem inside the paragraph
> is a mainlined image: it shoots right into the vein, into the blood, so
> to speak, of meaning, and the reader takes it in before arming himself
> or herself against it. (Phillips, "'Cheers'" 37)

Critics of flash fiction, a relatively new literary form,[1] have preoccupied themselves with definitional questions: What is it? What are its constituent features? What do we *call* it? Indeed, any bibliography of the emerging body of scholarship dealing with the form would be dominated by efforts to pin the genre down—whether by naming it or by specifying the precise length restrictions to which a work within the genre must conform.[2] Moreover, scholarly efforts in this direction have led some observers to the point of exhaustion or exasperation, with one observer asking, "Who the hell cares?" (James 129), and proclaiming, "We have wasted too much time already floundering on this issue" (131). Although *flash* seems to be the established term, I ally myself with scholars who find special value in the form's unsettled and even "protean" nature (Casto, "Myth-ing Link" 24).[3] I therefore investigate a subset of texts within this burgeoning and exciting genre: nanofiction. If pieces of flash can be meaningfully measured in terms of number of words as opposed to number of pages or chapters, then works of nanofiction can be sensibly quantified by an even smaller unit, the number of characters required to render them.

Beyond the need to label the underlying concept, the term itself is unimportant. The point, rather, is that these works reside near the extreme of what flash can accomplish, for it is difficult to imagine a text being shorter while still having literary qualities. Artist, illustrator, and collagist Lou Beach has emerged as an early master of this form of flash, in what has been described as "a concerted series of experiments in miniaturization" (Bradfield 13), with a published collection of untitled Facebook status updates composed and posted during a period when that social media platform limited user posts to, as his anthology's title indicates, *420 Characters*.[4] Ranging from eerie and haunting to wry and witty, Beach's nanofictions offer glimpses into what flash can accomplish at its absolute briefest: "Just because a story is short, even really, really short, doesn't mean that it can't contain multitudes" (Bradfield 13). Indeed, perhaps only poems like Ezra Pound's extraordinarily compact "In a Station of the Metro" or a six-word fiction like the piece apocryphally attributed to Ernest Hemingway—"For sale: Baby shoes, never worn"[5]— could subsist in greater brevity without loss of literary richness in both signification and resonance. And extreme and limit cases can be instructive to study; like vaster worlds compressed into the abstract realm of test tubes and like the outlandish and improbable hypotheticals popular among law school professors, they permit us to explore at the boundaries what might be essential at the core.

To say that this essay will place several of Beach's works under the microscope is to invoke a metaphor that is fitting on at least two levels. First, because the works are remarkably short, the microscopic perspective of close reading—a keen focus on minute textual details—is an appropriate one to adopt. As I tell my students, a well-constructed text is like the TARDIS from *Doctor Who*: bigger on the inside than it appears to be on the outside. Indeed, the smaller the text appears to be on the outside, the more significant each individual authorial choice becomes and the greater the impact of each choice upon the work as a whole.[6] As we unpack the implications of each textual detail in a piece of flash, it is almost as if we are witnessing an instance of the old sight gag: scores of clowns emerging impossibly from a Volkswagen or a phone booth. This level of attention fosters a sharper sense of how texts work and a greater aptitude for the skill of close reading. Second, the microscopic perspective implies an endeavor that involves testing and investigating. If, as I suggested, nanofiction is a limit case akin to a test-tube version of flash, then the act of placing a few pieces under the microscope promises to reveal something about the form more broadly understood: what it does particularly well and why it has become so appealing to readers. Ultimately, I hope to contest the common view that works of flash must recount actual narratives or tell complete stories, that "anything less than a third of a page is likely to be a mere summary, or perhaps a joke," rather than a bona fide piece of flash (Thomas and Shapard 12).[7] To the contrary, I contend that the requirement of narrative overlooks what flash has in common with verse or with the prose poem, genres to which it is often compared.[8] In particular, flash possesses a special ability to capture an image or mood, a scene or persona, through an inconclusive effect of indirection, allusiveness, or suggestiveness that is pleasurable for flash's often sophisticated readership and that has been described as *impressionistic*.[9]

In order to perceive this feature of flash and of nanofiction more particularly—to understand that this effect is a key characteristic of much great flash, what it does especially well—consider this piece by Beach:

> She trusted grins, they were shot directly from the heart. Whereas smiles, oh, smiles could trick, be untrue, do you harm. Mendacious, twisted with bad intentions, like her father's, his mouth turned up at one corner like a beckoning finger, pulling his eye down into a squint. (5)[10]

This piece offers no plot, story, or narrative, even considering the most minimalistic conceptions of those notions. Taking plot as a simple series of physical actions (Ferguson 221), the central figure in the piece does not bodily engage with the world; she only thinks, feels, and recalls, and the barest physical action that the piece describes (the father smiling) is remembered, rather than enacted "live," in a sentence fragment that significantly contains no complete main verb to denote a central action.[11] Plot can be considered as a series of episodes, collections of scenes in which multiple speakers engage in dialogue (Friedman 171), but Beach's nanofiction contains none of these elements. The central figure may be said to speak only in the sense that Beach gives us access to the words or ideas that unfold in her mind through free indirect discourse—filtering a character's words or thoughts, which are not placed within quotation marks, through a third-person narrator—marked in this piece by Beach's use of the exclamation, "oh." To take another conception of plot from Norman Friedman, the extent to which a character undergoes change (174), Beach has again elected not to provide this element for his reader; in Friedman's terms, the story is "static" and "simply shows its protagonist in one state or another and includes only enough to reveal to the reader the cause or causes of which this states [*sic*] is a consequence" (174).[12] Just as minimalistic are Steve Moss and John M. Daniel's criteria for what constitutes a story: setting, character, conflict, and resolution (217). Although Beach's piece provides hints of conflict, or at least tension, between the central figure and her father, there is no resolution of this conflict or tension, only a statement that it exists. And even in Butler's account—that "the essence of a plot" requires, at a minimum, "yearning challenged and thwarted" (103)—Beach has chosen not to describe his character's inner drives or desires; to be sure, we can infer that she has had a troubled relationship with her father and further speculate that she might desire a better or healthier connection with him, but those would be merely inferences or speculations unsupported by concrete evidence from details of language in the text itself.

So if this work of nanofiction does not present its readers with a plot, narrative, or story, then what does it do? I contend that it paints in delicate outlines the figure of a person, or of her momentary thoughts at a singular, brief point in time, hinting through dense imagery and carefully deployed language that the woman has, at one point, been injured (or perhaps even molested) by a malicious father, summoning her toward him with a crooked finger, smiling in a distorted grimace, only the squint of an eye signaling his harmful and quite deliberate intent. The story begins with what Frank K. Stanzel calls "the referentless 'she,'" a cue that the reader will need "to adopt the point of view of the person to whom the [. . .] pronoun refers and to suspend for the time being his curiosity about who this person is, what he or she is called, and so on" (27).[13] The rest of the comma-spliced first sentence, emphasized with the onomatopoeic verb "shot," closely equates grins with spontaneity, the expression of emotion "directly from the heart." Smiles, on the other hand, are sharply distinguished from grins in the central character's mind by Beach's choice to insert a sentence break instead of continuing his first sentence with the conjunction, "Whereas." The final, verbless fragment, through its pulsing assonance of the repeated vowel sound in "twisted," "intentions," and "squint," serves to link those words or concepts, fusing them together in a subtle insinuation about the unspeakable memory to which the central character cannot give full utterance even in the privacy of her own thoughts.

By attending closely to Beach's choices of language—and especially good writers make especially meaningful choices—we have come to a deeper understanding not only of the piece's connotations but also of how Beach has generated those meanings, which go well beyond the mere denotations or dictionary definitions of the words that he has skillfully elected to deploy: we have, in Stanzel's words, attended "to their symbolic or metaphorical rather than their referential meaning" (23). This exercise in close reading enhances our appreciation for how texts work and offers pleasure for sensitive and sophisticated readers of flash fiction. It is the kind of attention to language that is ordinarily reserved for works of verse, suggesting that flash can have some of the qualities of poetry, and it is a method of reading that permits us to enjoy, by gaining access to, some of the inconclusiveness and suggestiveness of flash, verse, and prose poem. We have not, however, as some scholars of flash recommend, gone beyond the text itself to invent our own ending or to occupy with our own imaginings the silent spaces that Beach has left open in his work.[14] Instead—really reading *the lines* rather than trying to read *between them*—we have enjoyed "a radical resolution that leaves the reader anxious in a particularly satisfying way" (Banks 244), and we have savored the way that flash "should hang in the air of the mind like an image made of smoke" (Phillips, "Flash Theory" 226).

Two more examples from Beach's collection further illustrate my central points. The second piece reads as follows:

Critical Insights

"Open the goddam door, Ronnie! I mean NOW!" He's locked himself in there again, turned Slayer and Deathhammer up all the way, the cheap speakers distorting the already distorted to the point where I know the fish will pulsate and wobble in their water. The blue tetras Miriam got him after his release, to make the room cheery. The poor, poor little fish. (Beach 23)

Does this composition feature a story, plot, or narrative? Although it presents a somewhat closer case than the previous piece of nanofiction that I analyzed, it offers at best a very sketchy narrative, one so wispy that it is barely even there; whatever narrative dimension the piece possesses is subordinated to other features of the text.

Here we *do* see physical actions (Ferguson 221), which we can sequence in a fairly straightforward chronological order: Ronnie's release (from prison or jail? from treatment in rehab?—the details are left unstated); Miriam (presumably his mother) buying fish to make his room back home more welcoming; Ronnie locking himself in his room and playing loud, metal music; and finally, his father (again, an assumption) yelling at him to open his door. Significantly, however, only the last of these is an element of live action in the piece itself; the others are recounted obliquely through the father's memory so that the "action" of the piece begins *in media res*, in the middle of the sketchy narrative rather than at its beginning. Although the father also speculates about what the music might do to the fish and internally expresses sympathy for them through free indirect discourse, those are not physical actions but rather "adjustments of thought or feeling" that Ferguson considers to be aspects of impressionism (221), and the last of these thoughts— "The poor, poor little fish," which we will come to see as the most important element of the piece—provides no *physical* resolution to the action: Ronnie is still locked in his room, defiantly blasting music, and the family unit remains fractured, perhaps hopelessly so. As a consequence, the best argument that we could construct to support a claim that this text has a plot, as Ferguson conceives that notion, would be a rather tenuous one.

The same could be said on the issue of whether the piece contains Butler's "essence of a plot": "yearning challenged and thwarted" (103). In one sense, Beach definitely provides enough material for his piece to satisfy that definition. The text opens with the father's demand that Ronnie open his door, and it ends with the door remaining closed and locked; the father's desire has been thwarted. But in another sense, that argument seems rather unsatisfactory. After all, even a surface reading of the text reveals that there is more at issue, in narrative terms, than the question of whether Ronnie will *literally* "Open the goddam door." Rather, at stake in this piece is whether this apparently very troubled young man will find healing (that is, whether he will *figuratively* open his door) and whether the family of which he is a vital part will come together despite their obviously splintered and dysfunctional relationship. In other words, the deeper and more genuine yearnings that frame the piece do not find any literal resolution within its actual words; we are left in a state of doubt about whether those yearnings will be satisfied or thwarted.

On the other hand, judging the piece according to the other definitions of plot or story that we have considered, the text more clearly denies us a narrative dimension. It certainly lacks dialogue, the central condition for one of Friedman's two definitions of plot, for only one character speaks (or even thinks) during the piece, which therefore lacks "scenes" or "episodes" (171). Character change, Friedman's other conception of plot (174), is also notably absent: Ronnie has shown no signs of full recovery or rehabilitation, his family remains deeply divided, and his father's anger in the text's opening line has not been successfully modulated by the text's final sentence, in which the father very pointedly expresses sympathy for Ronnie's fish rather than for Ronnie himself. By the same token and for the same reasons, the piece fails to satisfy one of Moss and Daniel's preconditions for what qualifies as a story: resolution (217).

Whatever fragmentary narrative Beach offers in this work is overshadowed by what Beach *does* accomplish quite effectively: in just a few words (or characters, rather), Beach tenderly describes a family on the edge and offers a poignant diagnosis of the problems at its core. The piece opens in a moment of mutual rage. The father's profanity and the volume of his yelling voice, signaled by repeated exclamation points and the word "NOW" being rendered in all capital letters, is juxtaposed against Ronnie's own anger: Ronnie's aggressive and distancing action—he is "in there"—is something that has happened before, probably many times ("He's locked himself in there *again*"), and the names of the bands that he is playing so loudly ("Slayer" and "Deathhammer") strongly connote through their references to death and murder a singularly dangerous mental state. Gradually, however, Beach reveals much more to us in progressively gentler prose. The "cheap speakers" suggest a family that might have limited financial resources, a detail that finds counterpoint and pathos in its contrast with the blue tetra fish that Miriam has thoughtfully bought to welcome Ronnie home, for these are fish that require large and expensive aquariums in order to survive. The father's opinion that the music distorted by Ronnie's speakers is "already distorted" suggests a deep generational rift—the father is unable to understand Ronnie's choice on any level other than as a kind of perversion of normality and stability. Ronnie's painful insensitivity to his family is marked by the father's observation that this music is playing so loudly that it will cause the small fish, symbols of Miriam's love and care for Ronnie, to "pulsate and wobble." Most of this detail is painted for us in a long, grammatically complex and complete sentence that forms within the father's mind, an odd choice for representing a process of thought, which is ordinarily more disjointed and rambling. This choice suggests a kind of deliberation and self-consciousness that could be considered dangerous when coupled with the father's evident rage. But then the final sentences turn into fragments, implying that a growing sense of resignation or even wistfulness is overtaking the father's mind. The last sentence, "The poor, poor little fish," with its insistent repetition and emphasis on vulnerability and helplessness, tells us a great deal—that the same father who is capable of empathizing with fish is unable to find sympathy for his own son. Again, a careful and respectful attention to Beach's language, the actual words on the page, has given us a moment of pleasure inside the TARDIS of the text without requiring us to compose for ourselves an ending or resolution that Beach has clearly chosen to withhold.

As a final example of this kind of reading and of the pleasures that this particular kind of flash can deliver without the necessity of plot or narrative, consider this text:

> The prisoner of noise stood before the bathroom sink, fingers in his ears, head down, mouth wide open, willing the sounds in his head to spill into the basin—the yelps and booms, screeches, screams and howls, crashes and groans, explosions and roars and babel and bangs. What if they formed a hairball of din, clogged the sink, scared the children when they came in at night to pee? He closed his mouth, went back to bed. (Beach 27)

By most of the standards that we have been using to determine whether pieces of nanofiction possess plots, this text would most likely be found wanting. On one hand, we have two physical actions depicted "live" within the body of the piece—a man experiencing a moment of apparent madness, first attempting to get the noises in his head to spill out of his mouth and then giving up on the effort out of concern for his children's sensitivities to the resulting ugly mess—so Ferguson would probably describe the piece as a narrative (221). Because we have an example of a yearning or desire being thwarted, Butler would likely reach the same conclusion (103). But the text does not feature any dialogue (Friedman 171); the central character has not changed (Friedman 174), for he has only managed to tame an insane impulse for a moment rather than to overcome his madness; therefore, this nanofiction also withholds a sense of resolution (Moss and Daniel 217). Instead of these indicia of plot or narrative, we see a sketch of a character at a pivotal moment in time, rendered in distinctly poetic language. The importance of sound to the piece—for poetry is both oral (spoken) and aural (heard)—is signaled immediately in the subject phrase of the long first sentence: "The prisoner of noise." An effectively produced and grotesque image of vomiting is complemented by the sounds that the sentence simultaneously names and makes: "yelps and booms, screeches, screams and howls, crashes and groans, explosions and roars and babel and bangs." The parallel rhythms of the phrases "yelps and booms" and "screams and howls" is disrupted by the placement of the two-syllable single word "screeches" in between them, and the following phrase ("crashes and groans") is out of sync with that potential for a repeated rhythm; the result simulates the internal cacophony by which the figure is being tormented. Beach's strategy changes at the end of this sentence, however, with the phrase, "explosions and roars and babel and bangs." The use of polysyndeton—a succession of instances of the repeated word, "and"—emphasizes for us the unending nature of the noise to which the piece's character is subjected, as do the rhythm duplicated by the phrase's two halves ("explosions and roars" and "and babel and bangs") and the alliteration of the last two named sounds. All of these poetic devices contribute to a powerful depiction of psychosis.

Flash, especially nanofiction like Beach's, has solidified itself "as an avenue of experimentation" (Masih, "In Pursuit" xxvi), and a key element of that adventurous spirit can be the absence of narrative; as Pamelyn Casto has written, "This type of story is often rich in implication [. . .], compressed and highly charged. The best stories often speak to us obliquely" ("Flashes"). Many thinkers familiar with the form have observed its frequent similarities with verse: Casto says that flash is "read by serious readers as slowly and carefully as they might read good poetry" ("Myth-ing Link" 24), and Grace Paley advises that flash "should be read like a poem. That is slowly" (253). From the examples of Lou Beach's work at the limits of the form, readers in their encounters with flash should be open to close-reading strategies resembling those often deployed with poetic texts, for "above all else, [flash] must be an innovative, attention-grabbing exploration of that perennial mystery that is the origin and end of expression itself: language" (Johnson 233). As well, readers of flash should remain receptive to the lack of closure that plotless works often feature, instead of trying to fill the uncomfortable silences, for "*Unease*, whether humorous or sad," is often flash's goal (Chappell 227).

Notes

1. For a brief genealogy of the term *short short fiction* and some of its variants, see Masih, "In Pursuit." For glimpses into what might be described as the prehistory of the form, see Chantler 39; and Shapard 47.

2. See, for example, Al-Sharqi and Abbasi; Brown; Byrnes; Campbell; Casto, "Flashes"; Gerlach; Gilead; Guimarães; Gurley; Hazuka; Nelles; Shapard; and Wright.

3. See also, for example, Barenblat ("there are no distinguishing rules"); Casto, "Flashes" ("That which we call flash fiction, by any other name would read as bright"); James 130 ("These short forms are like [. . .] babies, bloody, slimy new living creatures tied to some unexplainable and unknowable future"); and Leslie 8 ("flash fiction at its best has ambiguity on its side").

4. For theories about the role of the Internet and other digital technologies in prompting innovations to flash, see Al-Sharqi and Abbasi 52; Batchelor; Chambers 57-59; Nelles 88; Penny 19; and Wright 333-34.

5. For a cogent reading of this piece, see Gilead. For an account of its actual origins, see Wright.

6. See, for example, Casto, "Myth-ing Link" 24 ("These highly charged stories often go well beyond their surface details and manage to expand in the reading"); Ferguson 227 ("the deletion of traditional plot elements also demanded a more attentive reading, one in which the reader is conscious of narrative technique and style as keys to meaning"); and Phillips, "'Cheers'" 36 ("great [flash] is intensely compressed, every line weighted precisely, every image firing on multiple levels").

7. Wright implicitly adopts this standard when he argues that the apocryphal Hemingway text does not qualify as a story (335-37). For other critics, scholars, and writers of flash who subscribe to this viewpoint, see Byrnes; Campbell; Chinquee; Gurley; Hazuka; Pieroni; and White. But see Al-Sharqi and Abbasi 52 ("Flash Fiction is not plot driven and precisely includes only essential information in a compressed manner"); Batchelor 79 ("the flash fiction piece isn't granted the luxury of developing a plot like a short story"); Leslie 8 ("Flash fiction is about a singular moment, a slice of life, a sketch"); and Masih, "In Pursuit" xi ("To say that a flash must contain all the

literary elements that a longer story does [. . .] would be argued against by the proponents of experimental flash who lean more toward slice-of-life sketches").

8. See, for example, Barenblat; Gerlach; Oates; and Stanzel. But see Butler 102 ("it is a short short story and not a prose poem because it has at its center a character who yearns"); Chinquee 112 ("I believe that a prose poem is more about language and poetics, whereas a flash carries more narrative and story"); and James 130 ("I don't want clear definitions of the prose poem or the short-short").

9. A text is *impressionistic* if it emphasizes characters' subjective feelings and experiences, their impressions, rather than an omniscient narrator's more objective sense of a concretely conceived reality that exists independently of the characters' subjectivity. For a more fully developed discussion of impressionism in short fiction, see Ferguson. But see Nelles 97-98 (arguing that "microfiction" is predominantly expressionistic).

10. Excerpts from *420 Characters: Stories* by Lou Beach are copyright 2011 by Lou Beach and used by permission of Houghton Mifflin Harcourt Publishing Company, all rights reserved.

11. In this sense, the piece is similar to Pound's "In a Station of the Metro," which also lacks a verb to denote an action completed or in progress.

12. But see Nelles 90 ("Microstories often do present a single scene or speech, but they are not normally restricted to small static actions").

13. Significantly, Stanzel goes on to note that this technique of language was "originally confined to lyrical usage" (27).

14. See, for example, Al-Sharqi and Abbasi 55 ("Readers can interpret the story in a variety of ways and season it with their perceptions and experiences"); Chantler 48 (a story "prompts the reader to create his/her own narrative"); Gerlach 79-80 ("a story is an invitation to construct explanations, explanations about causality, connections, motives"); and Guerrero-Strachan 274 ("lack of resolution obliges the reader to seek the missing links and forces him to provide the story's ending").

Works Cited

Al-Sharqi, Laila, and Irum Saeed Abbasi. "Flash Fiction: A Unique Writer-Reader Partnership." *Studies in Literature and Language*, vol. 11, no. 1, 2015, pp. 52-56.

Banks, Russell. "Afterwords: Toward a New Form." Shapard and Thomas, pp. 244-45.

Barenblat, Rachel. "Prose Poems or Microfiction?" *In Posse Review*, www.webdelsol.com/InPosse/barenblat.htm/. Accessed 12 June 2016.

Batchelor, Katherine. "In a Flash: The Digital Age's Influence over Literacy." *Cult Pop Culture: How the Fringe Became Mainstream*, edited by Bob Batchelor, vol. 2, Praeger, 2012, pp. 77-88.

Beach, Lou. *420 Characters: Stories*. Houghton Mifflin Harcourt, 2011.

Bradfield, Scott. "Social Network Stories." *New York Times Review of Books*, 1 Jan. 2012, p. 13.

Brown, Randall. "Making Flash Count." *The Rose Metal Press Field Guide*, edited by Tara L. Masih, pp. 68-75.

Butler, Robert Olen. "A Short Short Theory." *The Rose Metal Press Field Guide*, edited by Tara L. Masih, pp. 102-4.

Byrnes, Thomas E. "Essentials of the Short Short Story." Kamerman, pp. 3-8.

Campbell, Walter S. "The Short Short Story Form." Kamerman, pp. 57-62.

Casto, Pamelyn. "Flashes on the Meridian: Dazzled by Flash Fiction." *Riding the Meridian*, vol. 1, no. 1, www.heelstone.com/meridian/meansarticle1.html/. Accessed 20 May 2016.

_____. "The Myth-ing Link (Or, Linking Up to Myth)." *The Rose Metal Press Field Guide*, edited by Tara L. Masih, pp. 24-30.

Chambers, Aidan. "Sparks of Fiction." *Horn Book Magazine*, Mar./Apr. 2012, pp. 55-59.

Chantler, Ashley. "Notes towards the Definition of the Short-Short Story." *The Short Story*, edited by Ailsa Cox, Cambridge Scholars Publishing, 2008.

Chappell, Fred. "Afterwords: The Tradition." Shapard and Thomas, pp. 227-28.

Chinquee, Kim. "Flash Fiction, Prose Poetry, and Men Jumping out of Windows: Searching for Plot and Finding Definitions." *The Rose Metal Press Field Guide*, edited by Tara L. Masih, pp. 109-15.

Ferguson, Suzanne C. "Defining the Short Story: Impressionism and Form." *The New Short Story Theories*, edited by Charles E. May, Ohio UP, 1994, pp. 218-30.

Friedman, Norman. "What Makes a Short Story Short?" 1958. *Form and Meaning in Fiction*, U of Georgia P, 1975, pp. 167-86.

Gerlach, John. "The Margins of Narrative: The Very Short Story, the Prose Poem, and the Lyric." *Short Story Theory at a Crossroads*, edited by Susan Lohafer and Jo Ellyn Clarey, Louisiana State UP, 1989, pp. 74-84.

Gilead, Amihud. "How Few Words Can the Shortest Story Have?" *Philosophy and Literature*, vol. 32, no. 1, 2008, pp. 119-29.

Guerrero-Strachan, Santiago Rodríguez. "Realism and Narrators in Tobias Wolff's Short Stories." *Short Story Theories: A Twenty-First-Century Perspective*, edited by Viorica Patea, Rodopi, 2012, pp. 271-80.

Guimarães, José Flávio Nogueira. *The Short-Short Story: A New Literary Genre*. Strategic Book Publishing, 2012.

Gurley, Jason. "Flash What? A Quick Look at Flash Fiction." *Writing-World.com*, 2002, www.writing-world.com/fiction/flash.shtml/. Accessed 20 May 2016.

Hazuka, Tom. "Flash Fiction from Embryo to (Very Short) Adult." *The Rose Metal Press Field Guide*, edited by Tara L. Masih, pp. 31-35.

James, David. "Another Voice in the Wind: A Brief Rant on the Difference between Prose Poems and Short-Shorts." *Sentence: A Journal of Prose Poetics*, vol. 1, 2003, pp. 129-31.

Johnson, Charles. "Afterwords: The Tradition." Shapard and Thomas, pp. 232-33.

Kamerman, Sylvia E., editor. *Writing the Short Short Story*. The Writer, 1942.

Leslie, Nathan. "That 'V' Word." *The Rose Metal Press Field Guide*, edited by Tara L. Masih, pp. 7-14.

Masih, Tara L. "In Pursuit of the Short Short Story: An Introduction." *The Rose Metal Press Field Guide*, edited by Tara L. Masih, pp. xi-xxxviii.

_____, editor. *The Rose Metal Press Field Guide to Writing Flash Fiction: Tips from Editors, Teachers, and Writers in the Field*. Rose Metal Press, 2009.

Moss, Steve, and John M. Daniel. "How to Write a 55-Word Story." *The World's Shortest Stories of Love and Death*, edited by Steve Moss and John M. Daniel, Running Press, 1999, pp. 217-21.

Nelles, William. "Microfiction: What Makes a Very Short Story Very Short?" *Narrative*, vol. 20, no.1, 2012, pp. 87-104.

Oates, Joyce Carol. "Afterwords: Toward a New Form." Shapard and Thomas, pp. 246-47.

Paley, Grace. "Afterwords: Skippers, Snappers, and Blasters." Shapard and Thomas, p. 253.

Penny, Laurie. "The Great English Novel Is Dead: Long Live the Unruly, Upstart Fiction That's Flourishing Online." *New Statesman*, 18-24 July 2014, p. 19.

Phillips, Jayne Anne. "'Cheers,' (or) How I Taught Myself to Write." *The Rose Metal Press Field Guide*, edited by Tara L. Masih, pp. 36-40.

_____. "Flash Theory." *Flash Fiction International: Very Short Stories from around the World*, edited by James Thomas, Robert Shapard, and Christopher Merrill, Norton, 2015, p. 226.

Pieroni, Jennifer. "Smart Surprise in Flash Fiction." *The Rose Metal Press Field Guide*, edited by Tara L. Masih, pp. 65-67.

Shapard, Robert. "The Remarkable Reinvention of Very Short Fiction." *World Literature Today*, vol. 86, no. 5, 2012, pp. 46-49.

Shapard, Robert, and James Thomas, editors. *Sudden Fiction: American Short-Short Stories*. Peregrine Smith Books, 1986.

Stanzel, Franz K. "Textual Power in (Short) Short Story and Poem." *Modes of Narrative: Approaches to American, Canadian and British Fiction*, edited by Reingard M. Nischik and Barbara Korte, Königshausen & Neumann, 1990, pp. 20-30.

Thomas, James, and Robert Shapard. Editors' note. *Flash Fiction Forward: 80 Very Short Stories*, Norton, 2006, pp. 11-14.

White, Trentwell Mason. "The Mechanics of the Short Short Story." Kamerman, pp. 11-18.

Wright, Frederick A. "The Short Story Just Got Shorter: Hemingway, Narrative, and the Six-Word Urban Legend." *Journal of Popular Culture*, vol. 47, no. 2, 2014, pp. 327-40.

RESOURCES

Additional Works of Flash Fiction_____

Collections

Aciman, Alexander, and Emmett Rensin. *Twitterature: The World's Greatest Books Retold Through Twitter*. Penguin, 2009.

Allen, Roberta. *Certain People*. Coffee House Press, 1996.

Almond, Steve. *The Evil B. B. Chow and Other Stories*. Algonquin Books, 2006.

_____. *My Life in Heavy Metal: Stories*. Vintage, 2003.

Alwin, Gail, *Four Buses: A Collection of Short Stories and Flash Fiction*. Arial, 2012.

Arnzen, Michael A. *100 Jolts: Shockingly Short Stories*. Raw Dog Screaming Press, 2004.

Atwood, Margaret. *Good Bones*. Virago, 2010.

_____. *Murder in the Dark: Short Fictions and Prose Poems*. Virago, 1994.

_____. *The Tent*. Bloomsbury, 2007.

Barnes, Rusty. *Breaking It Down*. Sunnyoutside Press, 2007.

Barthelme, Donald. *60 Stories*. Penguin, 1993.

Beach, Lou, *420 Characters*. Houghton Mifflin Harcourt, 2012.

Beckman, Paul. *Peek*. Big Table, 2015.

Bernhard, Thomas. *The Voice Imitator*. U of Chicago P, 1997.

Borges, Jorge Luis. *Collected Fictions*. Translated by Andrew Hurley, Penguin, 1998.

_____. *The Book of Imaginary Beings*. Translated by Norman Thomas di Giovanni, Dutton, 1969.

Brautigan, Richard. *Revenge of the Lawn, Stories 1962–1970*. Simon & Schuster, 1971.

Brown, Fredric. *Nightmares and Geezenstacks: 47 Stories*. Bantam, 1961.

Brown, Randall. *Mad to Live*. PS Books, 2011.

Butler, Robert Olen. *Intercourse: Stories*. Chronicle Books, 2008.

_____. *Severance: Stories*. Chronicle Books, 2006.

Buttaci, Salvatore. *200 Shorts*. All Things That Matter Press, 2011.

Calvino, Italo. *Invisible Cities*. Translated by William Weaver, Harcourt Brace Jovanovich, 1978.

Carlson, Ron. *The Blue Box: Flash Fiction and Poetry*. Red Hen Press, 2014.

Chekhov, Anton. *Stories*. Modern Library, 2000.

Cherches, Peter. *Lift Your Right Arm*. Pelekinesis, 2013.

Chinquee, Kim. *Pretty*. White Pine Press, 2010.

_____. *Oh Baby: Flash Fictions and Prose Poems*. Ravenna Press, 2008.

Claffey, James. *Blood a Cold Blue*. Press 53, 2013.

Corin, Lucy. *One Hundred Apocalypses and Other Apocalypses*. McSweeney's, 2013.

Cortázar, Julio. *A Certain Lucas*. Translated by Gregory Rabassa, Knopf, 1984.

Czyzniejewski, Michael. *Chicago Stories: Forty Dramatic Fictions*. Curbside Splendor, 2012.

_____. *Elephants in Our Bedroom*. Dzanc, 2009.

DeWan, Christopher. *Hoopty Time Machines: Fairy Tales for Grown Ups*. Atticus Books, 2016.

Davis, Lydia. *Can't and Won't*. Picador, 2015.

_____. *The Collected Stories of Lydia Davis*. Picador, 2010.

Doyle, Roddy. *Two Pints*. Jonathan Cape, 2012.

_____. *Two More Pints*. Jonathan Cape, 2014.

Duncan, Gary. *You're Not Supposed to Cry*. Vagabond Voices, 2017.

Dybek, Stuart. *Ecstatic Cahoots: Fifty Short Stories*. Farrar, Straus & Giroux, 2014.

_____. *The Coast of Chicago*. Picador, 2004.

Edson, Russell. *The Tunnel: Selected Poems of Russell Edson*. Oberlin College Press, 1994.

Eggers, Dave, *Short Short Stories*. Penguin, 2005.

Etter, Sarah Rose. *Tongue Party*. Caketrain Press, 2011.

Faulkner, Grant. *Fissures: One Hundred 100-Word Stories*. Press 53, 2015.

Fish, Kathy. *Together We Can Bury It*. The Lit Pub, 2012.

_____. *Wild Life: A Collection of Undomesticated Flash Fictions*. Matter Press, 2011.

Fish, Kathy, and Robert Vaughan. *Rift: Stories*. Unknown Press, 2015.

Flick, Sherrie. *Whiskey, Etc*. Queen's Ferry, 2016.

_____. *I Call This Flirting*. Flume Press, 2004.

Forrest, Rosie. *Ghost Box Evolution in Cadillac, Michigan*. Rose Metal Press, 2015.

Freele, Stephanie. *Feeding Strays: Short Stories*. Stray Horse Press, 2009.

Gaffney, David. *Aromabingo*. Salt, 2009.

_____. *The Half-Life of Songs*. Salt, 2010.

_____. *More Sawn-Off Tales*. Salt, 2013.

_____. *Sawn-Off Tales*. Salt, 2010.

Gebbie, Vanessa. *Storm Warning: Echoes of Conflict*. Salt, 2010.

_____. *Words from a Glass Bubble*. Salt, 2008.

Gifford, John. *Wish You Were Here*. Big Table Publishing, 2016.

Giles, Molly. *Bothered*. Split Oak Press, 2013.

Golaski, Adam, *Color Plates*. Rose Metal Press, 2010.

Gonzalez, Ray. *The Religion of Hands: Prose Poems and Flash Fictions*. U of Arizona P, 2005.

Gordon, Karen Elizabeth. *The Red Shoes and Other Tattered Tales*. Dalkey Archive Press, 1996.

Gould, John. *Kilter: 55 Fictions*. Handsel, 2003.

Grass, Gunter. *My Century*. Trans. Michael Henry Heim. Harcourt, 1999.

Gray, Amelia. *Gutshot: Stories*. FSG Originals, 2015.

_____. *AM/PM*. Featherproof Books, 2009.

Guess, Carol. *Index of Placebo Effects: A Collection of Flash Fiction*. Matter Press, 2012.

Hall, Tina May. *The Physics of Imaginary Objects*. U of Pittsburgh P, 2010.

Hamilton, Mary. *We Know What We Are*. Rose Metal Press, 2010.

Haskell, John. *I Am Not Jackson Pollock*. Picador, 2003.

Hamilton, Mary. *We Know What We Are*. Rose Metal Press, 2010.

Hemingway, Ernest. *In Our Time*. 1925. Scribner, 1996.

Henderson, Kim. *The Kind of Girl*. Rose Metal Press, 2013.

Henning, Barbara. *A Swift Passage: Stories and Poems*. Quale Press, 2013.

Hershman, Tania. *My Mother Was an Upright Piano: Fictions*. Tangent, 2012.

_____. *The White Road and Other Stories*. Salt, 2008.

Heynen, Jim. *The Boys' House: New and Selected Stories*. Minnesota Historical Society Press, 2001.

Highsmith, Patricia. *Little Tales of Misogyny*. Virago, 2014.

Jemc, Jac. *A Different Bed Every Time*. Dzanc Books, 2014.

Kafka, Franz. *The Complete Stories*. Schocken Books, 1971.

Kawabata, Yasunari. *Palm-of-the-Hand Stories*. Translated by Lane Dunlop and J. Martin Holman, Farrar, Straus & Giroux, 2006.

Kelman, James. *If It Is Your Life*. Hamilton, 2010.

Keret, Etgar. *The Bus Driver Who Wanted to Be God and Other Stories*. Translated by Miriam Shlesinger et al., Riverhead, 2015.

_____. *Suddenly, a Knock on the Door*. Translated by Nathan Englander, Farrar, Straus & Giroux, 2012.

_____. *The Girl on the Fridge*. Translated by Miriam Shlesinger and Sondra Silverston, Farrar, Straus & Giroux, 2008.

Kerr, Calum. *Lunch Hour: A Flash-Fiction Collection*. Gumbo Press, 2014.

Kesey, Roy. *All Over*. Dzanc Books, 2007.

Kotzin, Miriam N. *Just Desserts: Flash Fiction*. Star Cloud Press, 2010.

Laskowski, Tara. *Modern Manners for Your Inner Demons*. Matter Press, 2012.

Lennon, J. Robert. *Pieces for the Left Hand: 100 Anecdotes*. Granta, 2005.

Lin, Kim Gek. *The Bugging Watch & Other Exhibits*. Tarpaulin Sky Press, 2010.

Litz, Cynthia. *Imprints: A Collection of Flash Fiction*. Matter Press, 2013.

Loory, Ben. *Stories for Nighttime and Some for the Day*. Penguin, 2011.

Lovelace, Sean. *How Some People Like Their Eggs*. Rose Metal Press, 2009.

Lutz, Gary. *Stories in the Worst Way*. Knopf, 1996.

Manguso, Sarah. *Hard to Admit and Harder to Escape*. McSweeney's, 2007.

Manickavel, Kuzhali. *Insects Are Just Like You and Me Except Some of Them Have Wings*. Blaft Publications, 2008.

Marcus, Peter. *Good, Brother*. Calamari Press, 2005.

_____. *The Singing Fish*. Calamari Press, 2005.

Martone, Michael. *Double-Wide: Collected Fiction of Michael Martone*. Quarry Books, 2007.

_____. *Memoranda*. Bull City Press, 2015.

Masih, Tara. *Where the Dog Star Never Glows*. Press 53, 2010.

Maugham, William Somerset. *Cosmopolitans: Very Short Stories*. Heinemann, 1936.

McMillan, Frankie *My Mother and the Hungarians: And Other Small Fictions*. Canterbury UP, 2017.

Moore, Dinty W. *Toothpick Men*. Mammoth Press, 1998.

Neal, Darlin'. *Elegant Punk: Stories*. Press 53, 2012.

_____. *Rattlesnakes and the Moon: Stories*. Press 53, 2011.

Nye, Naomi Shihab. *There Is No Long Distance Now: Very Short Stories*. Greenwillow Books, 2011.

Orner, Peter. *Esther Stories*. Houghton Mifflin, 2001.

Painter, Pamela. *Wouldn't You Like to Know: Very Short Stories*. Carnegie Mellon UP, 2010.

_____. *Getting to Know the Weather: Stories*. U of Illinois P, 1985.

Paley, Grace. *The Collected Stories*. Farrar, Straus & Giroux, 2007.

Phillips, Jayne Anne. *Black Tickets*. 1979. Vintage, 2001.

Pokrass, Meg. *The Dog Looks Happy Upside Down*. Etruscan Press, 2016.

_____. *Damn Sure Right*. Press 53, 2011.

Prinzi, Santino. *Dots, and other flashes of perception*. Nottingham Review Press, 2016.

Reeves, Craige. *Flash Fiction*. Vantage Press, 2005.

Rhodes, Dan. *Anthropology and a Hundred Other Stories*. Canongate, 2005.

_____. *Marry Me*. Canongate, 2013.

Robertson, James. *365: Stories*. Penguin, 2014.

Rogers, Bruce Holland. *The Keyhole Opera*. Wheatland, 2005.

_____. *49: A Square of Stories*. CreateSpace, 2013.

Rohan, Ethel. *Goodnight Nobody: Stories*. Queen's Ferry Press, 2013.

Schultz, Katey. *Flashes of War*. Apprentice House, 2013.

Scotellaro, Robert. *What We Know So Far*. Blue Light, 2015.

_____. *Measuring the Distance*. 1st World Publishing, 2012.

Shapard, Robert. *Motel & Other Stories*. Predator, 2005.

Shepard, Sam. *Days Out of Days: Stories*. Knopf, 2010.

Shua, Ana María. *Without a Net*. Translated by Steven J. Stewart, Hanging Loose Press, 2012.

_____. *Microfictions*. Translated by Steven J. Stewart, U of Nebraska P, 2009.

_____. *Quick Fix: Sudden Fiction*. Translated by Rhonda Dahl Buchanan, White Pine Press, 2008.

Smith, Claudia. *The Sky Is a Well and Other Shorts*. Rose Metal Press, 2007.

Smith, Curtis. *Beasts and Men*. Press 53, 2013.

Sosa, Alejandro Córdoba. *Two Hundred and One Miniature Tales*. Editorial Autores de Argentina, 2015.

Stohlman, Nancy. *The Vixen Scream and Other Bible Stories*. Pure Slush, 2014.

_____. *The Monster Opera*. Bartleby Snopes, 2013.

_____. *Searching for Suzi: A Flash Novel*. Monkey Puzzle, 2009.

Swann, David. *Stronger Faster Shorter: Flash Fictions*, edited by Peter Blair and Ashley Chantler, The International Short-Short Story Press, 2015.

Tuite, Meg. *Lined Up Like Scars: Flash Fictions*, edited by Peter Blair and Ashley Chantler, The International Short-Short Story Press, 2015.

Valenzuela, Luisa. *Strange Things Happen Here: Twenty-Six Short Stories and a Novel*. Harcourt Brace Jovanovich, 1979.

Vandermeer, Jeff. *The Day Dali Died: Poetry and Flash Fiction*. Prime Books, 2003.

Vaughan, Robert. *Diptychs + Triptychs + Lipsticks + Dipshits*. Deadly Chaps, 2013.

_____. *Flash Fiction Fridays*. Lulu, 2012.

Wideman, John Edgar. *Briefs: Stories for the Palm of the Mind*. Lulu, 2010.

Williams, Diane. *Vicky Swanky Is a Beauty*. McSweeney's, 2012.

_____. *This Is About The Body, The Mind, The Soul, The World, Time and Fate*. Grove Weidenfeld, 1990.

Williams, Joy. *Ninety-Nine Stories of God*. Tin House, 2016.

Yourgrau, Barry. *The Sadness of Sex*. Delta, 1995.

_____. *Wearing Dad's Head*. Gibbs Smith, 1987.

Anthologies

Ackerman, Forrest J., editor. *Ackermanthology: 65 Astonishing, Rediscovered Sci-Fi Shorts*. Sense of Wonder Press, 2000.

Asimov, Isaac, Martin H. Greenberg, and Joseph D. Olander, editors. *100 Great Science Fiction Short Short Stories*. Doubleday, 1978.

Baines, Elizabeth. *Balancing on the Edge of the World*. Salt, 2007.

Beckel, Abigail, and Kathleen Rooney, editors. *Brevity & Echo: An Anthology of Short Short Stories*. Rose Metal Press, 2006.

Budman, Mark, and Tom Hazuka, editors. *You Have Time for This: Contemporary American Short-Short Stories*. Ooligan, 2007.

Chantler, Ashley, editor. *An Anatomy of Chester: A Collection of Short-Short Stories*. Chester Academic Press, 2007.

_____, editor. *Prize Flights: 20 Stories from the Cheshire Prize for Literature 2003*. Chester Academic Press, 2004.

Clark, Amy, Elizabeth Ellen, Kathy Fish, and Claudia Smith. *A Peculiar Feeling of Restlessness: Four Chapbooks of Short Short Fiction by Four Women*. Rose Metal Press, 2008.

Colen, Elizabeth J., John Jodzio, Tim Jones-Yelvington, Sean Lovelace, and Mary Miller. *They Could No Longer Contain Themselves: A Collection of Five Flash Chapbooks*. Rose Metal Press, 2001.

David, Jack, and Jon Redfern, editors. *Short Short Stories*. Holt, Rinehart and Winston of Canada, 1981.

Fles, Barthold, editor. *The Best Short Short Stories from Collier's*. World Publishing, 1948.

Forman, K. Scott, Kona Morris, and Nancy Stohlman, editors. *Fast Forward: A Collection of Flash Fiction*. Flash Forward Press, 2008.

Gingher, Marianne, editor. *Long Story Short: Flash Fiction by Sixty-Five of North Carolina's Finest Writers*. U of North Carolina P, 2009.

Goldschmidt, Pippa, and Tania Hershman, editors. *I Am Because You Are: An Anthology of Stories Celebrating the Centenary of the Theory of General Relativity*. Freight Books, 2016.

Goodman, Roger B., editor. *The World's Best Short Short Stories*. Bantam, 1967.

Hazuka, Tom, editor. *Flash Fiction Funny: 82 Very Short Humorous Stories*. Blue Light Press, 2013.

Howe, David J., and David B. Wake, editors. *Drabble Who?* Beccon, 1993.

Howe, Irving, and Ilana Wiener Howe, editors. *Short Shorts: An Anthology of the Shortest Stories*. Bantam, 1983.

Huang, Harry J., editor and translator. *An Anthology of Chinese Short Short Stories*. Foreign Languages Press, 2005.

Hubler, Richard G., editor. *The World's Shortest Stories: An Anthology*. Popular Library, 1962.

Kerr, Calum, and Valerie O'Riordan, editors. *Jawbreakers: A Collection of Flash Fictions*. CreateSpace, 2014.

Laskowski, Tara, editor. *SmokeLong Quarterly: The Best of the First Ten Years, 2003–2013*. Matter Press, 2014.

Lay, Graeme, editor. *The Third Century: New New Zealand Short Short Stories*. Tandem Press, 1999.

Masih, Tara, and Stuart Dybek, editors. *The Best Small Fictions 2016*. Queen's Ferry, 2016.

_____, and Robert Olen Butler, editors. *The Best Small Fictions 2015*. Queen's Ferry, 2015.

Mills, Mark, editor. *Crafting the Very Short Story: An Anthology of 100 Masterpieces*. Prentice Hall, 2003.

Monaghan, Nicole, editor. *Stripped*. PS Books, 2011.

Moore, Dinty W., editor. *Sudden Stories: The Mammoth Book of Miniscule Fiction*. Mammoth Books, 2003.

Morris, Kona, Leah Rogin-Roper, and Stacy Walsh, editors. *The Incredible Shrinking Story: A Collection of Flash Fiction*. Flash Forward Press, 2011.

Mukherjee, Wanda Wade, and Sharlene Baker, editors. *Women Behaving Badly: Feisty Flash Fiction Stories*. Paper Journey Press, 2004.

Neufeld, Josh, and Sari Wilson, editors. *Flashed: Sudden Stories in Comics and Prose*. Pressgang, 2016.

Pagan, Patricia Flaherty, editor. *Up, Do: Flash Fiction by Women Writers*. Spider Road Press, 2014.

Perkins-Hazuka, Christine, Tom Hazuka, and Mark Budman, editors. *Sudden Flash Youth: 65 Short-Short Stories*. Persea, 2011.

Qi, Shouhua, editor and translator. *The Pearl Jacket and Other Stories: Flash Fiction from Contemporary China*. Stone Bridge, 2008.

Richmond, Michelle, editor. *Flash in the Attic: 33 Very Short Stories*. Fiction Attic Press, 2013.

Roberts, Jessy Marie. *Daily Flash 2011: 365 Days of Flash Fiction*. Daily Flash Publications, 2010.

Schuster, Anne, and Maire Fisher, editors. *Women Flashing: A Collection of Flash Fiction from Women's Writing Workshops*. Women's Writing Workshops, 2005.

Shapard, Robert, and James Thomas, editors. *New Sudden Fiction: Short-Short Stories from America and Beyond*. W. W. Norton, 2007.

_____. *Sudden Fiction: American Short-Short Stories*. G. M. Smith, 1983.

_____. *Sudden Fiction (Continued): 60 New Short-Short Stories*. W. W. Norton, 1996.

_____. *Sudden Fiction International: 60 Short-Short Stories*. W. W. Norton, 1989.

Shapard, Robert, James Thomas, and Ray González, editors. *Sudden Fiction Latino: Short-Short Stories from the United States and Latin America*. W. W. Norton, 2010.

Stern, Jerome, editor. *Micro Fiction: An Anthology of Fifty Really Short Stories*. W. W. Norton, 1996.

Swartwood, Robert, editor. *Hint Fiction: An Anthology of Stories in 25 Words or Fewer*. W. W. Norton, 2011.

Thomas, James, Denise Thomas, and Tom Hazuka, editors. *Flash Fiction: 72 Very Short Stories*. W. W. Norton, 1992.

Thomas, James and Robert Shapard, editors. *Flash Fiction Forward: 80 Very Short Stories*. W. W. Norton, 2006.

Thomas, James, Robert Shapard, and Christopher Merrill, editors. *Flash Fiction International: Very Short Stories from Around the World*. W. W. Norton & Company, 2015.

Ziegler, Alan, editor. *Short: An International Anthology of Five Centuries of Short-Short Stories Prose Poems, Brief Essays, and Other Short Prose Poems*. Persea Books, 2014.

Novels/Novellas-in-Flash

Bell, Matt. *Cataclysm Baby*. Mud Luscious Press, 2012.

Cisneros, Sandra. *The House on Mango Street*. Vintage Books, 1991.

Hall, Tina May. *{All The Day's Sad Stories}*. Caketrain Press, 2009.

Holland, Tiff. *Betty Superman*. Rose Metal Press, 2011.

Holland, Tiff, Aaron Teel, Meg Pokrass, Chris Bower, and Margaret
Patton Chapman. *My Very End of the Universe: Five Novellas-
in-Flash and a Study of the Form*. Rose Metal Press, 2014.

Robison, Mary. *Why Did I Ever*. Counterpoint, 2002.

Salesses, Matthew. *I'm Not Saying, I'm Just Saying*. Civil Coping
Mechanisms, 2013.

Teel, Aaron. *Shampoo Horns*. Rose Metal Press, 2012.

Literary Journals

A-Minor Magazine   https://aminormagazine.com
Editor-in-Chief: Nicolette Wong

Bartleby Snopes   http://www.bartlebysnopes.com
Managing Editor: Nathaniel
Tower

Blink Ink   http://www.blink-ink.org/
Managing Editor: Sally Reno

Cease, Cows   http://ceasecows.com
Editor-in-Chief: Susannah Jordan

Cleaver Magazine   http://www.cleavermagazine.com
Founding Editors: Karen Rile and
Lauren Rile Smith

The Collagist   http://thecollagist.com
Editor-in-Chief: Gabriel Blackwell

Crack the Spine   http://www.crackthespine.com
Editor: Kerri Farrell Foley

decomP   http://www.decompmagazine.com
Editor-in-Chief: Jason Jordan

Dogzplot Editor-in-Chief: Jesse Eagle	http://dogzplot.blogspot.com
Fiction Southeast Editor-in-Chief: Chris Tusa	http://fictionsoutheast.org
Flash: The International Short-Short Story Magazine Editors: Peter Blair and Ashley Chantler	http://www.chester.ac.uk/flash.magazine
Flash Fiction Online Editor-in-Chief: Suzanne Vincent	http://flashfictiononline.com/main
Flash Frontier: An Adventure in Short Fiction Founding Editor: Michelle Elvy Editor: James Norcliffe	https://www.flash-frontier.com/about/
Frigg Editor: Ellen Parker	http://www.friggmagazine.com
JMWW Editor-in-Chief: Jen Michalski	http://jmwwjournal.com
The Journal of Compressed Creative Arts Managing Editor: Randall Brown	http://matterpress.com/journal
Matchbook Editors: Brian Mihok and R. B. Pillay	http://www.matchbooklitmag.com

New Flash Fiction Review
Editor-in-Chief: Meg Pokrass

http://newflashfiction.com

Nano Fiction
Editor: Kirby Johnson

http://nanofiction.org

Pithead Chapel
Editor-in-Chief: Keith Rebec

https://pitheadchapel.com

Prick of the Spindle
Editor-in-Chief: Cynthia Reeser

http://prickofthespindle.org

SmokeLong Quarterly
Editor: Tara Laskowski

http://www.smokelong.com

Spelk
Editor: Gary Duncan

https://spelkfiction.com

3 AM Magazine
Coeditors-in-Chief: Andrew
Gallix and David Winters

http://www.3ammagazine.com/3am

Vestal Review
Coeditors: Susan O'Neill and
Mark Budman

http://www.vestalreview.org

Wigleaf
Editor: Scott Garson

http://wigleaf.com

Word Riot
Publisher: Jackie Corley

http://www.wordriot.org/

Bibliography

Editors' note: The titles featured here are criticism and writing guides.

Allen, Roberta. *Fast Fiction: Creating Fiction in Five Minutes*. Story Press, 1997.

Blair, Peter. "Flash Fiction." *Writers' and Artists' Yearbook 2016*. Bloomsbury, 2015, pp. 248-51.

Brown, Randall. *A Pocket Guide to Flash Fiction*. Matter Press, 2012.

Casto, Pamelyn. "Flash Fiction." *Books and Beyond: The Greenwood Encyclopedia of New American Reading*, edited by Kenneth Womack, vol. 2, Greenwood Press, 2008. pp. 385-399.

Chantler, Ashley. "Notes Towards the Definition of the Short-Short Story." *The Short Story*, edited by Ailsa Cox, Cambridge Scholars, 2008, pp. 38-52.

Galef, David. *Brevity: A Flash Fiction Handbook*. Columbia UP, 2016.

Hershman, Tania. "Writing Flash Fiction: Liberation through Constraint." *Writing Short Stories: A Writers' and Artists' Companion*, edited by Courttia Newland and Tania Hershman, Bloomsbury, 2015, pp. 198-202.

Kerr, Calum. *The World in a Flash: How to Write Flash-Fiction*. Gumbo Press, 2014.

Masih, Tara L., editor. *The Rose Metal Press Field Guide to Writing Flash Fiction: Tips from Editors, Teachers, and Writers in the Field*. Rose Metal Press, 2009.

McDowell, Gary L., and F. Daniel Rzicznek, editors. *The Rose Metal Press Field Guide to Prose Poetry: Contemporary Poets in Discussion and Practice*. Rose Metal Press, 2010.

Rourke, Lee. *A Brief History of Fables: From Aesop to Flash Fiction*. Hesperus, 2011.

Shields, David, and Elizabeth Cooperman, editors. *Life is Short—Art is Shorter: In Praise of Brevity*. Hawthorne Books & Literary Arts, 2016.

Williams, Tony. "Flash Fiction." *The Handbook of Creative Writing*, edited by Steve Earnshaw, 2nd ed., Edinburgh UP, 2014, pp. 315-23.

Wilson, Michael. *Flash Writing: How to Write, Revise and Publish Stories Less Than 1,000 Words Long*, Virtualbookworm.com Publishing, 2004.

About the Editors

Michael Cocchiarale is an associate professor of English at Widener University, where he teaches American literature, creative writing, and composition. With Scott D. Emmert, he is coeditor of *Upon Further Review: Sports in American Literature* (2004), *Critical Insights: American Sports Fiction* (2013), and *Critical Insights: American Short Story* (2015). He is also the author of *Still Time* (2012), a collection of short stories.

Scott D. Emmert is a professor of English at the University of Wisconsin—Fox Valley, where he teaches composition, literature, and film. With Michael Cocchiarale, he is coeditor of *Upon Further Review: Sports in American Literature* (2004), *Critical Insights: American Sports Fiction* (2013), and *Critical Insights: American Short Story* (2015). With Steven Trout, he coedited *World War I in American Fiction: An Anthology of Short Stories* (2014).

Contributors

Randall Brown is the author of the award-winning flash fiction collection *Mad to Live*. His work appears in *The Rose Metal Press Field Guide to Writing Flash Fiction, The Norton Anthology of Hint Fiction,* Salem Press's *Critical Insights: American Short Story, Best Small Fictions 2015,* and *The Norton Anthology of Hint Fiction.* He blogs regularly at FlashFiction.net and has been published and anthologized widely, both online and in print. He is also the founder and managing editor of Matter Press and its *Journal of Compressed Creative Arts.* He received his MFA from Vermont College and teaches in Rosemont College's MFA in Creative Writing Program.

Pamelyn Casto has taught online courses in flash fiction and in haibun. She has written articles on flash fiction for *Writer's Digest* and *Fiction Southeast* (online). Her essays on flash fiction are included in *The Rose Metal Press Field Guide to Writing Flash Fiction: Tips from Editors, Teacher, and Writers in the Field* (edited by Tara L. Masih) and in *Books and Beyond: The Greenwood Encyclopedia of New American Reading* (edited by Kenneth Womack). She served as administrator for an online flash fiction critique workshop for over fifteen years and currently publishes *Flash Fiction Flash,* a monthly online newsletter for flash literature publishing news, markets, and contests.

Matthew Duffus has published fiction, nonfiction, and poetry in a variety of journals, both in print and online, including *Beloit Fiction Journal, Natural Bridge,* and *New Ohio Review.* He is Instructor of English Composition at Gardner-Webb University, in Boiling Springs, North Carolina.

Robert C. Evans is I. B. Young Professor of English at Auburn University at Montgomery. He earned his PhD from Princeton University in 1984. In 1982, he began teaching at AUM, where he has been named Distinguished Research Professor, Distinguished Teaching Professor, and University Alumni Professor. External awards include fellowships from the American Council of Learned Societies, the American Philosophical Society, the National Endowment for the Humanities, the UCLA Center for Medieval and Renaissance Studies, and the Folger, Huntington, and Newberry libraries. He is the author or editor of more than thirty-five books and of more than three hundred essays, including recent work on various American writers.

Kristen Figgins is a writer of fabulism, whose work has appeared in such places as *Dunes Review*, *Zoetic Press*, *The Gateway Review*, *Puerto del Sol*, *Sleet Magazine*, *Hermeneutic Chaos*, *Sakura Review*, and *The Whale Road Review.* Her first chapbook, *A Narrow Line of Light*, is available for purchase from Boneset Books and her novella, *Nesting*, is forthcoming from ELJ Publications in the Summer of 2017. She is a lecturer at the University of Texas of the Permian Basin.

Megan Giddings has an MA from Miami University and an MFA from Indiana University. She is the spotlight author in *Best Small Fictions 2016.* Her flash fiction has been published in magazines such *Quarterly West*, *New South*, *Black Warrior Review*, and *Wigleaf.*

Laura Hatry is a PhD candidate at the Universidad Autónoma of Madrid, with a thesis entitled "Power, Violence and Politics in Latin American Film and Literature." Her research focuses mainly on cinematographic adaptations of Latin American literary works as well as Argentine literature, and her work has been published in many specialized journals and books. She has also translated books and essays from and to Spanish, English, and German and has participated as a speaker in international conferences in Spain, England, Italy, Germany, the United States, and Argentina. Her work as a visual artist has been shown at exhibitions in the United States, Spain, France, Germany, Canada, Switzerland, and the United Arab Emirates.

Santino Prinzi is the Co-Director of *National Flash Fiction Day* in the UK, the Flash Fiction Editor of *Firefly Magazine*, a First Reader for *Vestal Review*, and a reviewer of flash fiction collections for *Bath Flash Fiction Award.* His debut flash fiction collection, *Dots and other flashes of perception*, is available from The Nottingham Review Press. In 2016 he graduated from Bath Spa University with a first-class degree in English literature with creative writing, and he is currently studying for an MA in English literature from the University of Bristol. His short stories, flash fiction, and prose poetry have been published or is forthcoming in various places online and in print. To find out more follow him on Twitter (@tinoprinzi) or visit his website: https://tinoprinzi.wordpress.com.

Eric Sterling earned his PhD from Indiana University in 1992. He is Distinguished Research Professor of English at Auburn University at Montgomery, where he has taught for twenty-three years. He has published extensively on Jewish literature and the Holocaust. He has published four books, including *Life in the Ghettos during the Holocaust* (Syracuse University Press) and *Arthur Miller: Dialogues* (Rodopi Press), along with seventy refereed articles.

David Swann is the author of *The Privilege of Rain* (Waterloo Press, 2010), which was shortlisted for the Ted Hughes Award for New Work in Poetry, and based on his experiences as a writer-in-residence in a high-security prison. He has also published a chapbook of flash fiction, *Stronger Faster Shorter* (Flash International Short Story Press, 2015), and a collection of short stories, *The Last Days of Johnny North* (Elastic Press, 2006). His poems and stories have won many awards, including two successes in the National Poetry Competition and eight in the Bridport Prize (including first prize for flash fiction in 2016). He is a former journalist for publications in the UK and Holland and now teaches in the Department of English & Creative Writing at the University of Chichester, United Kingdom.

Julie Tanner is a recent MA graduate from Goldsmiths, University of London, where she specialized in modern American literature. For her dissertation, she produced a handbook on Lydia Davis called "Now that I have been here for a little while, I can say with confidence that I have never been here before." She is interested in short fiction, specifically the interplay between form and feeling, and intends to pursue this line of research during graduate studies, focusing on Davis and other authors.

Laura Tansley's writing has been published in a variety of places including *NANO Fiction, New Writing Scotland, PANK, Short Fiction* *in Theory and Practice*, and *Flash*. She placed second in National Flash Fiction Day's Micro Competition in 2015 and has been shortlisted and won several flash fiction competitions. She is coeditor of the collection *Writing Creative Non-Fiction: Determining the Form* and has contributed chapters to several collections on creative practice. She graduated with a PhD in short-short forms and feminist expressions in 2012. She lives and works in Glasgow, Scotland.

Jarrell D. Wright, originally from Beckley, West Virginia, received his BA with high honors from the College of William and Mary and earned a JD from the same institution. He practiced law with the firm of Eckert Seamans in Pittsburgh, Pennsylvania, before returning to academia, earning his PhD in English at the University of Pittsburgh, where he focused on Renaissance devotional literature and recreation. He teaches flash in courses targeted to undergraduates at the University of Pittsburgh, has led an inquiry devoted exclusively to the form in a course for senior citizens, and has written on the practice of close reading for *TeachingCollegeLit. com*. Randy Laxton and their two dogs, Mya and Jack, support him in his teaching, research, and writing.

Index

Lessing, Doris 150
L'Heureux, John 72
Lightman, Alan 16
Lish, Gordon 147, 148, 155, 161, 191
Lispector, Clarice 11
Loory, Ben xx
Lovelace, Sean xxii, 230
Lutz, Gary xx, xxiv
Lyons, Martyn 90

MacQueen, Clare 13
Mallarmé, Stéphane 4
Manguso, Sarah 152, 153, 159
Mansfield, Katherine 153, 159
Markus, Peter 15, 20
Martone, Michael xx, 227
Marx, Patricia xxi
Masih, Tara xxiii, xxiv, 12
May, Charles 33
McNeal, Tom 42
McQueen, Latanya xxi
melodrama 179
Merrill, Christopher xix, 13, 22, 220, 232
Merwin, W. S. 5, 6
metafiction 33, 116, 164
metaphor xxiii, 14, 29, 34, 61, 62, 63, 125, 148, 207
micro fiction 44, 45
Miller, Mary xxii, 230
Mills, Mark 11, 25, 38
minute stories 8, 18
Miriam 211, 213, 226
Monson, Ander xxi
Monterroso, Augusto 115, 125
Moody, Rick 147, 159
Moore, Dinty W. 10, 32
Moore, Lorrie 11

Mose, Gitte 18, 27
Moss, Steve 209, 220
Mousavi, S. Habib 27, 28, 30, 36, 39
Mousavi, S. Mohammad Ali 28, 39
Mu, Aili 33, 36, 37, 39
Munro, Hector Hugh 5
Murakami, Haruki 16
Muscarella, Steve 15

nanofiction 21, 206, 207, 208, 209, 211, 214, 215, 235
Needlers, Howard 43
Nelles, William 90
neologisms 123, 124
Nixon, Richard 202
Nobokov, Vladimir 11
Nold, Lisa 28

Oates, Joyce Carol xv, 82
Oberfirst, Robert 7
Olander, Joseph D. 8, 18, 229
Old Man and the Sea, The xiii
onomatopoeia 209

Paccchioni, Federico 26
Paley, Grace 215
Pasco, Allan H. 25
pataphysics 123
Perozo, V. M. Perez 42
Phillips, Jayne Anne 5
Pieroni, Jennifer xvi
podcasts 14
Podgorsek, Russell 15
point of view vii, 53, 54, 55, 56, 57, 58, 63, 64, 106, 150, 209
Pokrass, Meg xxii, 233, 235
Pollastri, Laura 115